A Decade of Devolution

E. BLAINE LINER
Editor

Jack A. Brizius
Stephen B. Farber
R. Scott Fosler
John Stuart Hall
Harold A. Hovey
Daphne A. Kenyon
and Charles J. Orlebeke

A Decade of Devolution: Perspectives on State–Local Relations

THE URBAN INSTITUTE PRESS
Washington, D.C.

Library of Congress Cataloging in Publication Data

A Decade of Devolution: Perspectives on State-Local Relations/E. Blaine Liner, editor.
1. State-local relations—United States.   2. Intergovernmental fiscal relations—United States—States.   3. United States—Politics and government—1977–
I. Liner, E. Blaine.

| JS348.D43 1989 | 353.9'293—dc20 | 89-31871 |
| | | CIP |

ISBN 0-87766-463-3 (alk. paper)
ISBN 0-87766-464-1 (alk. paper; casebound)

All Urban Institute books are printed on acid-free paper.

Printed in the United States of America.

9 8 7 6 5 4 3 2

Distributed by
            University Press of America
4720 Boston Way   3 Henrietta Street
Lanham, MD 20706   London WC2E 8LU ENGLAND

THE URBAN INSTITUTE is a nonprofit policy research and educational organization established in Washington, D.C., in 1968. Its staff investigates the social and economic problems confronting the nation and government policies and programs designed to alleviate such problems. The Institute disseminates significant findings of its research through the publications program of its Press. The Institute has two goals for work in each of its research areas: to help shape thinking about societal problems and efforts to solve them, and to improve government decisions and performance by providing better information and analytic tools.

Through work that ranges from broad conceptual studies to administrative and technical assistance, Institute researchers contribute to the stock of knowledge available to public officials and private individuals and groups concerned with formulating and implementing more efficient and effective government policy.

Conclusions or opinions expressed in Institute publications are those of the authors and do not necessarily reflect the views of other staff members, officers or trustees of the Institute, advisory groups, or any organizations that provide financial support to the Institute.

CONTENTS

Text Tables

Text Figures

The Urban Institute's State Policy Center was charged by its advisory board of five former governors (Bruce Babbitt, Richard Lamm, William Milliken, Richard Riley, and Dick Thornburgh) to examine how states and localities were adapting to the major changes in fiscal and service responsibilities resulting from the return of responsibilities previously lodged at the federal level. This devolution of responsibilities has been occurring in cycles since the first Nixon administration. However, the pace and magnitude of devolution quickened with the beginning of the Reagan administration, providing states and localities opportunities not only to reassert their administrative capacities but to take on new responsibilities. Our particular interest focuses on the principles called into play by the states and their subdivisions as they re-sorted responsibilities among themselves and between themselves and federal agencies. Several chapters address this question from both theoretical and pragmatic points of view. In this sense, the book may serve as a guide and reference for decisionmakers as they continue to think through the allocation of powers and duties of the various levels of government.

Services provided by state and local governments generally are examined in terms of efficiency (quality of services and economical use of public funds) or equity (equal access to public services, fair distributions of tax loads and electoral processes, and access to power). The approach used here follows this general framework. Included are discussions that hinge upon the concepts of efficiency and equity as they affect decision making in the current realignment of the state-local system.

The chapters provide a perspective on federalism, with a close focus on the state-local components as they have evolved during the 1980s—a period of rapid transitions in the relationships among federal, state, and local governments. The theme that runs through them is the notion that when major transitions occur, the redistribution of power and authority that accompanies them should be decided according to principles that form a sound and logical correlation between governmental functions or services being provided and the appropriate levels of government to control, pay for, and deliver those services.

Critics of the intergovernmental system find a misalignment between the levels of government and the appropriate control and management of the functions. The most common complaint is overreaching by the federal level into matters that seemed to be entirely local in nature. The devolutionary initiatives of the Reagan administration curbed federal activism and provided states with the opportunity for rethinking and re-sorting these alignments. The re-sorting is not yet complete. In fact, it is unlikely that there will ever be a final, perfect resolution of the question of who should be in charge of what and where. But the principles underlying the division of power within a system of intergovernmental management such as that found in the United States are important, and they need to be kept in sharp focus when rapid re-sorting of functions is occurring. This need for a rational resolution of who delivers which services is the underlying reason for the advisory panel of governors' encouraging The Urban Institute to explore the principles behind the allocation of power.

The subject of state-local relations assumed magnified importance during the 80s because of the withdrawal of federal financial assistance and the continued issuance of federal cost-increasing mandates. The withdrawals were initiated immediately upon arrival of the Reagan administration at magnitudes substantially greater than those of earlier administrations, and the mandates were viewed as attempts by the federal level to continue some measure of control, or assurance, that the federal standards or requirements would be continued, even at others' cost. The transfer of responsibility, generally without a transfer of money, was theoretically made easier by the Economic Recovery Tax Act of 1981, which, while reducing federal taxing levels, left the door open for states and localities to increase their taxes proportionately to pay for the devolved functions. This change forces choices at the state and local levels, choices about which services should be provided by which level and, therefore, which level should increase taxes to pay for the service in a realigned, re-sorted system.

The book is organized into two sections. Part One concerns the allocation of responsibilities among the various levels of government, particularly since 1978, the peak year of federal financial assistance to states and localities, and up to 1988, the final year of the Reagan presidency. Included in these first six chapters is an examination of two states, Illinois and Arizona, and their recent experiences with devolutionary impacts, which in some ways were not at all what was expected.

Part Two sets forth a theoretical framework for making decisions about allocation of power among levels of government. Each chapter hinges on questions of who pays, who delivers the service, and who controls. Those who are in the throes of making decisions about the "best" allocation of responsibilities will benefit not only from the pragmatic examples of Part One but will also find the theoretical basis for allocations contained in Part Two helpful in sorting out which levels should be assigned which services.

The study of the relationship between states and localities is a hands-on exercise in specifics. In chapter 1, E. Blaine Liner summarizes the major influences that underpin the devolutionary philosophy and outlines the setting within which the devolutionary actions of the last decade took place. In chapter 2, Stephen B. Farber examines federalism and state-local relations by reviewing past and current events that bear directly on the division of roles and responsibilities of the various units of government. Farber discusses prospects for a reform agenda for federalism in the Bush presidency. Chapter 3, written by Jack A. Brizius, then presents a comprehensive view of the fiscal landscape of state and local governments, the backdrop of reality against which any decisions about re-sorting functions and services must blend. Next, chapter 4, by R. Scott Fosler, outlines the relationship between economic health of states and localities and their ability to provide service systems. The discussion is included both as an exploration of the interaction of local-state-national-international economies and as a reminder of how critical the economic picture is to any government's ability to serve its citizenry at any level of expectation.

The next two chapters present case studies of the evolution of state-local relations in the 1980s in two states: Illinois is discussed in chapter 5, written by Charles J. Orlebeke, and Arizona's experiences are presented in chapter 6, written by John Stuart Hall. Both provide surprising evidence of the resiliency of the structure of state and local governments; in spite of dramatic shifts of responsibilities, the basic structure of governments remains more or less unchanged. Growth of special districts, privatization, and recourse to user fees are shown to have been employed as ways to continue services without structural realignments of the basic system.

The next three chapters, by Harold A. Hovey, take the reader from a review of the logical approaches facing decisionmakers as they rethink the proper division of services among the levels of government (chapter 7) to specific alternatives or choices that can be made for the major functions of government (chapter 8) and then to the theoretical framework for making decisions about financing (chapter 9) by using need and fiscal capacity as determinants for decision making.

In chapter 10, Daphne A. Kenyon establishes a framework for assessing proposed reforms or revisions in state policies that affect local taxing and borrowing. The chapter also sets out several reform proposals.

The entire effort was made possible by grants to The Urban Institute from the J. Howard Pew Freedom Trust and the Aetna Life and Casualty Foundation, to which the editor and authors are indebted. The encouragement of James McGann at the Pew Charitable Trusts was critical to the undertaking. The State Policy Center at the Institute benefited from the advice given on this study by its advisory board and by several reviewers, particularly John Shannon, former director of the Advisory Commission on Intergovernmental Relations and now a senior fellow at The Urban Institute; Jed Kee, George Washington University; and Steven Gold, National Conference of State Legislatures. Susan Kalish provided editorial assistance in the preparation of the first draft. The authors and the editor welcome the opportunity to express our appreciation for their work on several drafts of the manuscript to Gail Shur and Theresa Owens.

E. Blaine Liner
Editor

Part One

JURISDICTION, AUTHORITY, AND DEVOLUTION

Chapter One

SORTING OUT STATE-LOCAL RELATIONS

E. Blaine Liner

We should . . . know over which matters local tribunals are to have jurisdiction and when authority should be centralized; for example, should
one person keep order in the market and another in some other place, or
should the same person be responsible everywhere? Again, should offices
be divided according to the subjects with which they deal, or according to
the persons with whom they deal. I mean to say, should one person see to
good order in general, or one look after the boys, another after the
women, and so on?

—Aristotle, *Politics*

These words, written more than 2000 years ago, suggest that decisionmakers have struggled with the logical and proper assignment
of responsibilities among different segments and levels of government since ancient times. In this country, from the writing of the
Constitution to the present day, separating or sorting out the appropriate public functions among our three major levels of government—federal, state, and local—has preoccupied philosophers,
politicians, academics, jurists, practitioners, and citizens. This perennial dilemma becomes acute in times of rapid change in the character of American federalism, such as marked the decade of the
1980s, the decade of devolution.

During the 1980s, rapid changes occurred in the way the federal
government carries out its functions. Influenced by conservative political philosophy and economic pressures, policymakers reversed a
50-plus-year trend of centralization and federal activism. Observers
may argue as to how sudden or thorough the change actually was,
but it is evident that many responsibilities previously lodged at the
federal level were allocated to the states or localities in the 1980s.
This new climate of *devolution* brought new powers and opportunities to these levels of government, but it also necessitated many
changes in the traditional relationships that had evolved—not only
between the states and the federal government but also between states

and the local governments within them. Old arrangements as to what tasks state or local governments would carry out, which level would control different services, and particularly which level would pay for different services—no longer worked. Moreover, devolution has often left states and localities with federal mandates to provide services in such areas as water treatment, housing, and indigent health care without the funding to pay for them. Caught in a fiscal squeeze, states and localities have often encountered serious organizational and political obstacles to provide all the services they are now expected to deliver.

The intergovernmental system is highly complex, interconnected, and interdependent. Because it is, states and localities working to re-sort their roles face a problem as complex as getting solid color faces to appear on all six sides of the Rubik's Cube, with each level of government working its side of the cube more or less independently of the other but at the same time.

This book brings together the perspectives of several experts on how states and localities are adapting to the major transitions in fiscal and service responsibilities in the devolutionary environment of the 1980s. It presents case studies of two states and analyzes in detail state-local relations in the major areas of tax and fiscal policy, economic development, and intergovernmental systems. It focuses particularly on the principles that states and their subdivisions employ or could employ as they re-sort responsibilities among themselves and between themselves and federal agencies. Thus, it is hoped that this book will serve as both a practical and a theoretical guide for decisionmakers as they continue to work through these adjustments.

A DECADE OF DEVOLUTION

American federalism has been in a state of transition since before the ink dried on the Constitution. However, most of the change has been incremental rather than dramatic, glacial rather than revolutionary. But the 1980s brought major changes in the relations among the federal government, the states, and substate units such as municipal or county governments. As the decade unfolded, it became apparent to governors, mayors, and other elected officials that a bit of drama had been introduced to intergovernmental affairs for the first time since the 1930s. In 1978, federal aid to states and localities peaked at the all-time high of $85.5 billion and has been in decline since then.

Federalism has evolved over the past 200 years into a much more centralized national government than was anticipated by the Founding Fathers. Especially since World War II, the major trend in American federalism has been toward centralization of power at the federal level and a tendency for the federal government to take on new responsibilities. For example, the administration of Franklin Delano Roosevelt established Social Security and an alphabet soup of new federal agencies to carry on the war effort and to solve pressing domestic problems that were not being addressed successfully by the states and local governments. The Eisenhower administration in the 1950s initiated a massive interstate highway system, provided federal housing programs, and established extensive educational, medical, and pension programs for veterans. During the 1950s and 1960s, an activist federal government created agencies and programs to act aggressively to defend the civil rights of minorities, assist handicapped people, protect the environment, ensure basic nutrition, help states support dependent children, and so on. As a result, states were increasingly in the position of administering federal funds to implement federal programs in accordance with federal guidelines and controls. Frequently cities could approach the federal government directly for programs and funds, bypassing the states entirely.

In the 1970s, many voices began to criticize federal activism and the extremely complex, heavily regulated character of intergovernmental regulations that had developed. The Advisory Commission on Intergovernmental Relations (ACIR) issued frequent warnings about the congested intergovernmental system during the 1970s and finally, in 1985, supported a turnback of responsibility and revenue to the states and localities. ACIR was chiefly concerned with the continuing trend toward centralization of responsibility nationally and the accompanying trends resulting in weakened and dependent states and localities.

Some devolution of responsibilities from the federal level to the state occurred in every administration since President Richard Nixon's first term in the early 1970s. However, the pace quickened with the beginning of the Reagan administration. In 1980, Reagan campaigned on a platform of limiting the role of federal government, which became a central objective of his first term. In his first inaugural address, President Reagan said:

It is my intention to curb the size and influence of the Federal establishment and to demand recognition of the distinction between the powers granted to the Federal government and those reserved to the states or to the people. All of us need to be reminded that the Federal government did not create the states: the states created the Federal government.

For an understanding of what types of changes confronted states and localities in the 1980s, it is useful to identify the recent milestones of devolution, beginning with events in the 1960s (see figure 1.1). Stephen Farber provides a more detailed discussion of these turning points in chapter 2.

How did all these changes affect the budgets of states and localities, which had grown increasingly dependent on federal aid in the 1960s and 1970s? Figure 1.2 shows the rise and fall of federal aid as a percentage of state plus local outlays between 1958 and 1988, then projects the trend between 1988 and the end of the century. According to these ACIR estimates, federal aid increased from 11 percent to about 26 percent of state-local budgets between 1958 and 1978. The percentage of federal funds in state and local budgets then fell quite sharply from that high point, declining to about 17 percent by 1988. If trends continue as expected, federal aid will fall to about 13 percent of state-local outlays by 1998.

The total dollar value of federal aid to states and localities dropped from $106 billion in 1980 to $90 billion in 1987 (in constant 1982 dollars). The fall in federal aid to date is quite clear. The trend projected in figure 1.2 would result in federal aid to states and localities returning to the percentage level of 40 years ago.

Reduced Funding versus Elimination of Federal Programs

What happened to federal programs over the same period is more complex, however. The Reagan administration found much more success in cutting the budgets of domestic programs than in eliminating them. Two factors account for this outcome: the Congressional process, which tends to exact compromises from opposing forces, and the legendary ability of bureaucracies, once they have been established, to maintain their existence. Instead of program elimination, the administration often had to settle for fiscal retrenchment. The result was lowered funding levels; lowered growth rates in funding when reductions were not possible; tightened aid-triggering formulas and eligibility criteria; and, when feasible, devolution of federal functions to states and localities.

The administration did succeed in eliminating the 14-year-old General Revenue Sharing (GRS), which was a major local assistance program, and Urban Development Action Grants (UDAG). But a surprisingly large number of programs survived on reduced budgets, even several that had been presumed easy targets for elimination in the beginning. For example, just as in 1981, the President's FY 1989 budget called for the elimination of six of the survivors: the Appalachian Regional Commission, the Economic Development Administration, Tennessee Valley Authority's economic development programs, Housing Development Action Grants (HoDAGs), Section 312 rehabilitation loans, and Section 108 loan guarantees. The National League of Cities recently defended these programs by pointing out that their elimination would reduce overall federal spending by no more than 0.001 percent (*Nation's Cities Weekly* 1988).

The Reagan administration came to Washington in 1981 with a philosophical bias toward devolving substantial amounts of federal spending and taxing to the states and localities. It experienced some success in implementing this objective. However, as the administration cut spending in many areas, it sharply increased spending in other areas, such as defense. This increased spending, along with the tax cuts, increased the already large federal budget deficit. Moreover, the 1980s brought disturbances in the internal and external economic picture, producing serious deficits in the international balance of trade. These events created substantial constraints on federal spending, constraints that are expected to last well into the next decade. This situation implies that even a change of philosophy about federal activism in the White House would not much alter the devolutionary climate we see today. As the political philosophy undergirding devolution continues to gain strength in both political parties and as budget and trade deficits continue to soar at the national level, the subnational levels of government will take on still greater responsibilities.

The Impacts of Devolution on State and Local Governments

For the most part, states and localities welcomed devolution and the opportunity to move toward center stage. In general, states were eager to increase their control over the functions they carry out and most of them have been well-prepared to do so. The administrative capacities of these units have developed in scope and sophistication over the last 30 years, partly due to grant-in-aid programs provided by the federal agencies. That management capacity remained underutilized until events in the 1980s increased state and local responsibilities. Certainly there is a strong sentiment in state houses

Figure 1.1 MILESTONES OF DEVOLUTION

Block grants in the 1960s. Generally, during the Johnson years, categorical grants proliferated—some 240 new federal aid programs were enacted. Federal assumption of the principal role in solving domestic problems increased and the federal control expanded, frequently bypassing the states. However, two block grants were enacted: the Partnership for Health Act (1967) and the Omnibus Crime Control and Safe Streets Act (1968). These block grants consolidated funding for several specialized (categorical) programs within a service area and left states substantial discretion as to how to allocate that funding. With block grants, the federal level maintained control of policy and finance while recipients were charged with administration and implementation.

Nixon's new federalism. A flirtation with regionalization of federal agencies resulted in federal regional councils that had special powers to shortcut procedures, to demand coordination of disparate federal agencies, and to solve emergency or disaster-related problems on the spot. This arrangement brought federal regional executives into closer contact with state and local officials, reenforcing the apparent drift of decisionmaking back to a more local environment. Barfield (1981, p. 71) pointed out that the sorting out of functions among the governments reached a brief consensus during the Nixon and Ford administrations. The consensus held that income transfer programs for individuals would be continued by the federal level (Social Security, Medicare, food stamps) but service functions (education, community development) would be best provided by states and localities.

Block grants under Nixon. Three block grants were enacted in 1974: the Comprehensive Employment and Training Act (CETA), the Housing and Community Development Act (instituting the Community Development Block Grant ([CDBG] program)), and Title XX of the Social Security Act. GRS was enacted as part of the theme of returning federal funds (and power) to local governments. This program alone was providing $4 billion each year to local governments to use at their discretion before it was terminated in 1986.

Carter's devolutionary initiatives. During 1978, the second year of the Carter administration, federal intergovernmental aid reached its peak at $85.5 billion. The real dollar decline in federal aid, which continues today, began during 1979. One of the targets for cutting aid during the Carter years was the state portion of GRS, which was eliminated in 1980. New programs such as the Urban Development Block Grants (UDBG) program were routed around the states, directly to municipalities that qualified. Cost sharing by states became critical to obtain federal funds for

---

continued

large projects that in earlier years would have been financed entirely by the federal level—such as major water supply projects in the western states. The Carter hit list of major western water projects to be eliminated from his first budget had forced the issue, and counterproposals of cost sharing with states and others who wanted these projects became critical to obtain federal attention.

Reagan's block grants. In 1981, President Reagan and Congress consolidated 54 categorical programs into nine block grants worth $7.2 billion. These programs were in the areas of health services, social services, low-income energy assistance, substance abuse and mental health, community services, and community development. In 1982, Congress replaced CETA with the state-oriented Job Training Partnership Act (JTPA) and the federal highway program with the Surface Transportation Assistance Act. In general, these programs gave states greater discretion in allocating funds, but with reduced levels of federal assistance. Political forces, however, moderated both the cuts and the state bias to some extent.

Reagan's regulatory relief. From its inception, the Reagan administration pushed for regulatory relief in intergovernmental relations. The block grants replaced complex federal regulatory codes with much simpler guidelines; some regulations were rescinded or relaxed, and others became more flexible. Regulatory relief affected many areas: education, eligibility for health care, roads, and handicapped access, for example. Redirection of agency objectives and budgets to reflect the more conservative philosophies in power was achieved within months of Reagan's inauguration.

The Omnibus Budget Reconciliation Act (OBRA) of 1981. The first tangible encounter with the Reagan administration's comprehensive package of reforms was initiated by the introduction of OBRA. Vested interests, Congressional committees, and federal agencies were able to envision how they were to fare under the conservative philosophy of Reagan's first budget. The central themes were budget cuts (except for defense), elimination of agencies or programs of a social, economic, and regulatory nature, and simultaneously with OBRA, tax reductions across the board of 25 percent. In terms of intergovernmental relations, the states were recognized as principal decisionmakers and shapers of many domestic policy interests. This early theme continued throughout the Reagan presidency— shifting spending and taxing authority to the states whenever feasible.

The Economic Recovery Tax Act (ERTA) of 1981. Reagan's 1981 tax reform package, signed into law the same day as OBRA, cut federal income taxes and thus reduced the amount in the federal treasury to pay for domestic programs. It was argued that cutting federal taxes gave states and

continued

Figure 1.1 Continued

localities the opportunity to initiate new taxes, if they saw fit, to replace federal funding cuts. The principal message, however, was that supply-side economics would be responsive to the tax cuts and would generate far more economic activity than otherwise. The increased economic activity would then yield even more taxes in future years, even at lower rates.

Reagan's swap and turnback proposal. In 1982, President Reagan proposed to reorder intergovernmental relations through a $47 billion program to return programs and revenue sources to states and localities. He also proposed to "swap" funding responsibilities for two major programs: Medicaid would be federalized but food stamps and Aid to Families with Dependent Children (AFDC) would be state financed. Congress declined to adopt this proposal, and future similar proposals received even less consideration.

The demise of direct local financial assistance. GRS: The elimination of this 14-year old program in 1986 cut direct federal financial ties to four-fifths of all local governments. During its final year of operation, $4 billion was disbursed to the nation's local governments. For those communities whose only tie to the federal government was the annual GRS payment, the death of the program also meant a release from many federal cross-cutting rules and regulations, the strings that had been attached to those who received federal monies.

UDAG: Plagued by early assertions of being tilted to northeastern communities because of its eligibility criteria and by charges that its primary beneficiaries were major hotel and restaurant chains and many other urban service businesses, UDAG was eliminated during 1988, when it was pitted against the National Aeronautics and Space Administration's budget in an either/or proposition by Congress. UDAG lost. Both GRS and UDAG had been major sources of development and operations funding for local governments.

Executive Order 12612. This 1986 order required federal agencies to accord states the maximum flexibility in administering federal programs and to avoid preemption of state policies. All federal agencies must now submit proposals to the Office of Management and Budget with a "federalism assessment" certifying compliance with the order.

Gramm-Rudman-Hollings Act. In 1986, Congress attempted to address a growing federal budget deficit by setting up a mechanism to make automatic across-the-board cuts if total federal appropriations exceeded a preestablished limit. Gramm-Rudman-Hollings effectively capped spending on federal programs and federal installations in every state.

Figure 1.2 THE RISE AND DECLINE OF FEDERAL AID, 1958–88—AND 1998? (AS A PERCENTAGE OF STATE-LOCAL OUTLAYS)

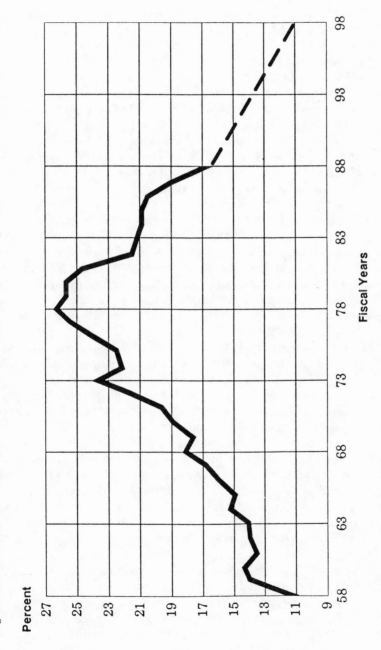

Fiscal Years

Source: Advisory Commission on Intergovernmental Relations 1988, p. 13.

and municipal councils that the 1980s brought a welcome reduction in federal controls and in burdensome and overly rigid regulations. The other side of the bargain, however, calls for increases in local taxes to fill the gaps caused by federal funding reductions in these areas—a task often easier to explain than to execute.

Some supporters of devolution saw it as a way to cut back government services and involvement at all levels because they assumed that states and localities would have little interest in picking up the slack left by federal reductions and cuts. But, there have been surprises. As Nathan, Doolittle, and Associates (1987) observe, states found that they often possessed the ability to permit fiscal replacement of federal cuts during the eighties, and consequently many expanded the span and scope of the state governments, much beyond what would otherwise have occurred. Expansionary state governments were not expected by many administration supporters. The real test of need for a service has become whether the states and localities continue the service with their own dollars. Illinois, for example, initiated its Build Illinois program to inject $2.3 billion into Illinois communities in the form of infrastructure assistance. Other states responded by developing rainy day funds by spinning off several functions, such as prisons, to the private sector and by instituting intensive management improvement efforts.

Bowman and Kearney (1986), in broader fashion than Nathan, Doolittle, and Associates, confirm that the states have indeed made progress in the minds of the public and the media, and in fact have become a principal innovator and manager in the intergovernmental system. Many localities, especially smaller cities, have not had the resources to provide extensive innovations, however.

In spite of the evidence, states and localities generally hesitate to move to the center stage of *full* fiscal and programmatic control, especially as the total costs of replacing federal aid have become clear. Unfunded mandates and cost shifting from one level to another have created problems for states and localities. Whether the functional area is Medicaid, road financing, or housing or whether the issues emerge as part of a taxpayers' revolt, such as Proposition 13 in California, states and localities face a fiscal squeeze.

To add to the pressure, some state and regional economies experienced declines, especially early in the decade. Currently, several larger states face deficits that resulted from optimistic revenue projections after the federal tax revisions of 1986. Particularly in these states, taxpayers had sold capital gains properties during 1986 to beat the deadline of increases in the capital gains tax effected by the

1986 Tax Reform Act. Several states reported revenues from capital gains during 1986 at twice normal levels. Projecting that one-shot windfall into 1988 and 1989 has brought about most of the current deficits, particularly in California and Massachusetts. The short-term windfall has now become the long-term shortfall.

Being backed into a corner from which the only way out is a tax hike is bound to trigger the cautionary instincts of the seasoned politician. Few elected officials relish the role of author of the next tax increase. In political affairs, as in personal circumstances, getting what one wants may not be as important as what getting it leads to. In this case, getting the responsibility for a service ultimately means raising the taxes to pay for it. Many states and localities have already increased taxes or plan to do so. One of the central tenets of devolution is that the tax-paying capacity that once went to federal income taxes has now been released for states and localities to absorb. However, the theoretical notion that federal tax reduction facilitates a corresponding increase in state and local taxes is not a simple proposition politically.

The trends of the 1980s drastically changed the funding picture for cities, where needs for social services tend to be most concentrated. Direct federal aid to cities, as well as federal aid through the states to the cities, has fallen sharply. The National Conference of State Legislatures (NCSL) studied this problem because most state officials were besieged by local authorities to provide them with more flexibility and discretion in local financial affairs. The 1987 report of the NCSL study committee called for a loosening of the traditional tight reins states hold over local finances. With services provided at the state and city levels not lower now than in 1980, cities have taken cost-cutting measures, such as the elimination or reduction of a service, tightening eligibility criteria, privatizing or contracting out the service, or shifting the service to another jurisdiction. Despite these moves, cities have had to increase revenues, mainly through the politically unpopular moves of hiking property taxes and user fees.

STATE-LOCAL RELATIONS: COMPLEXITY IS A GIVEN

Fiscal relationships between the 50 states and more than 83,000 local governments in the United States are diverse and complex. They have always been so. First, the size and wealth of different states and different localities within a state vary enormously. For example, state expenditures in 1985 in California were $46 billion, more than three times those of Pennsylvania and more than 22 times those of Nebraska. The population of New York City surpasses that of 42 states. Substate levels of government range from cities of hundreds of thousands or millions to villages of a few souls. Illinois ranks as the 14th largest nation in the world when its population and gross state product are included in international comparative statistics.

Climates, economies, histories, ethnic influences, political traditions, historical division of labor between states and localities—all these differ from state to state. Jack Brizius explains in chapter 3 that the historical ebb and flow of relative political and fiscal strength among states and localities have created a "geological landscape" of fiscal relations, where strata laid down in past decades or centuries influence what can be done in the present.

To add to the complexity, states and local governments choose to leave the actual provision of many services to nonprofit agencies or private businesses that carry out publicly funded activities under contract. Private soup kitchens, special education schools, hospitals, prisons, and other institutions may thus become, in a sense, part of the system of intergovernmental relations.

As Daphne Kenyon points out in chapter 10, state policies affect local government finances in a great variety of ways. States restrict local taxing powers by placing limits on property taxes and by limiting the types of taxes that localities may levy. States may limit the amount of debt a locality can issue; they also dictate the volume of certain types of tax-exempt debt allowable under federal law. On the other hand, by creating bond banks or issuing debt on behalf of their localities, state policies may enhance local borrowing power. States may dictate standards for local educational, health, and welfare facilities. They may prescribe standards for personnel systems, accounting procedures, and the types of officials elected for local units. They may follow the practice of the federal government in imposing unfunded mandates on localities. Or states may leave many matters to local home rule.

Relations between cities and counties and their states have varied over time from bad to good, depending upon legislative and gubernatorial postures toward local government as much as the reverse. Some of the battles between substate units and the state legislature have been newsworthy, even legendary. For example, conflicts between Chicago, the state legislature, and downstate Illinois assumed classic proportions in past years, and is reviewed by Charles J. Orlebeke in chapter 5.

During recent years, several efforts have been made to fashion more positive relations. The National Governors' Association and the National League of Cities began discussions along this line in 1986. The NCSL has formed a standing committee to deal with state-local relationships. The Committee for Economic Development (CED) (1986), calling for a better understanding by leaders at both levels that they are part of a system or partnership, has urged more discussions of mutual interests and cooperative actions. CED refers to the levels of government as being in "a delicate web of interrelationships," one that could become paralyzingly tangled without thoughtful attempts at reconciliation of differences. In May 1988, four influential interest groups issued a joint policy on behalf of communities that would apparently bypass the states in an attempt to restore direct federal-local assistance. The National League of Cities, National Association of Counties, National Association of Regional Councils, and United States Conference of Mayors all approved the "restoration of direct federal-local relationships" as part of their election-year pressure on both presidential candidates. The National Governors' Association responded by rejecting this approach.

Thus it is no simple matter to sort out state-local relationships in ordinary times, let alone to make major changes in response to the series of shock waves brought by devolution.

Some observers believe that this extreme complexity in itself is a sign that something is wrong with the intergovernmental system. As evidence, they point out that the division of powers in the Constitution implies a system in which each level of government would be self-sufficient, carrying out, controlling, and raising the revenues to pay for the functions reserved to it. The Founding Fathers, who hammered out *The Federalist Papers*, the Bill of Rights, and other early amendments to the Constitution, viewed the states as the cornerstone of government. Powers not expressly given to the federal government were reserved to the states, with localities not even mentioned in the Constitution. This simple vision seems to have been very much in the minds of the Founding Fathers, but it barely resembles the complex, intertwined system of responsibilities that characterizes American federalism in this century. Whether things were simpler in earlier days does not matter much now; there were no simple answers to the central questions about who provides which service or who pays for it then, and few appear likely now.

Some criticize the entire concept of intergovernmental aid, arguing that such transfers from one level of government to another should be considered a de facto finding of a mismatch between resources and responsibilities. Others consider this a highly debatable proposition, arguing that higher levels of government may be the first to detect a need for action, may have more fiscal capacity to address a need, or be more responsive to certain issues than entrenched local power structures. According to this line of thinking, lower levels may generally be best suited to carry out programs, but higher levels should offer financial or other incentives or impose sanctions to induce lower levels to act on matters that would otherwise not be addressed. Proponents cite the racial progress made in local jurisdictions in the Deep South under the prodding of an activist federal government during the civil rights era as an example of this dynamic.

Much of the theoretical discussion of state-local relations proceeds on the assumption that clear lines can be drawn between what is or should be local, what is or should be state, and what is or should be federal. This is not necessarily the case. For example, there may be a national interest in education, but that interest may extend only to some basics, not to what is taught every minute of every day in every classroom in the nation. The state may have to intervene to force some communities to recognize that their choices have an impact on others, but the state need not necessarily tell either set of communities exactly what policies to pursue. Harold A. Hovey points out in chapter 9 that there are logical ways to sort out these questions.

If there is a consensus on these issues at the moment, it is most likely that the system of governance has become excessively intertwined and complex and that simplification in any meaningful form is a risky undertaking that will yield as many surprises as expected outcomes.

STATE-LOCAL RELATIONS: AN ANALYTICAL APPROACH

We can cut through this complexity, diversity, and uncertainty, however, by applying some principles that, even though we may not be aware we are using them, govern decisions about sorting out state and local roles and responsibilities. Moreover, although generalizations about state-local relations must be drawn cautiously, the experience gained in the 1980s makes it possible to identify certain guidelines for structuring effective relationships between different levels of government.

Separating Service Provision, Control, and Finance

To realign state-local relationships effectively, leadership must be able to separate three different elements of responsibility: who performs a function, who controls the performance, and who pays the bill. What does being responsible really mean? Does it mean performing a service but not necessarily setting standards or paying for it? For example, for many years state police enforced the 55-mile-per-hour limit on all federal and state highways, although many states felt that such a low limit was inappropriate on some interstate segments. Another example is the federal government's mandate that localities meet federal air pollution standards, but with no funding provided for achieving these federally dictated levels of control. Blistering attacks on the practice of unfunded mandates have been directed by municipal officials, particularly at the Clean Water Act's expensive impact on localities not in compliance. Who is really in charge in each of these examples? From the point of view of a locality that provides a service, four theoretical possibilities exist:

- ☐ local control and local funding
- ☐ local control but no local funding
- ☐ no local control and local funding, and
- ☐ no local control and no local funding.

In real life, these theoretical possibilities are often not yes-or-no propositions. For example, a local funding share could vary from a small to a large percentage of total funding. It is useful to consider these elements separately. As Hovey points out (chapter 7), in the hurly-burly world of state and local politics, there is a tendency to consider together these three decisions, although they are not inherently linked. When these considerations are automatically linked in practical discussions, meaningful options are often ignored.

Merging the three questions creates impossible dilemmas. There are enormous differences in financial capacities among states and among localities within states. The tax base of Maryland is much stronger than that of Arkansas, for example. Different states and communities also have widely varying levels of need. For example, big cities tend to have a higher proportion of poor people than the suburbs that surround them. To provide anything close to equitable levels of services among communities requires mitigating these disparities.

In the past, concerns about inequity led to consolidating jurisdictions, shifting functions to a higher level of government, and/or increasing the amount of aid from higher levels of government. But if we link control and performance of a service with paying for it, we can only impose increasingly more control on localities as we funnel resources from higher levels to address disparities of capacity and need. This course of action produces a continuing migration of power away from local governments to consolidated units, states, and the federal government, a pattern that prevailed during much of the 1960s and 1970s.

A similar dilemma presents itself if we want to maximize voter control and the flexibility to accommodate differing local tastes and conditions. To accomplish those goals, we should place functions at the smallest level of government possible. But if we link performance of a function with control, then the smaller governmental units must proliferate their services, a situation that may violate economies of scale and the goal of efficiency. If local control can come only with the ability to finance, the result would be extreme variation in local taxing and service provisions.

The way out of these dilemmas is to sort out service provision, control, and financing and to consider each separately when analyzing or structuring responsibilities between states and localities.

Separating Redistributive and Economic Efficiency Goals

At a theoretical level, policies that boost the economy and thus increase the tax base will most efficiently fund expanding government services. A larger economic pie provides more tax money to aid the poor and spreads the tax bite among more taxpayers, making it less onerous for all. Thus, theoretically at least, policies that aid the poor at the expense of economic efficiency ultimately damage the poor as well as the rich.

Under political combat conditions, however, this theory does not always prove correct. Sometimes, politically acceptable ways of redistributing income necessitate paying a price in economic efficiency. But even if society is willing to pay such a price to achieve a more equitable redistribution of resources, both rich and poor have an interest in watching that price and attempting to keep it as small as possible.

RESTRUCTURING STATE-LOCAL RELATIONS

Guidelines for the Federal Role in State-Local Relations

Although this book concentrates on state-local relations as deter-mined by state and local officials, these officials have to acknowledge the presence, and in some cases the necessity, of federal influence, control, and dollars.

Some achievements are simply beyond the combined efforts of state and local officials of states that are appreciably poorer than other states. We may picture a state rescuing a poor rural county or fiscally distressed central city as something like a sleek, well-pow-ered Coast Guard cutter saving a drowning swimmer. The image of assured rescue does not fit, however, when the state's situation re-sembles that of a nearly swamped, leaky scow and the nearby waters are filled with the drowning. Put another way, if the total economic pie of the state is too small to allow fulfillment of the reasonable expectations of state citizens, much less national averages or stan-dards, no amount of cooperative recutting of that pie by the state or local leadership will solve the problem.

The federal government can use both tax and spending policies to deal with the disparities in resources and need among states. In tax policy, the federal government needs to fund clearly national func-tions, such as defense, and other functions it chooses to pursue through progressive taxes, such as the income tax, that are roughly related to ability to pay. However, any national tax system that draws higher per-capita tax payments from citizens of richer states than from citizens of poorer states will automatically decrease inequalities among the states.

In spending policy, the federal government should base direct outlays, particularly grants, on indicators of need, especially needs that are disproportionately higher in the poorer states and carry a large price tag. Highest on this list are means-tested federal programs such as AFDC, Medicaid, food stamps, low-income energy assis-tance, commodity distribution, and subsidized housing. Programs targeted at populations eligible for such programs will automatically redistribute income away from the more affluent states and toward the less affluent ones. Certain program characteristics, however, tend to reward the states that can best afford higher payment and service levels. Lower eligibility thresholds and more extensive services tend to undo the equalization that otherwise results from targeting need. Some indicators of need perform a redistributive function exceptionally well: disadvantaged students in elementary and secondary schools, numbers of low-income recipients seeking grants for higher education, and populations meeting a nationally uniform means test. Less appropriate and effective but still redistributive indicators of need include population, student counts, and counts of selected populations, such as the illiterate.

Federal aid allocations based on factors other than these will not necessarily produce the desired income redistribution. Examples include basing assistance on the presence or absence of military bases, national forests, leased grazing rights, mineral exploitation on public lands, miles of interstate highways, and the like.

Federal policy can also compensate for economic differences among the states by targeting the location of federal facilities and procurement and by adopting programs or policies that explicitly aim to stimulate the economic development of particular regions. The Tennessee Valley Authority of the 1940s, which stimulated economic development in Appalachia, was such a program. Insofar as such policies strengthen the economies of less developed states, they reduce state-to-state disparities and lessen the need for future redistributive actions.

Nothing in the federal policy prescriptions described above needs to increase costs. State and local officials, of course, prefer policies that increase aid for some (or all) while not cutting aid for any. But the emphasis on federal redistributive assistance could be accommodated within a mildly increasing, stable, or even declining federal aid environment.

Federal action (or inaction) on the regulatory front, such as grant conditions, also affects state-local relations, whether federal dollars rise, fall, or remain the same. The federal government provides some programs directly to substate units, such as school districts and cities, if needs within the jurisdiction justify it. As we have seen, there has been a tendency to reduce the number of these federal-local direct assistance efforts in recent years. Examples of direct assistance include impact aid for education, CDBG, and UDAG. Other programs target local areas, but some aspect of the state's situation affects overall allocations to communities within the state. Statewide indicators of need determined total state allocations under GRS in the past, and they still determine federal highway fund totals today. Similar criteria affect fund allocation for small city demonstration activities in CDBG. When block grants to the states consolidate many previously separate smaller programs, for example, in elementary and secondary education, the states may exert more influence on how funds are divided than do local communities.

It is not easy to resolve the question of whether the federal government should continue to reduce its direct links with cities and other local governments. On one hand, many local officials—perhaps most—feel that they will receive better treatment from direct federal allocations than if allocations are influenced by state policy. On the other hand, many state officials might be more likely to address areas targeted by federal programs if there were no federal-local pipelines touted as solving those problems.

Many state and local officials resist federal mandates as unnecessary intrusions on their flexibility to respond to local conditions. In addition, unfunded federal mandates drive up state and local costs with no real accountability to taxpayers at any level of government. States find it difficult to avoid passing on unfunded mandates to localities. For example, in social services, the states must incorporate federal mandates in their instructions to local governments administering these programs in order to remain in compliance with the federal rules.

We should not leave the subject of federal influence on the relationship between states and localities without noting that subfederal units often emulate federal approaches to problems. For example, soon after the federal Department of Transportation was created, most states also formed departments of transportation out of smaller highway, bridge, road-crossing, airport, and other narrow-function agencies. More recently, many states created clones of the federal approach to housing (Stegman and Holden 1987).

Guidelines for State-Local Relations

State tax policies, like federal ones, tend to equalize resources among local areas to the extent that revenues are spent for programs providing general statewide benefits. This statememt is true even if the bulwarks of the state tax system are sales taxes and flat rate income taxes. Even though a sales tax may in itself be regressive, taking a greater proportion of the income of a poor family than a wealthy one, the sales tax still raises more per capita from rich communities than from poor ones. The more progressive the state tax system and the larger the proportion of state-local tax revenue provided by the state, the larger the redistributive impact of state tax policy.

Structuring user charges presents a particular problem for state and local policymakers. For example, states typically finance high-way construction and maintenance by the gas tax, which is a user charge in which revenues rise with the intensity of gas consumption and thus of highway use. When state taxes fund this service entirely, as in Delaware, or states cover a sufficient share of local road costs through revenue sharing, the user charge roughly pays for the function. But where the state sharing is inadequate to cover local costs *and* no option exists to levy additional user charges at the local level, localities can make up the gap only by dipping into local general funds, typically local property taxes. Thus too low a level of state sharing for one function can distort the entire structure of local tax systems.

The variation in need among local jurisdictions is typically much greater than among states. State and federal funding of the major income-tested programs such as Medicaid and AFDC compensates for some of this variation. However, some states require local cost sharing in these programs, and many require local contributions to general assistance. Caseloads for these programs tend to be concentrated in central cities and poor rural areas, with few cases in suburban communities. State assumption of these costs is particularly helpful in overcoming imbalances of needs among communities within a state.

There are also massive mismatches between needs and resources among school districts. Often the new residential suburb feels this mismatch most severely because of limited commercial and industrial property and a proliferation of new homes occupied by young families with school-age children. Such districts may require new home construction even while a neighboring district may have excess classroom capacity. State foundation programs work reasonably well to handle disparities in school operating costs, particularly if the level of assets is reasonably high in relation to statewide average spending. States may need an equivalent revenue structure to deal with school construction, particularly when state policies, such as limits on local debt as a percentage of property valuation, limit the ability of localities to raise taxes to provide for their own needs. State loan programs are the most appropriate means for dealing with indebtedness limits and temporary imbalances of classroom capacity and needs. Grant programs for construction, the equivalent of those covering operating costs, are appropriate for permanent imbalances of need and local tax capacity.

Substantial mismatches between needs and resources also occur among a state's counties, towns, townships, cities, and villages. An extreme form of mismatching occurs when one jurisdiction, in fact, provides services to nontaxable residents and former residents of other jurisdictions. For example, central cities may provide uncompensated services to commuters, such as arts performances or mass transit. These types of situations can be handled by changes in local taxing authority and the scope of governments providing services— for example, the city and suburbs can share regional mass transit system costs. Imbalances of needs and resources also occur when certain service-consuming classes of people, such as the homeless, congregate in central cities. In this case, the state may provide need-targeted aid programs or assume some program responsibilities.

We can apply the same cautions for structuring state mandates to localities as we did for federal-state mandates. Generally, mandates that require increased local funding should be funded by the level of government creating the mandate.

One possible exception to this rule lies in the many state prescriptions for the processes of local government: how personnel systems, accounting, and auditing shall be set up; how the local decision-making bodies shall be organized; whether meetings are open; and which officials must be elected. A strong case can be made for home rule in all these matters in many states. However, states with large numbers of local governments that cannot reasonably afford full-time public servants in central control and financial administrative capacities may find it essential to impose statewide standards.

Structuring Local Tax Policies

One of the knottier problems of state-local relations concerns local taxing authority. States and local governments must make changes in their traditional tax arrangements to bring about better alignments between resources and responsibilities in an era of devolution. For example, states often need to give more taxing authority to local governments, and conversely, local governments must find the political will to levy higher taxes. But vexing questions remain. To what extent should states relax their caps on property tax rates and other local taxes? How much can state-level actions create equity within a state?

Although the subject is controversial, a consensus probably exists on certain points:

□ No amount of local taxing authority will provide a tax base for a jurisdiction that has inadequate property, sales, and income on which to base taxes reasonably competitive with its neighbors. More logical solutions include state assumption of functions, consolidation, tax-base sharing, regional special districts, and state aid.

□ To reduce administrative costs to the collecting governments and thus reduce the total tax bill, revenue collections that piggyback on a state tax base are much preferred over local taxes applied to a different base. This principle may not apply, however, in a few states with sales taxes that differ in their base from the state tax and among municipalities with income taxes based on something other than taxable income used for a state tax. Normally, piggyback taxes should be administered by states, with funds remitted to local communities.

□ Major disparities among communities in local tax rates typically indicate a problem that no amount of local tax flexibility will readily solve.

Many of the improvements to be made in state-local relations do not necessarily result in major changes in state spending. Examples of inexpensive state policies include:

□ To promote efficiency, states should practice neutrality toward the way in which local governments select service providers. This suggestion includes open doors for contracting with private suppliers, contracting with other local governments, and cooperating with other governments collectively to provide services.

□ States should practice neutrality toward the size of governments. State policies that reward smallness or largeness per se should be reexamined.

□ State policies should not prevent local governments (or consortia of local governments) from offering different service levels among and within jurisdictions. For example, a single regional landfill can provide a central solid waste disposal function, with participating jurisdictions exercising freedom of choice on the subject of frequency of collection. Another example is to subdivide the responsibility for decisionmaking among sub-units within a municipality or school district.

References

Advisory Commission on Intergovernmental Relations (ACIR). 1988. *Intergovernmental Perspective* 14(1):13. Federalism in 1986–87: Signals of a New Era. Robert Gleason.

ACIR. 1986. *Devolving Federal Program Responsibilities and Revenue Sources to State and Local Governments*. Washington, D.C.: ACIR.

Barfield, Claude E. 1981. *Rethinking Federalism: Block Grants and Federal, State, and Local Responsibilities*. Washington, D.C.: American Enterprise Institute for Public Policy Research.

Bowman, Ann O'M., and Richard C. Kearney. 1986. *The Resurgence of the States*. Englewood Cliffs, N.J.: Prentice–Hall.

Committee for Economic Development (CED). 1986. *Leadership for Dynamic State Economies*. Washington, D.C.: CED.

Loomis, Louis Ropes. 1943. Aristotle: On Man in the Universe. In *Politics*, bk. 4. Roslyn, N.Y.: Walter J. Black.

Nathan, Richard P., Fred C. Doolittle, and Associates. 1987. *Reagan and the States*. Princeton, N.J.: Princeton University Press.

Nation's Cities Weekly 11(9) February 29, 1988. Housing, CDBG, UDAG Again Put in Jeopardy. Marvin McGraw.

Reagan, Ronald. 1981. Inaugural Address. 20 January 1981. Washington, D.C.: Government Printing Office.

Stegman, Michael A., and J. David Holden. 1987. *Nonfederal Housing Programs*. Washington, D.C.: Urban Land Institute.

Chapter Two

FEDERALISM AND STATE-LOCAL RELATIONS

Stephen B. Farber

Changes in American federalism during the Reagan presidency were dramatic rather than apocalyptic. Although the president's efforts to shift power and responsibility away from Washington had a number of important effects, they were not as successful as proponents hoped and opponents feared. Therefore it is no simple matter for those concerned with establishing appropriate state-local relations to answer the questions: where do we stand and where do we go from here?

To address these questions, this chapter first reviews the fate of President Reagan's federalism initiatives from the perspective of state-local relations, identifying what happened to major proposals—which were implemented and which were limited or rejected by opposing forces. It then sums up the current status of the federalism debate. With this state-federal analysis as background, the next section identifies major points of conflict between states and localities today and explores the views of various national organizations concerning these issues. The last section reviews several recently proposed reform agendas for state-local relations.

THE OUTCOME OF REAGAN FEDERALISM INITIATIVES

All the major federalism initiatives of the Reagan administration raised issues central to state-local relations: the block grants launched in 1981, the State of the Union swap-and-turnback plan of 1982, the continuing program of regulatory relief, and the federalism executive order of 1987. Some local officials felt a fundamental concern that Reagan's federalism, with its emphasis on devolution and increased state authority, would terminate the federal-local relationship that they have nurtured in recent decades and place them, without recourse, at the mercy of indifferent state legislatures and rigid state bureaucracies.

Block Grants

In his first term, President Reagan secured passage of 11 block grants, which involved seven functional areas and accounted for about 15 percent of fiscal year 1984 grants-in-aid. During the Johnson administration, two block grants had been enacted (the Partnership for Health Act in 1967 and the Omnibus Crime Control and Safe Streets Act in 1968). President Nixon had added three more (the Comprehensive Employment and Training Act [CETA], the Housing and Community Development Act, and Title XX of the Social Security Act in 1974), in addition to General Revenue Sharing (GRS) in 1972 (Williamson n.d.). A number of the Reagan block grants were relatively small, permitted only limited flexibility, or were merely revised versions of previously enacted block grants. Nonetheless, they represented a significant shift in the direction and philosophy of federal assistance: not only did the number of consolidated programs increase, but Reagan's consolidations gave more control to the states than did earlier block grants. The original CETA legislation, for example, bypassed the states (except for balance-of-state programs) through a system of prime sponsors who were responsive to local officials. Reagan's Job Training Partnership Act of 1982 (JTPA) replaced CETA with a program that was oriented far more to both the private sector and the states.

In 1981, Reagan proposed that 85 categorical programs costing $16.5 billion be consolidated into seven block grants. Congress ultimately consolidated 54 programs into nine blocks with budget authority of $7.2 billion and with numerous restrictions on flexibility. Congress reduced funding by an average of 12 percent, far less than the 25 percent the president requested (Nathan, Doolittle, and Associates 1987, p. 57).

From the standpoint of state-local relations, most of the 1981 block grants did not represent cataclysmic change. States generally gained greater discretion in the allocation of funds, but they were already playing the central role in programs covered by six of the block grants: Alcohol, Drug Abuse and Mental Health; Preventive Health and Health Services; Maternal and Child Health Services; Primary Health Care; Social Services; and Low Income Energy Assistance. The Elementary and Secondary Education block grant generally preserved previous funding arrangements, although it gave states greater authority to allocate funds among local districts. The Community Services block grant made states, instead of the Community Services Administration, the funding agent for local community action agencies, but it also limited state flexibility.

A major battleground in state-local relations was the Community Development Block Grant (CDBG). Many local officials viewed the proposal to allocate 30 percent of the funds to the states for distribution to small cities as the first step toward elimination of direct federal-local funding of the entitlement jurisdictions (those with populations of more than 50,000). Both the U.S. Conference of Mayors and the National League of Cities were opposed institutionally to the small-city CDBG proposal and sharply questioned the states' capacity to take over the small-city programs from the Department of Housing and Urban Development (HUD) area offices. The administration countered by winning the qualified support of a small number of Republican mayors and of the National Association of Counties and the National Association of Towns and Townships.

The new small-city CDBG and the eight other 1981 block grants were enacted as part of the Omnibus Budget Reconciliation Act (OBRA) devised by David Stockman, Director of the Office of Management and Budget (OMB). But for this bold strategic decision to package all the massive program and budget changes together for an up-or-down vote, many individual elements of OBRA might well have been defeated. It is certainly arguable, for example, that on their own, the block grants could not have withstood the unremitting attacks of the iron triangles—bureaucrats in federal agencies, Congressional authorizing committees, and interest groups. (In a farewell speech on domestic policy, Reagan redefined iron triangle, substituting the press for executive branch bureaucrats as part of his attack on the "Washington colony.") Although the president was at the height of his power in 1981, it may well be that his block grants, already weakened in negotiations with Congress, survived mainly because of the anomalous OBRA package, which passed the House of Representatives by just six votes.

Congress adopted two additional block grants in 1982: the JTPA and a section of the Surface Transportation Assistance Act, which Reagan signed in early 1983. But Congress rejected his proposal to consolidate another 46 categoricals into seven new block grants and to expand three existing blocks. JTPA, as noted, brought about significant change from the perspective of state-local relations because it vested far greater authority in the states than did past employment programs. Local officials, finding scant political support for retention of CETA, decided not to oppose JTPA flatly, but to make the best possible deal for themselves in the new legislation and then to implement it to their best advantage.

In 1983, following the demise of his swap-and-turnback initiative in 1982, the president proposed four mega-block grants of the kind advocated by Republican leaders such as Senator Pete Domenici (R-N.M.), then chairman of the Senate Budget Committee. The 1983 proposals provided for consolidation of 34 programs worth $21 billion: a State Block Grant, worth $11 billion, combining 22 health, social services, education, and community development programs; a Local Block Grant, worth $7 billion, combining GRS and the entitlement portion of CDBG; a Transportation Block Grant, worth $2 billion, combining six programs; and a Rural Housing Block Grant, worth $850 million, combining four programs. But Congress, preoccupied with budget deficits and other battles, declined even to hold hearings on the mega-blocks. Subsequent proposals, such as a Science and Education Block Grant in 1985, also received little or no consideration from Congress.

Ultimately, then, the Reagan block grants altered state-local relations considerably less than some local officials had predicted or feared. The state-oriented changes in CDBG and JTPA clearly shifted significant power to the states. It is also clear that the education, community services, and other block grants increased state authority. But the efforts of local officials and interest groups to limit the increase in state discretion had a significant impact, not just on Congress, but on the administration as well. The administration's proposal for a Local Block Grant in 1983, which would have bypassed states and secured the direct federal-local link for GRS and CDBG entitlement funds, indicates the influence of local officials.

The 1981 block grants reflected the Reagan administration's commitment to both fiscal retrenchment and state-oriented decentralization. But as Nathan, Doolittle, and Associates (1987, p. 86) observe, major cutbacks in services were in fact forestalled by several factors: carryover funds, restored federal funding in 1983, federal and state fund shifts from other programs, and state and local replacement funding. Similarly, both the legislative process and the practical implementation of the new block grants softened the powerful state bias of the original Reagan block grant proposals.

The 1982 Federalism Initiative

Reagan's federalism initiative was the centerpiece of his 1982 State of the Union address. In a "single bold stroke," he proposed to reorder intergovernmental relations through a $57 billion program that would return programs and revenue sources to states and localities over an eight-year transition period. More than 40 education, transportation, community development, and social services programs would be turned back and financed initially by a $28 billion trust fund created from excise taxes and the windfall profits tax. In addition, in a swap, the federal government would pay for Medicaid while the states would assume the costs of food stamps and Aid to Families with Dependent Children (AFDC).

The federalism initiative proved too sweeping for the political process of 1982, or perhaps any year, to absorb. Several factors contributed to its demise. On income security, the gap between the president and the governors on the proper locus of responsibility for AFDC simply could not be bridged, and the administration was unable to produce a plan for federalizing Medicaid. In addition, the scope and complexity of the trust fund and turnback proposals raised a host of technical and financial questions. Finally, the increasingly severe recession, a second round of proposed OMB budget cuts, and the 1982 elections created an inhospitable economic and political climate for the sweeping federalism initiative (Farber 1983, pp. 36–38).

State-local relations also played a role. White House officials, alerted by the block grant experience of 1981, attempted to reassure local officials that the new plan would ensure pass-through of federal funds to localities and provide other safeguards. But many local officials saw the plan as the beginning of the end of the federal-local relationship. Seattle Mayor Charles Royer argued that the plan was based on the totally erroneous notion that all states had the competence of the California that Reagan knew as governor. As it turned out, local officials did not have to mobilize to defeat the proposal because many other determined foes quickly appeared and the plan found virtually no friends once the going got tough.

Regulatory Relief

The administration's efforts to ease federal regulations began on Reagan's second day in office with the creation of the Task Force on Regulatory Relief chaired by Vice President Bush. Executive Order 12291, signed within a month, set forth the standards for the new regulatory order: demonstrated need, benefits exceeding costs, and selection of the most cost-effective solution and most responsive unit of government (Williamson n.d.).

Of the initial 119 regulatory reviews reported on in August 1982, 24 directly involved states and localities. The administration made it a top priority to provide greatly simplified regulations to implement the new block grants. The president enjoyed making announcements, such as how 318 pages of Health and Human Services regulations for several categorical programs had been reduced to only 6 pages for the block grant that consolidated them.

But more substantive changes were also in the works. The administration rescinded proposed regulations for bilingual education and school dress codes. New rules provided greater flexibility in fields ranging from accounting requirements for the school lunch program to eligibility determinations in health care. In transportation, the Federal Highway Administration relaxed its reporting requirements, and—in a far more controversial area—the Department of Transportation eased the Carter administration's stiff requirements that localities modify their public transit systems to accommodate the handicapped fully. Similar changes were ordered in regulations administered by HUD, the Environmental Protection Agency (EPA), and other agencies. Executive Order 12372, signed in July 1982, attempted to give greater weight to state and local priorities in the administration of federal programs and to reduce the role of federally mandated state plans and planning agencies. Simultaneously, OMB rescinded its Circular A-95, which had provided for an intergovernmental grant review process (Williamson n.d.).

These changes were generally consistent with the long-term complaints of many state and local officials concerning burdensome federal regulations. On some issues, such as the public transit regulations for the handicapped, state and local officials had vigorously argued their opposition to the Carter administration's approach. The National Governors' Association (NGA) had worked with the Carter administration to simplify grant requirements. NGA produced reports with titles such as *Federal Roadblocks to Efficient State Government*, based on state surveys and work with the White House Office of Intergovernmental Affairs, and a "Green Book" on regulatory reform issues, requested by OMB Director James McIntyre. As evidence that concern with federal regulation continued, New Hampshire Governor John Sununu revived these efforts and made them his top priority when he became NGA chairman in August 1987.

But the Reagan administration's regulatory relief efforts also had their limits. They left the system of congressionally mandated crosscutting requirements for individual federal grants largely intact, and they did not address many of the federal mandates on states and localities. At the same time, the administration became intrusive in areas it deemed important. In the *Baby Doe* case, for example, it attempted to regulate state and parental rights concerning life-support systems. And despite the administration's strong philosophical bias against preempting state or local policies, other priorities evidently weighed more heavily in some of its decisions, especially on such matters as a national minimum state drinking age of 21, national standards for product liability, and the value of overriding locally designed affirmative action plans.

From the perspective of state-local relations, the administration's regulatory relief initiative did not have the divisive force of its federalism initiative. Although the executive orders clearly reflected the administration's state-oriented approach to decentralization, they were implemented in a manner responsive to some long-held concerns of localities.

The Executive Order of 1987

In November 1986, the Domestic Policy Council's Working Group on Federalism, chaired by Assistant Attorney General Charles Cooper, released its report, *The Status of Federalism in America*. Six years into the Reagan administration, the report railed against "an expansive, intrusive, and virtually omnipotent national government." It called for new restraints on Congress, and perhaps a constitutional amendment, to restore state authority. The report took particular umbrage—as had many state and local officials—at the Supreme Court's 1985 decision in *Garcia v. San Antonio Metropolitan Transit Authority*, which upheld broad congressional authority to regulate the wages and working conditions of state and local employees.

The Status of Federalism clearly reflects the philosophy of Attorney General Edwin Meese and other top administration officials— and also their frustration in having secured so few substantial changes during their years of greatest influence. The report's discussion of self-imposed congressional restraints and constitutional amendments was theoretical. But its proposals for executive branch restraint were put into practice through Executive Order 12612, which was signed on October 26, 1987. The order requires federal agencies to observe strictly the constitutional principles of federalism, to accord states maximum flexibility in administering federal programs, and to void or minimize preemption of state policies. Agency proposals sent to OMB for review are supposed to contain federalism assessments certifying compliance with the executive order.

From the perspective of state-local relations, the definition of states in the executive order is of particular interest. "States," the order says, "refers to state governments, including units of local government and other political subdivisions established by states." Here, in the view of some local officials, was the essence—and the fundamental problem—of Reagan federalism: it was so completely oriented to states that local governments had no independent identity. Indeed, at the beginning of the Reagan administration, a domestic adviser to the new president told a group of mayors: "It's our view that cities are not mentioned in the Constitution" (Groups 1987). (Supreme Court Justice William J. Brennan, Jr., made much the same observation in *Community Communications v. City of Boulder.*)

Other Federalism Initiatives

A variety of approaches to federalism were advanced during the Reagan years. Local officials, for example, called for a federalism that retained direct federal-local links, especially those developed during and since the Johnson administration. State officials argued that the federal government must take the primary role in income security programs, and they expressed a willingness to take greater responsibility for other grants-in-aid in exchange. These state proposals parallel those of the Advisory Commission on Intergovernmental Relations (ACIR), which in the late 1970s published extensive analyses of the "overload" in the federal system and the need to "decongest" it.

The December 1985 report of the Committee on Federalism and National Purpose, chaired by Senator Daniel Evans (R-Wash.) and Governor Charles Robb (D-Va.), took the same general approach. Formed after the demise of Reagan's swap-and-turnback initiative of 1982, the committee attempted to find a middle ground for reform on which liberals and conservatives could agree. The Evans-Robb report called for a revenue-neutral realignment of responsibilities, with federal primacy in AFDC and Medicaid and state primacy in most community development, local infrastructure, and social services programs. To ease fiscal disparities, it proposed fiscal capacity grants for the poorest states as well as targeted local revenue sharing. To implement the report's recommendations, Senator Evans introduced a sweeping legislative proposal, the Federalism Act of 1986, and a successor bill in 1987.

The Evans-Robb report drew predictably mixed reviews. Brookings Institution scholar Paul Peterson and his colleagues (Peterson, Rabe, and Wong 1987) wrote that the proposals "constitute the most thoughtful, coherent reform of the federal system since the emergence of the modern system of federal grants." State officials found it consistent with their long-held views on federalism; indeed, in 1986, the National Association of State Budget Officers arrived at similar conclusions after a two-year study. But NGA, while sympathetic, sensed little or no support in the administration or Congress for the plan and opted instead to focus on initiatives in education, welfare reform (i.e., work-welfare, which the Evans-Robb report also endorsed), and regulatory reform. The administration, for its part, found the ideas on devolution to its liking but saw no merit in the proposed shift to primary federal responsibility for AFDC. Congress was preoccupied with deficit reduction politics, and although the report said that its approach would ease the deficit problem, this argument gained few adherents.

The strongest reaction to the report and legislation came from local officials and lobbyists. The National League of Cities called the bill a "new threat to the federal-local partnership" that would have "devastating" effects on "every remaining city and town program." San Antonio Mayor Henry Cisneros, the league's thoughtful president, perceived "a very cynical plot to get the federal government out of the domestic business, other than welfare, completely, and do it at the expense of the cities, with the states gladly being part of this bargain." The National Neighborhood Coalition saw a divide- and-conquer strategy designed to "pit housing and community development advocates against health and welfare advocates, as both fight over the shrinking federal pie" (Peirce 1987). A former president of the National Association of Counties (Horsley 1986, p. 29), arguing that the plan treated states well and localities poorly, testified that it reminded him of a country western song: "She got the gold mine, and I got the shaft."

These criticisms were reminiscent of the war of words over the 1982 Reagan swap-and-turnback initiative. Senator Evans responded that the proposed reforms were sensible, badly needed, and the best way to address a range of serious problems. Governor Robb argued that critics were out of touch with improvements in state capacity and performance and that advocacy groups have as substantial influence on the political process in state capitals as in Washington. Congressman Tom Downey (D-N.Y.), lead House sponsor of the Evans bill, said that the plan offered far more protection to local interests than is afforded by a congressional budget process that is strangling grant programs year by year. None of these responses, however, proved convincing to the plan's critics.

FEDERALISM AND STATE-LOCAL RELATIONS TODAY

From the perspective of state-local relations, the important point about sweeping proposals to reform the federal system—from Reagan's swap-and-turnback initiative to Evans-Robb—is that they are on hold. American federalism is not given to apocalyptic change, especially when that change is not additive but instead forces hard trade-offs with apparent losers as well as winners. This fact accounts for much of the strong opposition of national *organizations* of local officials, and many individual officials, to the omnibus plans.

As for state officials, it should be acknowledged that it is one thing to rail against the federal colossus and quite another to sign on to genuine change. During the 1982 federalism negotiations, many governors made it clear that they would prefer to deal with the devil they knew, particularly because David Stockman's budget-cutting drive seemed to animate much of the administration's plan. A few governors, such as Maryland's Harry Hughes, wondered aloud what was so wrong with the current system. As California Governor Jerry Brown complained at the NGA winter meeting in 1982: "[The president] has got a lot of people talking about federalism who don't want to be talking about federalism. Look at me; I've been talking about it for three days" (Williamson n.d.).

Probably the only real opportunity for sweeping federalism reform in the Reagan years occurred in 1981, when the president was at the height of his power. But 1981 was the year for massive budget and tax changes. Beyond the block grants, there was apparently no room on the agenda for federalism. Even if the plan developed in 1982— or another less complex plan that could engender broader support— had been ready to go in 1981, it might well have been deferred for strategic reasons in favor of the budget and tax cuts. And even if a plan like the 1982 initiative had actually been included and rammed through the budget reconciliation process, it probably would not have survived over time. American federalism is remarkably resilient, but it cannot sustain an overhaul achieved simply through legislative fiat or legerdemain.

The 1981 budget and tax cuts, however, helped produce a different kind of change in federalism: incremental change that, as it happens, has often been consistent with the thrust of the omnibus plans. This de facto, or fend-for-yourself federalism, as Shannon (1987) calls it, has manifested itself in various ways. In economic development, federal funding has sharply declined, although the authorizing legislation remains defiantly on the books, while state programs have sharply increased. A similar shift has occurred in elementary and secondary education and also in water resources and sewage treatment. Some (but not all) state officials are pressing for a turnback of local road responsibilities and the trust fund revenue sources needed to finance them. Meanwhile, the basic state-federal income security programs—AFDC and Medicaid as well as food stamps and SSI—have not suffered the deep cuts inflicted on many grant programs. In fact, the income security programs were exempted from mandatory cuts under the Gramm-Rudman deficit reduction law. Moreover, the work-welfare law passed in 1988 made coverage for two-parent families mandatory (although incentives for higher benefits in low-benefit states, included in the House version of the bill, were dropped). In the Medicaid program, coverage for pregnant women and infants has been expanded.

Regulatory reform generally has not troubled the waters of state-local relations. The administration's intergovernmental regulatory relief efforts, as well as those of the governors, had a substantial state (rather than local) orientation, but not a divisive one. The administration's efforts in economic deregulation proceeded on a separate track. Indeed, in fields ranging from pesticides to product liability and from cable television to corporate takeovers, the business community sought the administration's support for federal preemption. These issues, however, have generally found state and local interests in relative harmony.

Conflicting Perspectives of States and Localities

The musical *Oklahoma*, as one expert observes, has a song about how farmers and ranchers will one day be friends. The same is not necessarily true, he says, about state and local officials. They can and frequently do get along quite well, both at home and in Washington. But a host of structural and fiscal factors often create tension between them.

Beyond these factors are basic issues of politics and control. In politics, competition among state and local officials for credit, advantage, and electoral support is not the exception but the rule. As for control, local elected officials, who by definition are neither wallflowers nor pushovers, understandably bridle at the numerous points of leverage and approval that state officials possess.

One graphic example of state-local struggle over control is in progress in Framingham, Massachusetts. The state's strong economy has made possible large increases in local aid, and Governor Michael Dukakis has given high priority to the needs of cities and towns. But Framingham officials accuse the state of arrogance and bullying on several issues. The state, seeking expansion room to help save the General Motors plant in 1985, seized the land by eminent domain after local officials balked. Local officials had wanted to place a snow dump and parking garage there. Over local objections, the state also shut down an incinerator that failed to meet emission standards, resulting in higher rubbish disposal costs. A local plan to turn an 88-acre hospital site into a geriatric center became the subject for another battle. The state insisted that to receive state funds, the plan had to include at least 31 units of affordable housing. Still another fight is expected over the intention of Framingham State College to expand its campus on open estate property despite the opposition of the abutting neighborhood. As one local official sees it, "The state complains about the federal government imposing its will, and then it turns around and acts the same way" (Framingham 1987).

Views of National Organizations on State-Local Relations

Washington is the home of most national organizations of state and local officials—the so-called Big Seven and their scores of affiliates. Included in the Big Seven are the National Governors' Association (NGA), National League of Cities (NLC), National Association of Counties (NACo), Council of State Governments, National Conference of State Legislatures (NCSL), U.S. Conference of Mayors (USCM), and International City Management Association.

These organizations maintain good relations but are frequently at odds. They work together effectively in creating institutions such as the State and Local Legal Center (although the organizations of attorneys general and local attorneys have both had differences with the Center). They also join forces on issues of common concern, such as intrusive federal mandates or restrictions on tax-exempt bonding authority (although here too strategic differences often emerge). They unite forcefully against particularly serious threats. For example, in response to the Treasury's massive 1985 report on the fiscal aspects of federalism, *Federal-State-Local Fiscal Relations*, they drafted a strong rebuttal report sharply contesting Treasury's rosy assessment of the state-local fiscal outlook and its negative view toward the deductibility of state and local taxes, tax-exempt bonds, and revenue sharing.

Sometimes their unity is less secure. On welfare reform, for example, all of them expressed support for congressional work-welfare legislation, but the municipal organizations were leery of having the cost paid, directly or indirectly, by cuts in city programs. On the taxation of mail order sales, the state and local organizations strongly support pending legislation that would provide new revenues, but until mid-1988, they remained deeply divided on how to allocate the revenues between states and localities.

The organizations are unmistakably at odds, however, when their fundamental interests are threatened. The national organizations of local elected officials, after all, were established to promote a direct federal-local link. They differ from one another, of course, in some important respects. NACo, for example, tends to be somewhat more conservative than the city groups and more supportive of the income security and social services programs that counties administer with states. But all the local organizations were happier in the Carter years, when local officials were an integral part of the administration's political strategy, than under Reagan, whose predilection for state authority was unmistakable.

NLC was particularly outspoken against the administration's federalism initiatives and budget policies. The league was vitriolic in its opposition to the 1981 proposal to have states administer the small-city portion of CDBG, even though one state municipal league openly expressed support for it. The league also precipitated a major cleavage among the Big Seven in 1980, when it announced its neutrality on renewal of the $2.3 billion state share of GRS. When the law was first passed in 1972 and extended in 1976, the groups jockeyed hard for advantage but ultimately remained united in their support, which greatly enhanced the bill's prospects. In 1980, NLC decided that given the strong opposition to the state share in the Carter administration and in Congress, the best way to protect the $4.6 billion local share, which in fact enjoyed almost universal support, was to abandon the state share. The league also hoped to recover a portion of the foregone state share in the form of an increase in the local share. This approach did not take account of the fiscal relationship between states and localities or the likelihood that the local share alone was unlikely to survive indefinitely. The local share, renewed in 1980 and again in 1983, faced growing pressure from deficit reduction efforts. In 1986, despite heroic local efforts and putative state support, the local share—like the state share in 1980—died.

One aspect of the revenue sharing battle of 1980 was particularly divisive in state-local relations. Given President Carter's personal animus toward the state share, his administration felt that he would support renewal only if it were conditioned on substantial reforms in state-local fiscal relations. To achieve these changes, the administration proposed to require each state to form a commission on local fiscal problems and to follow a detailed timetable and set of procedures, supervised by the Secretary of the Treasury, to address them. The draft plan was known as the Cooperative Federalism Act of 1980.

At the urging of NLC and USCM, the administration proposed that 9 of the 17 members of each federally prescribed state commission be chosen by "organizations representative of local governments." The governor and legislature were each to select four members, and of four public members, two were to be selected by the governor and two by the local members. The members, not the governor, would select the chair. Early drafts of the plan implied that if the governor and legislature failed to implement whatever the commission proposed, they might jeopardize continued payments of the state share.

Predictably, state officials found this draft plan intrusive and insulting—the reductio ad absurdum of the blame-the-states theory of federalism. Meanwhile, the national organizations of local officials delighted in their political clout with the Carter administration.

The plan quickly became moot, however, when nervous financial markets forced the administration to submit a revised budget for fiscal year 1981 in March 1980. The revised budget contained numerous spending cuts, and because the state share had been the last item included in the original budget, it was the first item eliminated from the revision. The battle over the commissions was thus never fully joined. One year later, as the state-centered federalism of the Reagan administration became the new order of the day in Washington, notions such as the state federalism commissions were suddenly out of date.

WHERE DO WE GO FROM HERE?

Prospects for Changes in Federalism

For several reasons, sweeping change in the federal system, in the spirit of the Reagan swap-and-turnback initiative, seems unlikely in the foreseeable future—as unlikely as a return to the peak federal aid flows of a decade ago. One reason is that American federalism seems to absorb incremental change far more comfortably than bold strokes, particularly when the strokes involve the politics of subtraction. Moreover, as Peterson and Hall (1986, p. 9) have noted, American federalism is given less to a clean, logical division of service responsibilities and funding than to imprecise, result-oriented collaborative arrangements. It was the latter approach that characterized the response of state and local managers to the fiscal retrenchment of the early Reagan years.

Sweeping change also seems unlikely because most community development, local infrastructure, and social services programs that would be terminated in a bold-stroke approach have proven to be hardy perennials, surviving year after year of determined efforts to uproot them. Even with Gramm-Rudman pressures in 1987, the administration's recurring effort to kill 40-odd categorical chestnuts worth about $3 billion was for naught. Although some observers have predicted the eventual demise through slow starvation of such programs, their iron triangle support makes it appear equally likely that they will outlast their opponents one way or another. The unexpected apparent termination of the Urban Development Action Grant program in 1988 appears to be more the exception than the rule.

No candidate for president in 1988 proposed the sweeping kind of federalism agenda that Reagan advanced vigorously as early as 1976. Among the Democratic candidates, only Bruce Babbitt, who withdrew from the race in February, had advocated the Evans-Robb philosophy. Democratic nominee Michael Dukakis, a strong believer in public-private partnerships, would have built on the Massachusetts partnership experience in such fields as housing, education, and especially economic development. One of his few explicit proposals for increased spending called for a $500 million regional development fund to supplement existing federal programs. Republican candidate Bob Dole's passion for deficit reduction seemed to suggest reduced funds, rather than no funds, for categorical programs. Republican nominee George Bush urged greater attention to education and the environment. He pledged in general terms to forge a new working relationship between the federal government and the cities, and the Republican platform contained language declaring that "urban America is center stage for our country's future."

To place city needs on the agenda of the presidential candidates, the NLC formed an Election '88 task force and invited all the candidates to its annual meeting in December 1987. The league's objective was to reforge a strong federal-local link. But only Jesse Jackson and Michael Dukakis bothered to appear at the league's meeting. Dukakis won the league's heart by averring that he "has had a love affair with cities as long as I can remember" and telling participants: "You should not be coming to Washington in 1989 hoping that a few crumbs will fall off the national table. You should be there as full partners in a national partnership for economic growth and economic opportunity in this country."

To drive home its central concern, the NLC, together with the national organizations of mayors, counties, and regional councils, issued a manifesto in May 1988 entitled "A Time to Restore the Federal-Local Partnership." NGA fired back: The "states must not be hampered in their ability to allocate precious resources among jurisdictions."

If sweeping change in federalism will not soon occur, what form will incremental change take? Conlan sees two quite different possible scenarios. One, a 1990s version of cooperative federalism, projects relative harmony and strength in the federal system based on a continuation of state and local dynamism and federal restraint. The other, cooptive federalism, projects serious problems for states and localities stemming from efforts by Congress, abetted by recent Supreme Court decisions, to impose ever more mandates without funding, to erect further obstacles to state and local tax and bonding authority and, in the words of Harvard Law School Professor Laurence Tribe, to "nibble away at state sovereignty, bit by bit" through the "tyranny of small decisions" (Conlan 1988, pp. 229–231).

Federalism in the Bush Administration

Although elements of both scenarios could well become visible during the Bush presidency, the administration seems disposed at its outset to embrace latter-day cooperative federalism: state centered and budget driven, as in the Reagan years, but like the new administration as a whole, less ideological and more pragmatic. Both philosophical and political imperatives support this view.

Bush set forth his philosophy of federalism in general terms in the fall 1987 issue of the *Cumberland Law Review*. In his article, he expressed support for devolution and restoring balance to the federal system, for maximum flexibility in federal regulations (he chaired the Reagan Task Force on Regulatory Relief), and for effective state-federal relations in such programs as Medicaid. He opposed extensive use of federal sanctions against states. On the other hand, he argued that there are some "legitimate areas of truly national concern" and cautioned that state regulation, while appropriate and desirable, should not interfere with national commerce (Shribman 1989, p. 21).

During the 1988 presidential campaign Bush's call for a kinder, gentler nation suggested a softening of social policy, but his pledge of no new taxes and his proposal for a flexible freeze in the budget implied real restraint in federal spending on intergovernmental programs. Bush's wish to be the education president would be carried out, it seemed, partly through small increases in programs like Head Start but chiefly through his bully pulpit to campaign—as he did at a White House conference just before taking office—for parental choice of public schools and other elements of the states' reform agenda. Bush's insistence that he is an environmentalist, his promise to address promptly such problems as acid rain and global warming, and his appointment of William Reilly to head EPA appeared to represent a major departure from the approach taken in the early Reagan years.

Bush made several general commitments to local officials during the campaign. He called for a presidential task force on urban affairs, increased support for community mental health centers and low-income housing, public-private partnerships to support single-room occupancy housing based on the Illinois model, and block grants to local authorities to fund homeless shelters under the McKinney Act. On economic development, his only specific commitment was to the urban enterprise zone legislation sought repeatedly by the Reagan administration but rejected consistently by Congress (Shribman 1989, pp. 21–22).

During the early primaries, in particular, Bush relied heavily on Republican governors, especially John Sununu of New Hampshire and Carroll Campbell of South Carolina, who helped save and secure his candidacy, and later James Thompson of Illinois. The close political ties between Bush and these and other Republican governors, such as convention keynoter Thomas Kean of New Jersey, suggest that governors will enjoy a favored position as the Bush administration begins. Moreover, it is clear that Bush is disposed to view states as powerful pillars, rather than the Peck's bad boys, of the federal system.

Bush strengthened these perceptions with the appointment of Sununu as White House Chief of Staff. Sununu's strong support for devolution and regulatory relief seems likely to be reflected in administration policies, although his interest in constitutional change—such as facilitating the states' capacity to amend the Constitution—seems likely to appear far lower, if at all, on the president's agenda. Bush's first meeting outside Washington after the election was with a bipartisan group of governors and governors-elect in Charlottesville, Virginia; he pledged to join forces with them on education, the environment, and other issues because "they, after all, are the ones on the cutting edge." Shortly thereafter, he met with Republican governors convening in Alabama. Although Bush selected only one governor to lead a cabinet department, former Pennsylvania Governor Dick Thornburgh, whom he retained as Attorney General, it was clear that both former and sitting governors, such as Lamar Alexander of Tennessee and George Deukmejian of California, might eventually play prominent roles in the new administration.

Although these political ties imply that the governors' views on federalism and domestic policy will receive a sympathetic hearing in the Bush administration, their views on budget policy, including cuts contained in Reagan's proposed fiscal year 1990 budget, are another matter entirely. In fact, as Bush struggles to redeem his campaign promises on fiscal policy, it seems possible that he might look to Republican governors for support just as Jimmy Carter looked to the Democrats in March 1980, when he decided to remove the state share of GRS from his fiscal year 1981 budget. Carter met with a group consisting of several big-city mayors and several governors—George Busbee of Georgia, Brendan Byrne of New Jersey, Bill Clinton of Arkansas, and Ella Grasso of Connecticut—to explain his decision and seek their support. Only Busbee and some of the mayors expressed reservations. Although NGA, then chaired by Otis Bowen of Indiana, had vigorously endorsed renewal of the state share, Byrne and Clinton told the Democratic party's Platform Committee in April 1980 that the states could do without GRS, proving an important lesson: political blood is thicker than institutional water. The Bush administration may give their Republican colleagues a chance to prove it again.

Local officials, for their part, were hopeful that Bush's designation of Jack Kemp (rather than a respected Republican mayor like William Hudnut of Indianapolis or George Voinovich of Cleveland) as HUD secretary would provide new energy and visibility, if not money, for HUD. Shortly before his appointment, Kemp urged that Bush pursue an antipoverty agenda for economic empowerment of the nation's poor and minorities. Such a course, he said, would have both political and practical benefits. Kemp, long an advocate of supply-side

economics and public-private partnerships, appears likely as secretary to press aggressively for adoption of a number of ideas on the
conservative antipoverty agenda, including enterprise zones, urban
homesteading, and tenant management and ownership of public
housing. He also seems likely to resist further draconian cuts in the
housing budget. But how these efforts can be reconciled with the
federal budget squeeze and how satisfied local officials will ultimately be with Kemp's enthusiasm and conservative agenda remains
to be seen.

With regard to block grants, the incoming Bush administration
appears likely to retain existing arrangements rather than accede to
criticisms made by the Coalition on Human Needs and other groups.
The coalition accuses states and localities of spreading block grant
dollars and services too thinly and neglecting pressing needs, com-
munity-based alternatives to public institutions, and representation
of beneficiaries on advisory boards.

Future Change in State-Local Relations

The states would find it difficult to relinquish the policy leadership
position, including the willingness to raise taxes, that the Reagan
years afforded—or required—of them. Whether or not you agree with
Reagan, says Governor Clinton, "he has made us important." "Our
time is now," asserts Governor Kean.

The critical question in state-local relations is: will the states'
enthusiasm for assuming a larger share of the state-federal burden
lead to a reenergizing of relations with their localities as well? Several
factors raise hopes for more positive and fruitful relations during the
remainder of the century. For one, the sharp decline in federal assistance, particularly the termination of revenue sharing in 1986, has
had a dramatic impact on many localities. Revenue sharing accounted on average for less than 3 percent of local budgets, but for
some hard-pressed jurisdictions, it represented far more: in Camden,
New Jersey, 11.2 percent; in Grey Eagle Village, Minnesota, 22.6
percent; and in McCreary County, Kentucky, 64.7 percent. As local
needs and revenue shortfalls become more pronounced, the imper-
ative of improved policies in state-local relations will become increasingly clear.

The national concern with economic competitiveness and its impact on education, job training, income support, and other state-local
systems will also drive the movement for better-ordered state-local
relations. Reforming these systems will be costly and will require

high standards of performance from both states and localities. A third factor is the improved fiscal and management capacities of the so-called altered states. Performance still varies widely among states and by field, and shortcomings are not hard to identify. But as ACIR and others have shown, in many areas states have demonstrated the capacity and the will to tackle the problems and opportunities created by Reagan federalism.

Views on the current state of state-local relations, of course, vary widely. Bowman and Kearney (1986, pp. 183–84) see "less adversarial" relations and "an evolving spirit of accommodation." They perceive both decentralizing trends (greater local authority and state reimbursement of mandates) and centralizing ones (greater state aid and assistance to urban areas). On the other hand, former Nevada Governor and Senator Paul Laxalt, after chairing President Reagan's Federalism Advisory Committee in 1981–82, said that he was stunned by the bitterness of local officials' complaints about their states.

Reform Agendas for State-Local Relations

Prescriptions for improved state-local relations are not hard to find. ACIR (1985), for example, has long recommended such measures as:

□ allowing localities to diversify revenue sources through local option taxes
□ avoiding unfunded state mandates on local governments
□ equalizing financial aid formulas to redress fiscal disparities
□ promoting consolidation of local jurisdictions and agreements among local jurisdictions to provide services jointly, and
□ providing for state assumption of welfare, court, and other costs.

Zimmerman (1983, p. 161), a strong advocate of greater local discretionary authority, has proposed a partnership approach to state-local relations that would involve:

□ constitutional prohibition or provision for a local veto of special legislation unless requested by the governing body of the concerned local units
□ constitutional devolution of all powers capable of devolution upon general purpose political subdivisions subject to preemption by general law
□ constitutional authorization for classified legislation provided there are no more than three classes of local governments and at least three political subdivisions in each class

□ constitutional requirement for the enactment by the state legislature of a code of restrictions upon local government powers
□ recodification of state laws clearly identifying powers totally or
partially preempted by the state legislature
□ partial or total state reimbursement of added costs associated with
state mandates
□ removal of constitutional debt, levy, and tax limits on local governments
□ creation of a state boundary commission
□ reservation to the state legislature of authority to establish areawide governments, and
□ state-established minimum levels of service provision in the most
important functional areas.

The NCSL Task Force on State-Local Relations (1987) undertook
the most serious and thorough national review of these issues in
recent years. (NGA gave top priority in 1974–75 to the question of
states' responsibilities to local governments and in the early 1980s
briefly had a standing Committee on State-Local Relations.) The task
force recommended that states should:

□ treat local governments as partners, not as another special interest
group, and local governments should abandon a go-it-alone attitude
□ create an organization devoted to state-local issues, such as a state
ACIR, and develop systems to monitor local fiscal developments
□ give localities more discretion in raising revenues, including sales
and income taxes
□ provide technical assistance to help local governments implement
user charges
□ make the property tax more acceptable by improving assessment
practices, adopting circuit breaker or other relief programs, and enacting truth in taxation provisions
□ loosen property tax limits
□ review mandates, eliminate or relax some of them, and in some
cases assume the cost of complying with them
□ sort out functions and assume major poverty-related costs from
local governments
□ develop new formulas for distributing state aid that target assistance to jurisdictions with the lowest fiscal capacity, and
□ provide other low-cost assistance, such as bond banks and insurance pools.

However sensible these NCSL proposals appear, they face two

obvious problems. First, the 50 state-local systems are enormously diverse: Hawaii has four local governments; Illinois has 6,643. The 83,000 substate units they embrace also exhibit great diversity. Second, it is difficult to assess specific state actions in terms of NCSL's reform agenda. Some state actions are fairly easy to categorize in this regard. For example, authorizations to fund local transportation projects through optional increases in the local sales tax (as in Arizona), transportation tax districts (as in Virginia), local gas taxes (13 states), or local impact fees on developers (half the states) appear generally positive. By contrast, Colorado's dumping of inmates on local jails without compensation and Texas's refusal to allow counties to regulate the impoverished *colonias* created by developers with minimal public services seem decidedly negative.

But the context and details of each of these state actions are unique, and they require careful review before definitive conclusions can be reached about their impact on state-local relations. For example, the Roemer revolution (led by Louisiana's new governor) has proposed to reduce state aid to localities sharply and thus to force the development of cheaper and presumably sounder local solutions. Some state actions that trample on local authority may serve other important public purposes—for example, Governor Kean's efforts to assert full state control over what he terms the corrupt and incompetent school system of Jersey City. The Roemer approach to state aid raises hard questions and may appear in other states faced with severe budget shortfalls. In late 1988, for example, New York Governor Mario Cuomo said that local governments expect too much from the state, which has lost the capacity to manage the three-fifths of the state budget devoted to local spending, and that localities would better control spending if they had expanded authority to raise their own resources. Local officials criticized Cuomo for attempting to transform the state deficit into a local deficit.

A recent report of New York's Commission on State-Local Relations (1987) clearly shows the importance of such definitional questions. Attempting to determine the principal sources of both cooperation and friction in state-local relations, the report found sharply divergent views not only between state and local officials but also among officials of different kinds of localities.

Such differences in perception are not surprising. Nor should tension and hostility in state-local relations be expected to vanish in a new era of good feeling or by some bold stroke. Improvement in state-local relations will come step by step, issue by issue, state by state. Proposals like those of the NCSL task force set useful benchmarks for this process.

Ultimately, state-local relations are likely to show truly dramatic improvement only when state and local officials come to believe that their constituencies face a common threat: a real or potential inability to compete economically with other regions or nations. This threat, if perceived as serious, may impel state and local officials to do more of what has too often eluded them: to subordinate their differences, view their universes as a single system, identify its deficiencies, and work as partners to confront them.

References

Advisory Committee on Intergovernmental Relations (ACIR). 1985. *The Question of State Government Capability*. Washington, D.C.: ACIR.

Bowman, Ann O'M., and Richard C. Kearney. 1986. *The Resurgence of the States*. Englewood Cliffs, N.J.: Prentice-Hall.

Commission on State-Local Relations. 1987. The 'State' of State–Local Relations. Nelson A. Rockefeller Institute of Government, Albany, 29 September.

Conlan, Timothy. 1988. *New Federalism*. Washington, D.C.: Brookings Institution.

Farber, Stephen B. 1983. The 1982 Federalism Negotiations: A View from the States. *Publius: The Journal of Federalism* (Spring): 36-38.

Framingham Feuds with State. 1987. *Boston Globe*, 20 November.

Groups to Press Candidates on Cities. 1987. *New York Times*, 14 December.

Horsley, John. 1986. *Hearing before the Subcommittee on Intergovernmental Relations of the Committee on Governmental Affairs, U.S. Senate*. 26 September.

Nathan, Richard P., Fred C. Doolittle, and Associates. 1987. *Reagan and the States*. Princeton, N. J.: Princeton University Press.

National Conference on Social Welfare (NCSW). 1985. *To Form a More Perfect Union*. Washington, D.C.: NCSW.

National Conference of State Legislatures, Task Force on State–Local Relations. 1987. Summary of Recommendations, 6 November.

Peirce, Neal R. 1987. Cities Attacking the Wrong Target. *Seattle Times*, 6 January.

Peterson, George E. and Carol W. Lewis, eds. 1986. *Reagan and the Cities*. Washington, D.C.: Urban Institute Press.

Peterson, Paul E., Barry G. Rabe, and Kenneth K. Wong. 1987. A Logical Reform Proposal for Federal Aid. *Seattle Times*, 1 January.

Shannon, John. 1987. The Return to Fend-for-Yourself Federalism: The Rea5 Mark. *Intergovernmental Perspective* (Summer–Fall).

Shribman, David. 1989. Among the Generalizations, Bush Gives a Few Signals to the States and Localities. *Governing* (January): 19–23.

U.S. Department of the Treasury, Office of State and Local Finance. 1985. *Federal-State-Local Fiscal Relations*. Washington, D.C.: Government Printing Office. p. xxvi–xxxi.

Williamson, Richard S. Forthcoming. *Federalism: Reagan's Efforts to Decentralize Government*. Lanham, Md.: University Press of America.

Zimmerman, Joseph F. 1983. *State-Local Relations: A Partnership Approach*. New York: Praeger Publishers.

Chapter Three

AN OVERVIEW OF THE STATE-LOCAL FISCAL LANDSCAPE

Jack A. Brizius

For the 50 state and more than 83,000 local governments in the United States, fiscal relations have always been diverse and complex. The complexity of these relations stems from the interaction of two fundamental facts about U.S. politics and constitutional structure:

☐ local governments are constitutionally creatures of the states, but
☐ political leaders at the state level must be responsive to political power within localities.

As Aronson and Hilley (1986) have observed, Justice John F. Dillon of the Iowa Supreme Court defined the constitutional position of states and localities more than a century ago:

Municipal corporations owe their origin to, and derive their powers and rights wholly from the legislature. It breathes into them the breath of life, without which they cannot exist. As it creates, so may it destroy. If it may destroy, it may abridge and control (p. 10).[1]

If Judge Dillon's characterization of state-local relations were the last word, state-local fiscal relations would be relatively simple. States would establish roles for local governments, make clear fiscal rules, and allocate functions and resources to local governments. Fortunately, however, political realities dictate that the fiscal relations of states and localities must be born of negotiation, usually on individual fiscal issues. As former House Speaker Tip O'Neill said, "All politics is local."

The current fiscal relations among states and localities, then, have evolved over many years of repeated negotiations on individual fiscal issues and in unique state political contexts. One may speculate, for example, that the reason why New York City pays a larger portion of Aid to Families with Dependent Children costs for its poor residents than Chicago is related to the historical political strength of governors, such as Rockefeller in New York, versus mayors, such as Daley in Illinois. School aid formulas are the product of repeated negotiations among local school officials, powerful teachers' unions (in some states), and state officials. The result of all these interactions is the system of state-local fiscal relations that exists today. This system may seem messy but, viewed as a whole, it is a system that can be understood and changed.

In setting the framework for this discussion of state-local fiscal roles and relations, one must constantly bear in mind the historical ebb and flow of relative political and fiscal strength among states and localities. These relations have not evolved on a national basis; their origins are rooted in the political traditions of each state. Even the number of local governments has been determined through a process of aggregating thousands of individual decisions made in the context of unique political environments in the states. Density of local governments also varies. Figure 3.1 illustrates the number of general purpose local governments per 10,000 population in each state.

Another barrier to generalization about state-local relations is not only the diversity in number and type of local governments but also their enormous variation in scale. In population and budget, for example, the city of New York and the county of Los Angeles are larger than most states. At the same time, the states of California and New York are more populous and wealthier than most nations.

Despite the diversity in the number and types of local governments, state-local fiscal relations do reveal national aggregate patterns, and state-local fiscal policies are influenced by national trends. State-local fiscal relations are markedly different today, for example, than they were before the property tax and spending limitation movement first gained national prominence in California. Patterns of state funding for schools have been buffeted by the conflicting pressures of property tax revolts and the national movement to seek equal educational opportunities for poor students.

Federal policies also affect state-local fiscal relations. By providing and then withdrawing large amounts of direct aid to local governments, for example, the federal government first undermined state influence on localities and then made local governments more dependent upon the fiscal largesse of the state capitols. The local addiction to federal programs, such as the Environmental Protection Agency's sewer and water grants or the Urban Mass Transportation Administration's urban mass transit grants, has created a demand for state funds as local governments seek help to ward off withdrawal

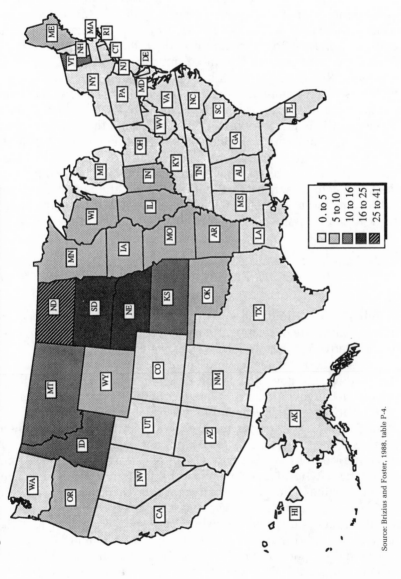

Figure 3.1 NUMBER OF GOVERNMENTS PER 10,000 POPULATION, 1987

Source: Brizius and Foster, 1988, table P-4.

pains from the federal government pull-out. As in the past, federal policies are changing state-local fiscal relations in direct, primary ways and as a result of the secondary effects of federal actions.

State-local fiscal policy, jolted by the devolution of federal responsibility for much of domestic policy, is likely to change significantly in the next decade. Moreover, economic changes, such as the shift to a more service-oriented economy, are interacting with the need for greater productivity in an increasingly competitive world economy. Resistance to taxes has been growing in a more conservative fiscal environment while demands for increased services seem not to be abating. Increased efficiency and effectiveness in delivering services will be necessary in both the public and the private sectors. Shifts in population across the state boundaries toward the South and West and the spreading of the population within large metropolitan regions are also changing the political and economic foundation of state-local fiscal relations. An examination of the evolution of broad patterns of state-local fiscal relations will help set the framework for a discussion of state-local fiscal relations in the future.

STATE-LOCAL FISCAL RELATIONS IN PERSPECTIVE

Two basic trends underlie the recent history of state-local fiscal relations nationally: a relative increase in state versus local revenues and a relative increase in local versus state spending.

Own-source revenues, composed primarily of taxes imposed by various levels of government, are now larger for state governments than for local governments. State governments raise more revenues than local governments do and they receive more federal aid.

As figure 3.2 shows, for most of this century local government receipts were larger than state government receipts, with the trend reversing around 1950. Since then, state government taxes have dominated the state-local revenue picture. By 1981, the ratio of state own-source revenues to local own-source revenues had stabilized at about 3:2. Local government tax revenues also are spread among cities, counties, school districts, townships, and special districts. (See figure 3.3.) In addition to own-source revenues, federal aid has been a substantial support for both state and local governments. Figure 3.4 depicts federal aid distributed to both state and local governments.

Although state governments raise more revenues than local governments, local governments actually spend more and employ more

Figure 3.2 STATE AND LOCAL RECEIPTS FROM OWN SOURCES

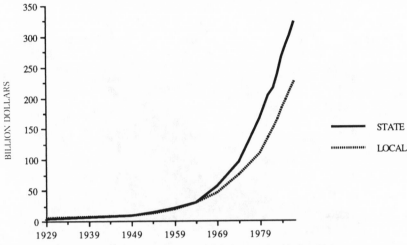

Source: Advisory Commission on Intergovernmental Relations. 1988. table 3. p. 26.

Figure 3.3 STATE AND LOCAL TAX REVENUES

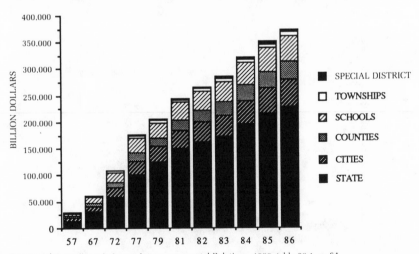

Source: Advisory Commission on Intergovernmental Relations. 1988. table 62.1. p. 64.

people. They are able to spend more because state aid pays for many services provided by local governments. For many areas of government enterprise, the state is the primary financier and the local gov-

Figure 3.4 DIRECT FEDERAL AID TO STATES AND LOCALITIES

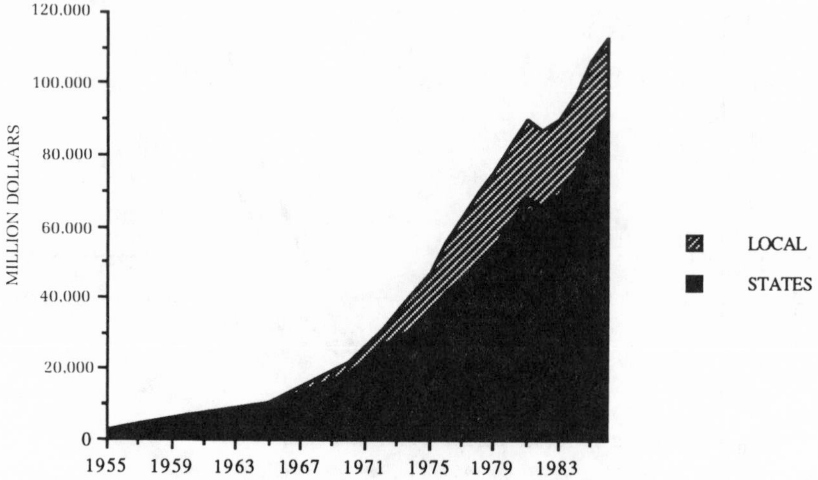

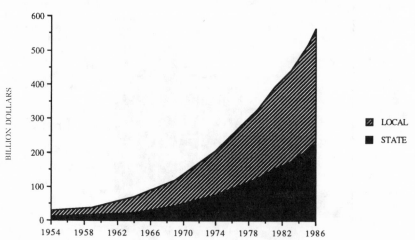

Source: Advisory Commission on Intergovernmental Relations. 1988. table 73. p. 81.

Figure 3.5 STATE AND LOCAL SPENDING AFTER INTERGOVERNMENTAL
TRANSFERS

Source: Advisory Commission on Intergovernmental Relations. 1988. table 2. p. 4.

ernment the primary service provider. Employment in state and local governments is another indicator of the historical trend toward more state revenue raising and more local service provision. Local government has always employed more people than state government.

Figure 3.6 STATE AND LOCAL EMPLOYMENT

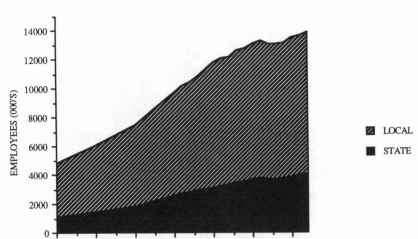

Source: Advisory Commission on Intergovernmental Relations, 1988, table 82, p.93.

Figure 3.5 depicts state and local spending from 1954 to 1986. Since the mid-1960s, local spending has outpaced state direct spending by a substantial margin. Employment in state and local governments reflects the same pattern. As the social programs of the late 1960s expanded, local employment rose dramatically and continued to rise; state employment has grown much more slowly. Figure 3.6 shows the relative numbers of state and local employees since 1954.

The difference between the spending curves and the own-source revenues curves for state and local governments represents the area in which federal and state aid combines to define much of the complex state-local and federal-local fiscal relationship. State aid to local governments flows through a variety of channels, just as federal aid flows to states and localities. As federal aid slowed, the importance of state aid and the state relationship for localities has grown. Figure 3.7 depicts the relative importance of federal aid as a percentage of state and local spending. Beginning even before the Reagan devolution, federal aid to states and localities as a percentage of spending had declined from a high of about 26.5 percent in FY 1978 to about 17.1 percent in FY 1988. Federal aid to states and localities declined over 23 percent in real terms from 1980 to 1985 (Advisory Commission on Intergovernmental Relations 1987). Federal aid is likely to play a smaller part in local budgets in the future, because the federal

Figure 3.7 FEDERAL AID AS A PERCENTAGE OF STATE AND LOCAL OUTLAYS

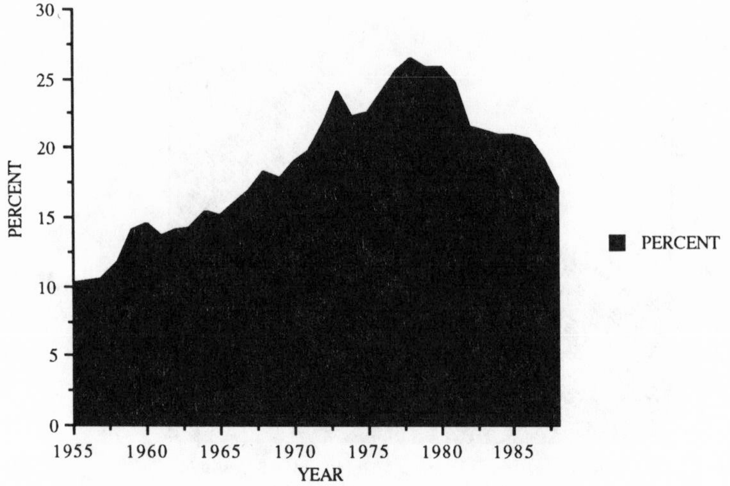

Source: Advisory Commission of Intergovernmental Relations. 1988. table 8. p. 15.

programs that continue to grow, such as Medicaid, are primarily state rather than local programs.

In the aggregate, the history of state-local fiscal relations can be characterized by a growing reliance by the state-local fiscal system upon the states' tax bases and the localities' ability to deliver services. The overall relationship, however, is defined by the interaction of many different funding and regulatory patterns arising from decisions in individual states about how best to finance a particular service. A closer look at state-local fiscal relations in several service areas illustrates how diverse these relations are in fact.

THE STATE-LOCAL FISCAL LANDSCAPE

Laying Down Fiscal Policy "Strata"

One way of looking at the current state-local fiscal landscape is to apply a geological analogy. The landscape on the surface is shaped by the strata underneath. Each stratum has a definite history and was laid down years ago under the conditions of the time. Some fracturing and movement has taken place since then, and individual strata may have been mixed or thrust upward to prominence. In any one geographical area, the landscape is unique, but it all developed in the context of larger geological processes acting on the local environment. Some of the "strata" are deeper and more solid than others, and occasional upwellings or erosion have caused seemingly anomalous features on the surface.

Like the geographical landscape, state-local fiscal relations have been shaped by years of laying down rules and formulas, defining funding patterns, and extending mandates for many strata of services provided by the state-local system. In any one state, the way these strata have been laid down differs from the ways they were laid down in other states. Each stratum representing a state-local fiscal relationship concerning a single service may be defined differently as well. Each is littered with "fossils," marks left by governors, legislators, mayors, and other politicians as they helped define state-local fiscal relations.

The diversity of fiscal responsibilities can be illustrated by a few examples. On the extreme end of local responsibilities lies New Hampshire, where local governments pay for over 80 percent of education costs, where there is no significant local property tax limitation, where no broad-based state income or sales tax is levied. In Texas, welfare costs are mostly paid by the state, but local education costs are largely borne by local governments. Texas does not levy a state income tax, but there is no local property tax limitation. In New Mexico, Mississippi, and Alabama, however, the state is the major fiscal actor. In these states, welfare costs are paid by the state government, over 70 percent of local education costs are borne by the state, and property tax limits have been enacted. A more mixed example is Indiana, where about 70 percent of education costs are paid by the state, a strict property tax limitation exists, state income and sales taxes are levied, and welfare costs are borne primarily by the state.

The diverse pattern of state-local fiscal relations has developed over many years, significantly influenced by national trends. Nationally, states have been paying increasingly larger percentages of local school costs, in part because they have constrained local property taxes and in part because local officials have successfully argued that state-mandated education reforms should be paid for by state taxes. Increasingly, state education aid formulas take into consideration local tax capacity as a result of both a national movement to ensure educational equity and several state court decisions. At the same time, many states have moved to require more local financial participation in infrastructure projects, such as water and sewer system construction and transportation improvements, as well as more local funding of housing and health care programs.

Federal requirements and new programs have dramatically changed the state-local fiscal landscape. The implementation of the Medicaid program in 1965, for example, drastically altered state budgets and influenced the states' abilities to finance welfare and other social services, many of them provided through localities. The federal government's tendency to start major programs directly with localities and then reduce aid places demands on states to develop new state-local fiscal cost-sharing programs, such as those now being implemented to finance water pollution control facilities. A new layer in the state-local fiscal landscape is being laid down right now because of the federal withdrawal from water and sewer funding.

Features in the State-Local Fiscal Landscape

In an effort to set the framework for a broader discussion of how the state-local fiscal relationship can be improved, it may be helpful to describe the major surface features of the national landscape. Several observations must be made, most important:

□ the revenue mix: how much of the total revenue of the state-local sector is collected by the state
□ state aid to local governments as a percentage of local own-source revenues, and
□ the state-local spending mix: the state percentage of state-local general spending from own-source revenues.

The Revenue Mix. State legislatures and governors control the access of local governments to the state tax base. Traditionally, property taxes have been the province of local governments, with sales and income taxes collected primarily by the states. States not only allocate access to the tax base, but they also set the rules for property assessment and rate changes, and in recent years they have imposed property tax limits on many local jurisdictions. In addition, although state legislatures historically have been parsimonious in allowing localities to levy sales and income taxes by local option, since 1980, many states have allowed local jurisdictions to collect these taxes, but with strict limits. In response to property tax limitations and strictures on the use of income, sales, and other broad-based taxes at the local level, many localities have ventured into a grayer area by imposing user fees for services, development fees, and other non-tax sources of revenues.

The allocation of taxing powers and pressures at the local level to keep taxes low has changed the revenue mix towards more state tax collection compared to local tax effort. Across the United States, for example, states collected about 61.1 percent of all the state and local taxes paid in fiscal year 1986. The percentage of state funds in total state and local tax revenues ranged from a low of 38.8 percent in New Hampshire to a high of over 79 percent in New Mexico and West Virginia. Figure 3.8 depicts the relative reliance of the states on state taxes in the state-local revenue mix.

State Aid for Locally Provided Services. Another indicator of the relative reliance of local governments on states for support in providing services is how state aid to local governments compares in size with local own-source revenue. This comparison reveals the extent to which many state governments use local governments to deliver services that the state supports or pays for in total. As figure 3.9 shows, total state aid as a percentage of local general revenue from local sources rose substantially from 1954 to about 1980, when it peaked, and it has trailed off in recent years. State education aid has continued to rise, but state aid to local governments for welfare, highways, and general government support has not risen as rapidly during the past five years. In addition, local receipts grew nearly as fast as state own-source revenues from 1980 to 1985 as local governments benefited from the revived economy and found new ways to raise revenues. (See figure 3.3.) Care must be taken in interpreting state aid figures, however, because these data do not reflect the allocation of service responsibilities among state and local governments. If a state has been paying 50 percent of locally administered welfare costs, for example, and then takes over the responsibility for providing welfare, the statistics will show a diminution of state aid even though the state is now paying for 100 percent of the previously local service. Because some states have taken full responsibility for the provision of services, such as courts, jails, and welfare, the statistics are probably slightly misleading.

The Spending Mix. After accounting for intergovernmental transfers, local governments spend far more than state governments. In 1986, for example, local governments spent nearly $335 billion. In contrast, state governments spent only about $228 billion. Examining the same information from the perspective of who finances state-local spending, rather than which level of government actually is the final pur-

Figure 3.8 STATE GOVERNMENT PERCENTAGES OF STATE AND LOCAL TAX REVENUES, 1986

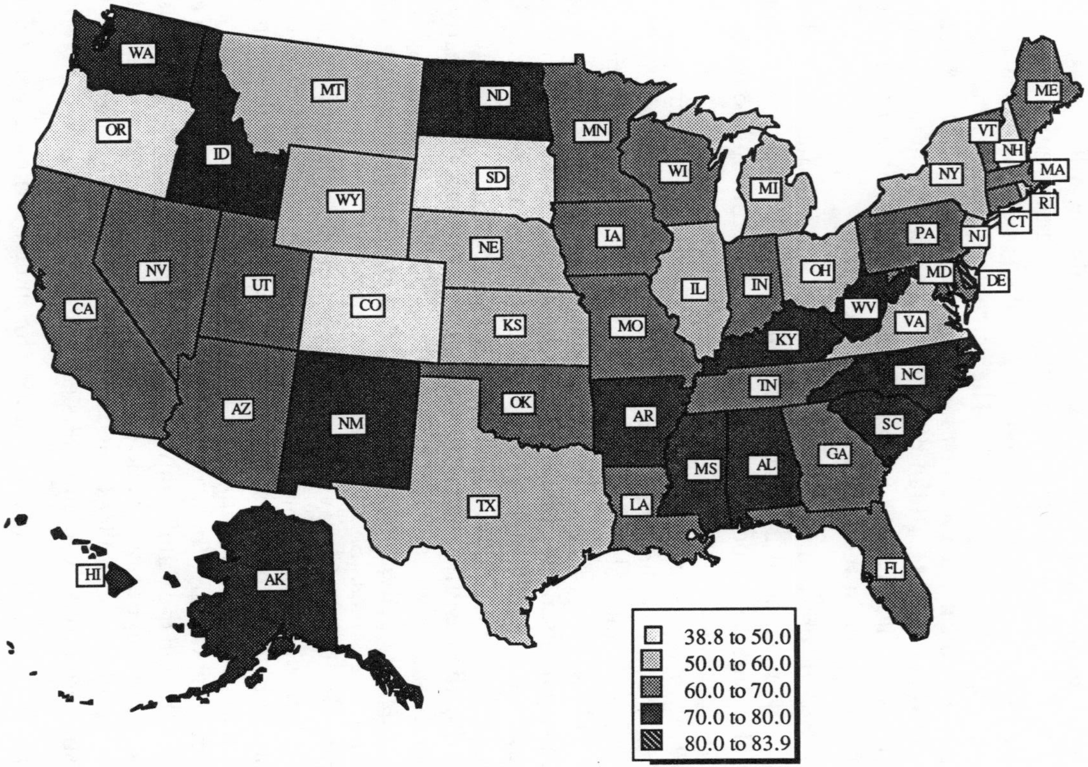

38.8 to 50.0	
50.0 to 60.0	
60.0 to 70.0	
70.0 to 80.0	
80.0 to 83.9	

Source: Advisory Commission of Intergovernmental Relations, 1988, table 68, p. 76.

Figure 3.9 STATE AID AS A PERCENTAGE OF LOCAL OWN-SOURCE REVENUES

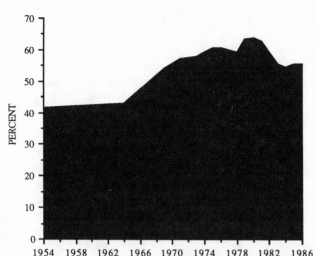

Source: Advisory Commission of Intergovernmental Relations. 1988. table 75. p. 83.

chaser of services, the picture is somewhat different. In fiscal year 1986, for example, the state share of total state-local general spending was about 57 percent. As figure 3.10 illustrates, state general spending as a percentage of total state-local general spending before transfers ranged from 44 percent in New York to 78 percent in Hawaii.

Within the broad category of general expenditures, the share of state financing of major service areas varies widely from state to state. In 1986, states financed about 83 percent of public welfare costs, 63 percent of highways, 52 percent of health and hospital expenditures, and 53 percent of elementary and secondary education costs. Table 3.1 shows the wide variation in the percentage of state-local general expenditures from own-source revenues for each of these functional areas. The variations are striking. New Hampshire pays for only about 7 percent of elementary and secondary education costs; neighboring Massachusetts finances over 46 percent of the same costs. Rhode Island, Georgia, Louisiana, Oklahoma, Pennsylvania, Utah, Vermont, Washington, and West Virginia pay for virtually all public welfare costs, and New York, Minnesota, and North Carolina provide less than 60 percent of total state-local public welfare spending.

The broad-brush picture of the state-local fiscal landscape that emerges from these indicators suggests that states raise more taxes

Figure 3.10 STATE PERCENTAGES OF STATE AND LOCAL GENERAL EXPENDITURES FROM OWN-SOURCE REVENUES, FY 1986

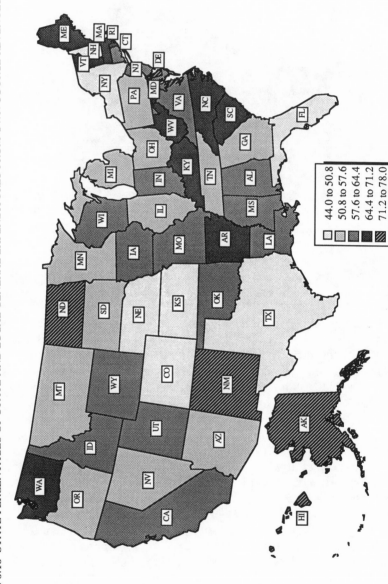

44.0 to 50.8
50.8 to 57.6
57.6 to 64.4
64.4 to 71.2
71.2 to 78.0

Source: Advisory Commission of Intergovernmental Relations, 1988, table 50, p. 49.

Table 3.1 STATE PERCENTAGES OF STATE-LOCAL GENERAL EXPENDITURES, FROM OWN-SOURCE REVENUES, FY 1986

Region and State	Total General Expenditure	Public Welfare	Highways	Health and Hospitals	Elementary and Secondary Education
New England	66%	93%	60%	81%	42%
Connecticut	61	86	62	93	42
Maine	65	97	61	70	55
Massachusetts	71	98	59	73	46
New Hampshire	47	54	58	97	7
Rhode Island	69	99	56	100	40
Vermont	68	100	64	95	38
Mideast	50	66	56	60	45
Delaware	72	99	76	100	75
Maryland	58	97	93	96	43
New Jersey	59	87	60	66	44
New York	44	45	36	51	45
Pennsylvania	57	100	74	88	48
Great Lakes	56	85	66	53	44
Illinois	55	92	67	55	43
Indiana	60	64	95	41	60
Michigan	54	90	64	56	35
Ohio	57	82	68	52	48
Wisconsin	59	78	43	56	38
Plains	56	74	59	49	47
Iowa	59	82	69	41	46
Kansas	49	95	52	53	46
Minnesota	56	58	49	49	58
Missouri	58	96	73	50	41
Nebraska	49	82	60	43	30
North Dakota	74	82	58	96	58

continued

Table 3.1 STATE PERCENTAGES OF STATE-LOCAL GENERAL EXPENDITURES, FROM OWN-SOURCE REVENUES, FY 1986

Region and State	Total General Expenditure	Public Welfare	Highways	Health and Hospitals	Elementary and Secondary Education
South Dakota	57	73	48	68	31
Southeast	59	92	73	43	61
Alabama	64	77	67	43	82
Arkansas	66	94	87	54	68
Florida	48	87	65	34	57
Georgia	53	100	60	24	61
Kentucky	71	94	81	60	77
Louisiana	61	100	63	55	60
Mississippi	60	91	63	31	65
North Carolina	67	52	85	61	70
South Carolina	68	85	80	56	65
Tennessee	54	88	75	36	55
Virginia	59	87	81	75	36
West Virginia	69	100	88	47	71
Southwest	51	84	62	45	56
Arizona	52	61	76	41	71
New Mexico	77	90	68	76	87
Oklahoma	61	100	76	50	69
Texas	46	89	55	42	49
Rocky Mountain	53	85	63	50	49
Colorado	46	84	52	52	41
Idaho	60	66	77	24	68
Montana	54	62	69	65	55
Utah	61	100	59	82	59
Wyoming	58	96	76	25	39

Region and State	Total General Expenditure	Public Welfare	Highways	Health and Hospitals	Elementary and Secondary Education
Far West[a]	62	92	56	49	72
California	62	91	52	49	75
Nevada	55	69	62	29	37
Oregon	54	85	82	72	30
Washington	67	100	54	45	80
Alaska	76	91	87	73	82
Hawaii	78	97	51	97	100
Total	57	83	63	52	53
Federal Aid as a Percentage of State-Local Expenditures	19	57	29	7	6

Source: Computations for 1986 based on ACIR Government Finance diskettes derived from data tape supplied by U.S. Bureau of the Census. Published sources: Census, Governmental Finances in 1985–1986 and State Government Finances, 1986. Computations were performed as follows: [State Direct Expenditures (GF, Table 13) plus State Intergovernmental Expenditure (SGF, 11) less State Intergovernmental Revenue from Federal (SGF, 7) less State Intergovernmental Revenue from Local (SGF, 7)] divided by [Total State-Local Direct Expenditure (GF, 13) less Intergovernmental Revenue from Federal (GF, 5)]. Local education data from National Education Association, Estimates of School Statistics, 1986–87 (revised 1987 by NEA).

a. Excludes Alaska and Hawaii.

than localities and provide substantial aid to local governments, which provide most of the services to the public. Funding of most services is shared, with states providing the bulk of welfare and highway funding and more than half the elementary and secondary education funding. Local governments have only a small role in higher education, although many community college systems are financed partially at the local level. Federal aid for a variety of services has been declining, at least in real terms, and this decline has put pressure on states and localities alike to make hard decisions about funding programs with shared responsibilities.

CHALLENGES IN STATE-LOCAL FISCAL RELATIONS

In statehouses and in local governments across the country, state and local officials are struggling to adjust to the decline in federal aid and are reevaluating the state-local fiscal system on a service-by-service, ad hoc basis, as they have in the past. Today's challenges to state-local fiscal relations, however, require a systemwide approach. Some of the challenges facing state and local officials include:

□ diminishing federal aid
□ disparities in need and fiscal capacities of different communities within the state
□ allocation of a shifting tax base
□ public demands for efficiency, and
□ unfunded mandates and cost shifting.

Diminishing Federal Aid. Although both states and localities have been hit hard by the decline in real federal aid, local governments have suffered more because they have been the more dependent upon the federal programs that have been reduced. As Gold (1988, p. 3) points out, between 1965 and 1978, federal aid to local governments rose rapidly. Federal aid as a proportion of local revenue from own sources rose from 4.5 percent to 25.8 percent for cities and from 1.6 percent to 19.2 percent for counties. By FY 1985, these percentages had dropped to 13 percent for cities and 9 percent for counties. Figure 3.11 corroborates this picture in terms of the decline in federal aid per dollar of own-source revenues of various local governments from 1978 to 1986.

Figure 3.11 FEDERAL AID PER DOLLAR OF OWN-SOURCE GENERAL REVENUES

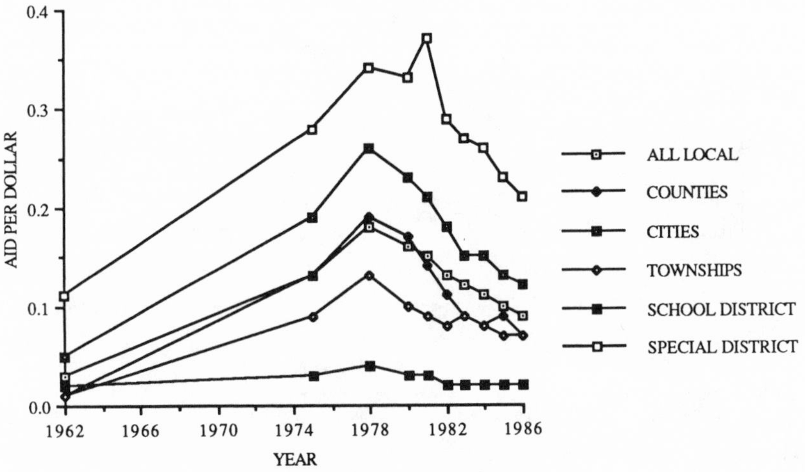

Source: Advisory Commission of Intergovernmental Relations. 1988. table 76. p. 84.

At the same time that local governments were undergoing withdrawal pains from federal aid, state aid as a percentage of local own-source revenues remained essentially static or declined somewhat. As figure 3.12 illustrates, state aid per dollar of own-source revenues for all local governments declined slightly from $0.58 in 1978 to about $0.54 in 1986. State aid to cities declined from $0.37 in 1978 to about $0.29 in 1986, while state aid to counties declined from $0.61 to $0.51. By contrast, state aid to school districts per dollar of own-source revenues increased from $0.97 in 1978 to $1.17 in 1986.

With both federal and state aid declining, local officials have increasingly looked to the state capitols for fiscal relief. As a result, many states have begun to address state-local fiscal relations as an issue in itself, partially separable from decisions made on individual issues such as school aid formulas. In Pennsylvania, for example, the governor and legislature set aside $500 million in the 1988 state budget to finance needed reforms in state-local funding before details of those reforms were worked out.

In most states, the immediate event that precipitated a new look at state-local fiscal relations was the loss of General Revenue Sharing, which affected not only the big cities but thousands of small and rural jurisdictions as well. The loss of federal housing aid to Phil-

Figure 3.12 STATE AID PER DOLLAR OF OWN-SOURCE GENERAL REVENUES

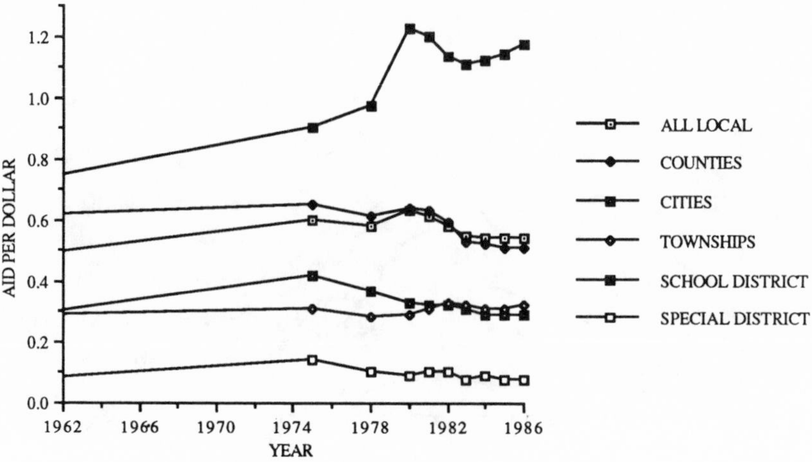

Source: Advisory Commission of Intergovernmental Relations. 1988. table 76. p. 84.

adelphia caused few legislators from rural Pennsylvania to lose sleep, but the loss of revenue sharing (which had often helped support small town fire-fighting units, for example) caused real concern among urban and rural legislators alike.

Fiscal Disparities. In the world of local government, all tax bases are not created equal. Major disparities exist in the tax capacity of local governments within every state. Because of primary reliance on the property tax, communities with low property values must assign much higher rates to property taxes than wealthier communities do to generate funds for services. Poorer communities are often the most resistant to property tax rate increases. As a result, citizens in poorer communities often receive fewer services than do those in wealthier areas.

In recent years, many state school aid formulas have been adjusted to provide at least some relief to poorer school districts, but few state aid mechanisms for other services have recognized the issue of fiscal disparities. Only one state, Wisconsin, has a full-fledged general aid program designed to reduce fiscal disparities, although New Jersey and some other states implicitly try to reduce disparities through urban aid or other special programs for local governments.

The difficulties in attempting to reduce fiscal disparities among localities have been well-illustrated through the many efforts to modify state school aid formulas. Some propose that states adjust levels of school aid so that local taxation at a fixed minimum rate, combined with state school aid, equals a minimum spending level for all students, regardless of whether they live in a rich or poor community. However, attempts to implement this reform often run up against an existing system that pays school districts according to the number of teachers and their salaries, or they have foundered when wealthier school districts discovered that they would lose funds under equalizing formulas. Where equalizing formulas have been enacted, they usually contain "hold harmless" provisions that stipulate that no school district will actually lose aid. These provisions may cost up to 10–20 percent more in total school aid, a considerable bite for many state legislators to swallow during times of fiscal austerity. Reducing fiscal disparities through other aid programs may run into similar difficulties and promise to be expensive.

Allocation of a Shifting Tax Base. As the economy changes, so do the state and local tax bases. The rise in spending on services, for example, has caused states to look at the option of expanding the sales tax to include services of lawyers, accountants, doctors, barbers, beauticians, and the host of other service providers. If the experience in Florida is any guide, this step will be a difficult—if inevitable— one for states to take. Local governments have been more successful in capturing the service tax base because many of them are able to levy occupation taxes or taxes on various service transactions.

Limitations on local property taxes have caused local governments to turn to a wide variety of user fees, development fees, licensing fees, and other sources of funds. This phenomenon is most widespread in California, but other states with strict property tax limitations also now employ user fees and other less traditional revenue sources. More important, local officials have asked state legislators to allow them to raise sales, income, or occupation taxes to reduce their heavy reliance on local property taxes. These local option taxes are spreading slowly, however, because state officials jealously guard their own tax base and sources of income.

The fiscal disparity issue interacts with the issue of broadening the local tax base as well. In a few states, for example, the legislature has allowed local school districts to levy nonproperty taxes in an attempt to reduce disparities in revenue capacity without large increases in state aid. Communities with few commercial or industrial properties can tax incomes rather than property and make up for the low property valuation per student. Local option sales taxes enable general local governments to broaden their tax bases and benefit from the fact that we save and invest little but spend a lot. It is likely that a continued rise in consumer spending coupled with slow increases in real property values will make the local option sales tax increasingly attractive to local officials.

State officials increasingly face demands from local officials for authority to tax income, sales, and other sources. At the same time, state legislators and others may find local option taxes a more attractive way of meeting local needs than raising state taxes and handing the funds back to local officials. In many states, the interaction of statewide property tax limitations, local resistance to property taxes, and increased demands for spending on education means that the state must commit itself to pay for nearly the entire cost of education improvement. In Indiana, for example, when property tax limitations were first enacted in 1974, state education aid accounted for only about 30 percent of local school costs. Today, the state share has grown to about 70 percent, and many state officials are wondering whether they have inadvertently undermined their own strongly held belief in local control of the schools. As school costs rise, the only way out of this dilemma may be to allow local taxing authorities to access nonproperty tax revenues.

Public Demand for Efficiency. A major part of the complexity and diversity of state-local fiscal relations results from the large number and different types of local governments. States deal with cities, counties, school districts, special districts of a bewildering variety and number, as well as townships and other local entities. These local governments were not designed to operate efficiently or to use economies of scale; they evolved to their present forms for a variety of reasons, only one of which was the desire for efficient delivery of services.

The goal of economic competitiveness and growing taxpayer resistance have combined to generate new calls for consolidation of local government, realignment of service responsibilities, tax-base sharing, and other actions to streamline local government. Streamlining local governments, the reasoning goes, will give states a better chance of addressing such issues as the improvement of education and diminishing federal aid, fiscal disparities, and the overall productivity of the state-local system. On the other hand, there is little evidence that within relatively low and relatively high thresholds, the size of governments significantly impedes efficient service delivery. (See chapter 8 for a discussion of the economies of scale.)

State officials may find issues of local government structure extremely difficult to confront, simply because there are usually substantial political reasons why the fragmentation or inefficiency of local governments has been allowed to develop. Kentucky, for example, has 120 counties, some of which have populations of fewer than 5,000 people. There are about 1,500 special districts in Kentucky as well. Most residents believe that fewer counties are needed, but virtually no one wants his or her own county merged with a neighboring jurisdiction. The urban county government in and around Lexington has proved successful in streamlining services and making government more efficient; yet outlying counties in Kentucky are extremely resistant to consolidation. Similar stories can be told about school districts in Nebraska and Mississippi, special districts in Illinois, and other local jurisdictions throughout the nation.

Mandates and Cost Shifting. When fiscal times are tough at one level of government and service demands continue unabated, lawmakers have a tendency to try to spur service increases without corresponding increases in spending and taxes. One approach is to require another level of government to provide services without providing the funds for them. States have always mandated certain levels of services by local governments, just as the federal government has attempted to mandate state service levels by tying grant programs to regulatory requirements. In recent years, however, groups such as the National Association of Counties, National League of Cities, and U.S. Conference of Mayors have objected strenuously to this practice of enacting unfunded mandates.

Local officials argue that imposing mandates without funding is unfair in the short run and is ultimately self-defeating. They point out that by imposing unfunded mandates, state legislatures may warp the priority-setting process of local governments. Fourteen states, most notably, California, Michigan, and Massachusetts, have passed laws restraining themselves from enacting unfunded mandates. Others require fiscal notes to pending legislation that examine the cost of new programs to both state government and local entities. Neither of these approaches appears to have substantially reduced the number of unfunded mandates, although it is possible that some further mandates may have been avoided through these requirements.

Similarly, local and state officials alike object to the practice of starting programs and shifting the costs of those programs to a different level of government—what one San Jose official has called the "shift and shaft" approach. The federal government is viewed as the greatest miscreant in cost shifting, but state officials are not without blame in this regard. The combined effect of unfunded mandates, cost shifting, and federal aid declines has squeezed local governments hard. Local officials are seeking redress of these grievances in their capitals, causing state officials to take a new look at state-local fiscal relations.

CRITIQUING STATE-LOCAL FISCAL RELATIONS

Criticizing local government is easy—a fact that probably explains its popularity. Local officials constantly face allegations of insufficient, inefficient, or too costly services. Roads have potholes and the snow is cleared too slowly. The police fail to control crime and criminals remain unprosecuted. The fire department and ambulance squads respond too slowly. The water supply system was not well-designed, so rationing is necessary in dry periods. The sewers back up, sewage treatment plants stink and inadequately treated sewage fouls the water. Schools are not educating children for a competitive international economy. Mass transit does not connect the right places or keep schedules, and subways and buses are not clean and safe. On top of that, taxes are too high.

State officials come in for their share of criticism also. Welfare payments are too high, promoting welfare dependency, or perhaps too low, depriving people of a minimum standard of decency in their lives and condemning their children to an environment of squalor. State universities have standards that are too high—making them an elite bastion—or too low, undermining the quality of education. The state parks are not well enough maintained, there are too few of them, they are located in the wrong places, and they prohibit (do not prohibit) snowmobiles and trailbikes where they should not (should).

For a policy decision to be criticized because of its state-local relations aspects, one of the following elements must be present:

☐ The decision is being made by the wrong government, such as a policy being made at the state level that should be made locally, or it is being made by a local government when it should be made at the state level or by some regional organization. Defining the right level is discussed below.

□ The decision is, in a legal sense, being made at the right level but is influenced improperly by forces emanating from other levels of government. Examples include local decisions that are distorted by state funding incentives or that overburden some bureaucratic procedures.

Criticisms of policies have no relevance to the issue of intergovernmental relations, however, if

□ the right level of government appears to making the decision and
□ the decision is made by processes generally agreed to be democratic in our society.

Thus, for those who agree that the municipality is the right level of government to provide urban fire protection, criticisms of high-cost, gold-plated fire departments or of low-budget, slow-response departments are irrelevant. The same criteria can be applied to states. For those who agree that the state is the right level at which to make the decisions and that a legislature is democratic, the criticism that welfare payments are too low is a criticism only of a state decision, not a criticism of state-local relations.

The most common criticisms of state-local relations concern the following issues:

□ size of government
□ voter control
□ separation of control and accountability
□ disagreements with policy outcomes
□ deviation from some optimal level of control
□ tax preference policies
□ concern with fiscal disparities, and
□ competition.

Size of Governments. Local governments may be criticized as too small, encompassing too few people. Sometimes the criticism suggests that a jurisdiction is below some threshold of service provision, such as being too small to support a fire department, a professional city manager, or foreign language instruction in the high school. The criticism may be that the government does not cover a large enough area to capture the benefits of resources and results of programs, such as single-city economic development programs that actually benefit the whole metropolitan area. Sometimes governments are viewed as too small because the constituency is too narrow: pupils are mostly black, elected officials are mostly black or white, or a particular firm, union, or ethnic group dominates its politics.

But governments are often criticized as being too large as well. This criticism is often directed at overlapping higher level governments for their supposed inability to reflect the local differences in taste and conditions. State officials make this criticism of the federal government, local officials make it of state governments, and municipal and township officials make it of county government. Sometimes the criticism is made of a single local government, such as a large city, city-county (e.g., New York City), or school district. These jurisdictions may be seen as fostering large bureaucracies and being unresponsive to local problems.

Voter Control. A multiplicity of governments is also seen as part of the problem of the long ballot. It is argued that average citizens have a limited ability to absorb information about candidates and issues— that they can be effectively mobilized to deal with a few issues and candidates but not with ballots offering dozens of issues and candidates. Such long ballots, it is argued, give rise to control by an informed minority and lead to the selection of candidates based on name recognition alone, including recognition of family names, which allows some candidates to win on the basis of notoriety or family connections.

If the long ballot is the problem, however, a multiplicity of governments is only one contributor. The other contributors are the number of officials to be elected (e.g., electing state and local auditors and prosecuting attorneys) and the number of propositions on the ballot (e.g., bond issues, tax levies, referenda, initiatives). But the opposite criticism is also made, that not enough offices or issues are on the ballot. For example, it is argued that popular control is lost when voters do not directly select school boards. Further, although at-large elections may simplify balloting in large jurisdictions, such arrangements may be faulted for diluting votes of minority groups or concentrations of poor people.

Separation of Control and Accountability. A constant criticism of governments at all levels is that apparently accountable officials often do not control the policy for which they are accountable. Some of this problem is built into the separation of powers among branches of governments, for example, when a governor or mayor is held accountable for the decisions of a state legislature or city council. But it also occurs as an issue in intergovernmental relations; officials who report to the local chief executive may be held accountable for granting or refusing welfare eligibility, even though their decisions are tightly controlled by state and federal officials.

Local officials often defend tax increases as having been required by state mandates, forced by federal mandates, or ordered by state or federal courts.

Disagreements with Policy Outcomes. Many people are more concerned with the policy choices made by governments than the niceties of which level of government selects the policy. For most citizens, any level of government that picks the wrong policy is the wrong level of government to be making the decision. If the 55-mile-per-hour speed limit is dictated by the federal government, those preferring 65 will want states to have the power to decide speed limits. But those who prefer 55 may perceive the appropriate level of decision making as the federal government.

Deviation from Some Optimal Level of Control. Since Plato and Aristotle, political thinkers and practical decisionmakers have been arguing over the appropriate size of the basic government policy-making unit. Contrasts between the Greek city-state and the Roman empire suggest that the issues were as difficult then as now.

Tax Policy Preferences. There is no inherent reason to confine particular forms of taxation to particular levels of government. School districts and municipalities as well as counties could levy income or sales taxes; states can, and some do, levy property taxes. But in most states there are traditions, even constitutional provisions, that result in association of a particular tax with a particular level of government. Most often the property tax is associated with school districts and other local governments, and sales and income taxes are seen as the primary state revenue sources. With this point in mind, proponents of particular tax policies (e.g., reducing property taxes) will also become proponents of expanding the power and financing responsibility of one level of government and reducing that of another.

Concern with Fiscal Disparities. Whenever any part of governmental financing responsibility is lodged in subnational governments, some governments will have higher-than-average needs in relation to their tax bases. This situation produces disparities in the level of services, in the tax rates, or in both. To some, these disparities are, per se, faults in the governmental arrangements.

Competition. Dividing government responsibilities into control by sub-units often leads to competition among them. Sometimes the critics argue that competition leads to overspending, such as an over-emphasis on athletics in high schools and state universities. Often neighboring jurisdictions vie with one another to attract new business enterprises by offering combinations of low taxes and low levels of social services. Such competition may lead to criticisms of undertaxing and underspending.

CONCLUSION: IMPROVING THE STATE-LOCAL FISCAL LANDSCAPE

In summary, the state-local fiscal landscape has been shaped by years of individual decisions on state-local allocation of tax bases, state aid formulas, and the most appropriate service delivery systems. Many criticisms have been leveled at the state-local system, but on the whole, the public appears to believe that it is better served by state and local governments than by the federal government. At the same time, the failure of many officials and the public to view the state-local landscape as a single system has led to many of the inefficiencies and inequities that fuel the criticisms of the relationship.

The problem of changing state-local fiscal relations is partly one of attitude: if state and local officials (and their respective lobbies) can stop viewing themselves as enemies in a zero-sum game and start working together to sort out roles and relationships with a systemwide perspective, we will have better state and local government. Although a great deal of rhetoric has been devoted to the need for a public-private partnership in improving government, more needs to be said about the advantages of a state-local partnership whose effectiveness (or lack thereof) has a lot to do with the satisfaction (or lack of it) that most people feel with their government.

Like the geological landscape, state-local fiscal relations do not change rapidly. It takes considerable digging to change the landscape. Those working on reforms must take care not to disturb too much of the underlying structure lest the system shift in ways that no one expects or wants. Nevertheless, by addressing the key issues of replacing federal aid, reducing fiscal disparities, allocating the shifting tax base, providing services more efficiently, and avoiding unfunded mandates, state and local officials can improve their relations and the system as a whole.

Note

1. For a full discussion of the historical balance of federal, state, and local power, see Aronson and Hilley 1986, pp. 11–20.

References

Advisory Commission on Intergovernmental Relations (ACIR). 1987. *Significant Features of Fiscal Federalism, 1986–87*. Washington, D.C.

Aronson, J. Richard, and John L. Hilley. 1986. *Financing State and Local Governments*. Washington, D.C.: Brookings Institution.

Brizius and Foster. 1988. *State Policy Data Book '88*. McConnellsburg, Pa.

Gold, D. Stephen. 1988. A Legislator's Guide to State-Local Relations. Preliminary draft. Denver: National Conference of State Legislatures.

Chapter Four

REVITALIZING STATE-LOCAL ECONOMIES

R. Scott Fosler

Public economic policy in the United States since World War II has been almost exclusively the responsibility of the federal government. Federal economic policy, in turn, has focused principally on macroeconomic management of the U.S. economy by using fiscal and monetary tools. Under this regime, state and local governments had little or no economic policy role, save the self-initiated recruitment of industry.

Economic forces that gained momentum in the 1970s and early 1980s—including restructuring of the economy, integration of the United States with the world economy, and the relative decline of U.S. economic strength—have fundamentally altered that old regime. These forces have diluted the effectiveness of federal macroeconomic policy tools and have exposed regions within the United States to prevailing world economic forces. The political responsibility for dealing with many of the consequences of these forces has fallen to state and local governments, in part because the federal government could not or has chosen not to address them. But the increasing state-local role is also due to the fact that state and local governments have powers and capabilities to address many of the factors that are important in the new economic environment, including human resources, knowledge and technology, capital, and the synergy of multiple economic factors.

As economic hardship visited each region of the United States—beginning with New England in the early 1970s, moving to the midwestern industrial belt in the late 1970s and early 1980s, and finding its way to the agricultural and mineral-rich heartland in the early to mid-eighties—the state and local governments in those regions discovered that they were unlikely to find adequate assistance from Washington but would be politically bound to act increasingly on their own in dealing with economic stress. In response, state and local governments initiated wide-ranging experiments to promote their economies.[1] Typically, jurisdictions fell back on the conventional remedy of recruitment, or "smokestack chasing," in search of new plants to replace the jobs lost by declining industry. But as they discovered the high costs and limits of this strategy, most expanded their economic programs to include a broad range of initiatives, such as providing capital, improving human resources, strengthening infrastructure, building the knowledge and technology base, and promoting entrepreneurship.

Most of these efforts have been incremental and piecemeal. And the jury is still out on their effectiveness. What is clear, however, is that the number, range, and intensity of these new efforts cumulatively constitute a fundamentally new economic role for state and local governments.

To understand the scope of the new state-local economic role, one must first understand the changes that have occurred in the world economy, the U.S. position in that economy, and the consequent shift in economic responsibilities within the intergovernmental system. This chapter discusses each of these points. It then outlines the new economic role for the state-local system as a whole. Herein lies the key to state-local relations for economic policy under the new regime: each state and its local governments comprise an integral political-governmental system whose harmony of interaction is a major determinant of the effectiveness of economic policy.

But although the state and local levels constitute an integral whole with respect to economic policy, each maintains unique dimensions within this partnership. This chapter describes these dimensions and the ways in which they are linked.

THE CONVENTIONAL MODEL OF ECONOMIC POLICY

The conventional model of economic policy responsibility in the United States rested on three major assumptions. First, the United States was a relatively closed economy in that it was not greatly affected by economic activity outside its borders. Exports and imports remained a relatively small share of the gross national product (GNP). Most important, because the United States was the largest, most dynamic, and in nearly all respects the leading economy in the world, it set the pace for the world economy. To the extent that U.S.

and world economies were related, U.S. economic performance and policy affected the rest of the world far more than the economic performance and policies of other nations affected the United States.

Second, the economy was defined by the activities of a competitive private sector, which responded to consumer demand through prices established in open markets. The appropriate role of government was to establish the context for private market operations through macroeconomic management to correct market failures and to provide a social safety net for those unable to provide for themselves.

Third, the responsibility for economic policy, such as it was, resided almost exclusively with the federal government. The tools of fiscal and monetary policy were under federal control, the legal basis for assuring competitive markets was predominantly federal, and the responsibility for providing the social safety net, although shared among the three levels of government, was nonetheless predominantly a federal role.

No explicit economic role was envisioned for state and local government under the conventional model. States and localities were free, if they desired, to sponsor economic development programs that consisted principally of recruiting businesses. Thus they were in direct competition with one another, the more so because the closed economy model held that all important business activity was located within the United States; consequently, one jurisdiction's gain in attracting investment from outside its borders was by definition another's loss. But this narrowly defined economic development function was quite small compared to the paramount responsibility of the federal government for economic policy.

The conventional model never operated in practice as it was understood in concept. For example, the federal government has always been more directly involved in microeconomic activities than is generally recognized. Defense procurement profoundly impacts the economy in general and specific industries and regions in particular, federal highway and housing policies affect the geographical contour of urban regions, the federal government sponsors research and other programs of economic importance, and federal tax policy influences economic activity in numerous particulars.

State and local governments are also more important economically than the conventional model would acknowledge. Their investments in education, transportation, and other infrastructure have always been important to economic development. And the sheer size of the state-local sector had reached a level by the 1970s that constituted a powerful macroeconomic force in its own right.[2]

New economic and political forces are now calling into question the assumptions underlying the conventional model, both in its definition of the economic importance of different types of government action under the old regime and in the appropriateness of conventionally defined roles under the new regime.

ECONOMIC RESTRUCTURING

Three powerful forces are reshaping the economy, with important consequences for government economic policy in general and the state-local role in particular.[3]

Transition in Traditional Incentives. First, industries that provided the main source of growth in the past are not likely to do so in the future. In some traditional industries, like automobile production, demand continues to grow. But because the numerous automobile manufacturers can easily satisfy demand, the industry in its conventional form is not likely to be the source of growth that it has been in the past. In the steel industry, producers face decreasing demands for many basic products. Lighter, cheaper, and more durable materials, such as plastics and ceramics, are replacing steel components in automobiles and many other products.

In the 1970s and 1980s, overcapacity also characterized agriculture, oil, forestry, and many other natural resource industries as well as ocean shipping, financial services, office buildings, and other service industries.

Companies in high-capacity industries face especially stiff competition because so many suppliers are pursuing a limited number of customers. One result is the high incidence of business cutbacks, employee layoffs, plant closings, and mergers and acquisitions.[4] The severity of impact varies from place to place, according to the community's dependence on industries in such markets. In the early to mid-1980s, the hardest hit areas were those dependent on traditional manufacturing, agriculture, and natural resources.

Many firms in these sectors have scaled back, modernized, or restructured their operations. The lower dollar value has helped to open global markets to many firms, and in early 1988, U.S. manufacturing plants were operating at above 85 percent capacity. To some extent, this level reflected the degree to which U.S. manufacturers cut back operations, moved overseas, or dropped product lines during the high-dollar years. This high-capacity utilization in certain industries may turn out to be a short-term phenomenon related to the fluctuating value of the dollar. Meanwhile, overcapacity continues in key manufacturing industries, such as autos, and it appears to be spreading among service industries.

New Technologies and Processes. A second powerful force is the emergence of new industries—and the transformation of existing industries—because of new technologies, processes, and changing consumer tastes.

The new technologies have created whole new industries in such areas as microelectronics and information, biotechnology, ceramics, and composite materials. In turn, robotics, microelectronics, and information processing are transforming other industries, many of them traditional. One of the most significant changes is the shift from the mass production of standardized items to smaller runs of more specialized products. Increasing product differentiation and "niche markets" reflect both rising consumer affluence and sophistication and the capability of new production technology and organization to conceive, produce, and market small quantities of specialized items and services profitably.

These new economic forces are partly responsible for the growth in service employment to support business and to satisfy new consumer demands generated by rising incomes. Between 1983 and the first quarter of 1987, U.S. employment increased 15.6 percent—14 million jobs. More than 70 percent of the new service jobs were in the managerial and technical categories that include doctors, lawyers, physical therapists, and sales and administrative personnel. By no means were they all hamburger flippers.[5]

The growth in service employment has not replaced manufacturing jobs so much as it has added to them. In 1987, the United States had 90 percent as many manufacturing jobs as it did in 1979 and about the same number as it had 20 years ago. Manufacturing employment remains relatively constant in actual numbers of jobs, but it has a lower proportion of total jobs because service employment has soared. There is also a dramatic change in the composition of manufacturing employment, with many old jobs giving way to new ones. This change has geographical impacts: much of the traditional manufacturing was in the Northeast and Midwest, but much of the new manufacturing has shifted to the South and West. The low dollar has afforded manufacturing firms in all regions the opportunity to boost output for both domestic and foreign markets, although the magnitude and endurance of this turnaround is threatened by sluggish demand.

Many of the jobs are being created in the newer medium-sized and expanding businesses. Over the past five years, 93 percent of the new jobs were created by the top 10 percent of companies ranked by growth (Birch 1987, p. 15). This, fact, in part, reflects the growing advantage of specialized products and services based on innovation, on flexible production, and on knowledge, skill, and technology.

Globalization. A third major force is the globalization of production, markets, finance, and technology. Multinational firms now manufacture products throughout the world, often drawing on suppliers in many countries. In addition, virtually every country is a potential sales target for producers from any other country. Merchandise trade among the industrial countries has grown from 12.7 percent of goods produced in 1960 to nearly 30 percent today.[6] The total value of world trade in goods and services now exceeds $3 trillion per year. Even if a U.S. company does not export, it still operates in a global market if its product is subject to foreign competition at home.

Capital and financial markets are closely linked through worldwide traders, as the ricocheting effect of collapsing stock markets in New York, Hong Kong, Frankfurt, and Tokyo so dramatically revealed in October 1987. The total volume of all domestic and foreign payments processed through New York's Clearing House Interbank Payment System totaled $1.5 trillion per day by 1987. And contrary to conventional economic theory, the flow of capital seems to be increasingly detached from international trade.

Technology (including knowledge and information) now flows freely and quickly from country to country. Companies and nations with the skills and networks can quickly take advantage of foreign technological developments and turn them into commercially successful ventures. As the United States has learned, being in the scientific or even technological lead is no guarantee of commercial success.

This growing global interdependence has been facilitated by rapid advances in transportation and communication technology, making the international movement of goods, people, and information fast, reliable, and inexpensive. For example, although California boasts a huge orange-growing industry, residents of San Francisco are just as likely to begin their mornings with orange juice from Newark, New Jersey, processed from oranges shipped through the ports of New York and New Jersey from Brazil.

All these trends toward globalization have been evident for many years, but each is accelerating and interacting with the others in an ever more complex fashion. The cumulative effect of these changes constitutes a significant change in character as well as quantity.

The Convergence of Trends. This period is not the first time that the United States has gone through a major transition from traditional to new industries. In some ways, the process of shedding, shrinking, or updating old industries and inventing and expanding new ones is a more or less permanent feature of capitalism, perhaps of industrial economies more generally.

Nor is it the first time that economic fortunes of different regions of the country have fluctuated. During the 1920s, the New England economy sank slowly into depression as its apparel and shoe industries atrophied; at the same time, the automobile industry was emerging as a powerful new economic force, turning the Midwest into the manufacturing center of the country. Such transitions are always turbulent, and they are especially painful for the companies, workers, investors, and regions that have a large stake in shrinking industries. Much depends on whether these stakeholders decide to transform the industries on which they depend, move into more promising industries, or simply attempt to protect or cling to what they have.

Today, however, the transition is even more challenging for the United States because it is occurring during a major transition in the global economy and a shifting international role. For example, U.S. automobile manufacturers and the regions that depend on them would have faced the problem of overcapacity even without international competition. But with aggressive and skillful foreign producers competing in markets that were already saturated, the competition is fierce. In these circumstances, even a slight advantage in cost, quality, marketing, or exchange rates can result in a major loss of market share.

Foreign competition is not confined to the traditional industries. It also has had a major impact in the new technology and service areas, where U.S. industrialists believed that they had a clear advantage. For example, the video cassette recorder (VCR) was invented by the American firms Ampex and RCA in the 1960s. But by 1986, all 13 million VCRs sold domestically were made in Japan or Korea. The United States enjoyed a $27 billion surplus trade balance in high-technology goods in 1981; by 1986, it had deteriorated to a $2 billion *deficit.*

The trade deficit reached a record $171 billion in 1987. By 1988, the cumulative trade deficits had produced a U.S. foreign debt of $400 billion, making the United States the world's largest debtor nation. Even if the U.S. balance of trade immediately turns for the better—and by the fall of 1987, it appeared that the lower dollar was finally beginning to make a dent in the U.S. trade balance—we will still face a growing foreign debt that could approach $1 trillion by the mid-1990s.[7]

How will these developments change the economic role of government generally in the United States, and what effect will they have in shifting economic responsibilities among the federal, state, and local levels?

THE FEDERAL ECONOMIC ROLE

The prevailing forces will seriously constrain the federal government's economic role in three ways.

The Relative Decline of the U.S. Economy. The U.S. share of world economic output has been shrinking. Following World War II, the United States held a commanding economic lead over the rest of the world, accounting for about 40 percent of world GNP. But as some other countries began to catch up to U.S. levels of productivity, the U.S. share of world GNP gradually declined, falling to 24 percent by 1986. At the same time, Japan's share soared more than fourfold from 2 to 9 percent.

There is nothing inherently wrong or threatening in the fact that other countries have improved their economic positions relative to the United States. After all, between 1945 and 1986, the U.S. economy grew threefold in absolute terms. The United States, moreover, continues to be the world's largest national economy. Nonetheless, with only 4.5 percent of the world's population and a smaller share of world economic production, the United States is not likely to have the same degree of influence and ability to shape international affairs and, therefore, to determine its own fate as it once did.

The Constraints of World Interdependence. The nation's latitude in shaping its economy will be further constrained by its increasing integration with the world economy. The U.S. ratio of exports and imports to GNP grew from 10.1 percent in 1960 to 21.6 percent in 1984. Because the United States is no longer a closed economy, its macroeconomic tools of fiscal and monetary policy no longer have the same effect in guiding the national economy.

In an integrated world economy with flexible exchange rates, the domestic impact of the fiscal stimulus intended through tax cuts or expenditure increases (or both) is diluted when consumers increase their purchase of imports. U.S. producers lose would-be customers to foreign producers and the trade deficit grows.[8]

The use of monetary policy as a policy tool is also more constrained, but for the opposite reason: it might have a stronger impact than intended. Higher interest rates intended to counter inflation, for example, could raise the value of the dollar and hurt U.S. exports. Lower interest rates intended to be expansionary, on the other hand, could lower the value of the dollar, thereby increasing the price of imports and potentially fueling inflation.[9]

We have seen the consequences of these international effects over the past few years. An expansionary fiscal policy and tight monetary policy combined in the early 1980s to drive up the dollar and worsen the trade deficit. The dollar then fell to below its 1981 levels. This situation increased the volume of U.S. exports, but not enough to compensate for the drop in the value of the dollar until 1987. Measured in dollars, the trade deficit remained largely unchanged until late 1987.

Meanwhile, because U.S. producers had cut back their domestic capacity during the high dollar years, they were not in a good position to take advantage of the lower dollar to increase their exports.

The revival of protectionism in recent years, both in the United States and abroad, is a reflection of national desires to reestablish control over economic forces that have a powerful integrating tendency.

The United States as Debtor. The third constraint on the federal government is that it is saddled with debt. Federal policy would have been challenged sufficiently to adjust to the shrinking relative size of the economy and global integration, but now the government will have to manage this transition from a weakened fiscal position. The chronic federal budget deficit, currently at about $160 billion per year, has produced a national debt of over $2 trillion, requiring $160 billion, 15 percent of the budget, just to service it every year.

This situation creates a dilemma for federal macroeconomic policy. Deficit reduction is important to boost savings, but it also risks cooling the economy or worse, reinforcing recessionary tendencies. Meanwhile, a tight money policy designed to curb inflation and sustain foreign investment risks choking economic growth and drying up liquidity, while an easier monetary policy risks fueling inflation and driving away the foreign investors the United States needs to finance its trade and budget deficits.

Implications for State and Local Governments. The changing federal economic role has important implications for state and local governments. Perhaps most important is the fact that the federal government can no longer be counted on to guide the country's domestic economy as it once did. The nation's economic future will be more directly and powerfully affected by the actions of foreign governments and by world market forces. State, county, and municipal governments will bear an increasing responsibility for assisting their local economies to compete directly in the world economy.

In time, the federal government should learn how to make better use of the formidable economic policy capability it can bring to bear under these new circumstances. Eventually, the United States, as a relatively less influential economic player, will likely adopt economic strategies other nations have used in similar circumstances to enhance their economic positions.[10] It is unlikely that the United States will ever again have the economic advantage it has enjoyed for the past half-century.

Even under favorable economic circumstances, state and local governments should expect no substantial new federal financial assistance. The real cutbacks in grants to state and local governments begun in 1978 are not likely to be substantially reversed. If anything, federal assistance will be curtailed even further as Congress and the president seek ways to cut the budget deficit.[11]

The demographic and political forces shaping the budget battle leave little room for maneuver by state and local officials. About 30 percent of the federal budget is allocated to defense, about 30 percent to support the elderly (including both Social Security and medical care), and about 15 percent to pay the interest on the national debt. Because the number of elderly is growing and the number of old elderly, who account for the highest proportion of medical costs, is growing especially rapidly, the outlays for elderly programs will continue to rise unless benefit levels or the number of eligible recipients is reduced. The defense budget (plus international affairs expenditures), despite its growth during the 1980s, is now 6.6 percent of GNP, smaller proportionately than in 1958, when it was 11.1 percent. It is unlikely that the federal budget will significantly increase as a proportion of GNP because the persistent deficit could have serious repercussions in financial markets, and political resistance to tax increases remains high.

As a consequence, additional federal expenditures for any domestic purposes, let alone grants to state and local governments, will confront difficult trade-offs: lower benefits for the elderly, further reductions in defense while relative U.S. strength in the world declines, further cuts in the remaining 25 percent of the federal budget (essentially, all federal executive agencies and programs for the nonelderly poor), a growing budget deficit, and higher taxes.

Because states and localities confront heightened economic responsibility when the United States is saddled with high debts, their burden is likely to be all the greater. There is no escaping the burden of those debts; the question is how severe the burden will be and who will bear it.

At the same time that these major economic forces are transforming the economy and placing greater economic responsibility on state and local governments, the federal government has been reducing its role across a broad range of government responsibilities. The consequence is a reduction in the resources available to state and local governments and a shift of responsibilities created by economic change to the states and localities.

THE STATE-LOCAL ECONOMIC ROLE

To summarize, the principal forces shaping the new state and local economic role are:

□ Economic restructuring is increasing the relative importance of economic factors affected by state and local actions.

□ Federal ability to guide the U.S. economy in its traditional manner has been reduced. The principal consequence for state and local governments is that the regional economies on which they depend are more exposed to world economic and political forces.

□ The burden on state and local governments is all the greater due to the political shift of responsibility from Washington and to the heavy U.S. debt in general.

What this adds up to, in historical perspective, is a sudden intensification of the economic importance of state and local governments. To be sure, the extent to which states and localities can determine their economic fortunes is limited. Their influence, at best, is marginal in an economic environment in which powerful international forces, national policies, and private sector decisions combine to determine the economic future. But the key point is: in today's rapidly changing and highly competitive economy, *marginal* determinants can be *decisive* in shaping a regional economy.[12]

Given these conditions, how can state and local governments maximize their potential economic leverage? Experience suggests three important features of the state and local economic role:

☐ Both state and local governments share a core of economically important powers and responsibilities that they exercise jointly, if not necessarily in a consciously coordinated fashion. The state and its local subdivisions are two dimensions of a single political-governmental system organized on a subnational territorial basis. Forces tend to blur the distinction between what is strictly a state and what is strictly a local responsibility insofar as their practical economic impacts are concerned.

☐ Although the state and local levels are closely related in a single political-governmental system, each has retained a unique definition and responsibilities for economic policy.

☐ If the full economic policy potential of the state-local system is to be achieved, the shared responsibilities and complementary dimensions of states and localities need to be integrated more systematically.

The core of economically important powers shared by state and local governments goes far beyond the narrowly defined economic development programs that focus on direct business promotion. It includes five principal areas of economic importance: building economic foundations, strengthening the process of economic development, improving strategic management, making key political choices of economic importance, and improving regional coordination and synergy.

Economic Foundations. The key to economic performance will continue to be a market-driven private sector. However, private sector performance will depend in part on the existence of economic foundations that are affected by state and local governments.[13]

The key economic foundations are enumerated below with their associated state and local government activities shown in parentheses:[14]

☐ a capable and motivated work force (primary, secondary, and higher education; training; employment security; labor relations)

□ sound physical infrastructure (transportation, water supply, energy, waste disposal)
□ well-managed natural resources (air, land, water, wildlife, forest, minerals)
□ knowledge and technology (universities, research institutions, public information systems)
□ enterprise development (capital, regulation, technical assistance, financial assistance, export promotion, recruitment)
□ quality of life (public services, environmental quality, amenities, aesthetics, social and political institutions), and
□ fiscal soundness (tax structures and levels, user charges and fees, spending policy, transfer payments).

The first priority for state and local governments is to provide high-quality services at minimal cost in those areas of governmental responsibility that affect these economic foundations. In a competitive world economy, small advantages can spell the difference between success and failure. Consequently, sound, effectively managed government that provides good schools, good transportation, and a high quality of life at reasonable tax rates is the first step toward making a regional economy competitive.[15]

Most of the conventional public services that affect these foundations are provided through joint administration of state and local governments. For example, education, which is generally recognized as key to economic competitiveness, is administered by a combination of state and local institutions. The effectiveness with which states, general purpose local governments, and school districts arrange and carry out their joint responsibilities for education affects not only the quality of public schools but the overall economic environment of the state (National Governors' Association 1986).

The importance of effective joint action holds true for all the traditional services of economic importance for which states and localities share responsibility. It is also true for many of the functions that have been initiated specifically for the purpose of economic development. For example, New York, like many states, authorizes its local governments (including cities, counties, towns, villages, and Indian reservations) to establish industrial development agencies for the purpose of issuing industrial development bonds (IDBs) to finance business and industrial projects. Real property taxes on facilities using IDBs may be waived, although local authorities frequently negotiate payments in lieu of taxes (National Association of State Development Agencies 1986, p. 450).

Some economic programs were initiated at the local level and then adapted for statewide use. Oregon's Marketplace is an import substitution program developed by the state on the basis of a successful program in Lane County. Businesses that purchase products outside their own jurisdictions are encouraged to trade with firms that produce the same products within their jurisdictions (*Economic and Industrial Development News* 1987, p. 2).

The Process of Economic Development. The conventional recruitment approach to economic development is a function that could be assigned to an office of economic development.[16] State and local officials are now coming to recognize that development is not a function, but a process by which resources are transformed into higher-value uses.

The process of economic development involves constant change that is reflected in the typical life cycle of a firm.[17] A business is started; it expands, matures, possibly relocates, regenerates or contracts, and may eventually fold. In any given year, numerous firms may be started and others terminated; some will expand and others will contract, a few businesses will come into a jurisdiction, and a few will leave (Birch 1979). It is the net sum of this churning—not simply how many firms are attracted to the jurisdiction—that determines overall economic vitality and the number and quality of new jobs.[18]

The conventional recruitment approach focused on only one stage in the business life cycle: relocation. Under conventional economic development programs which consist of financial incentives to attract firms, the principal issue in state-local economic policy relationships is the degree of responsibility and authority each level has for recruitment. For example, the Texas Property Redevelopment and Tax Abatement Act authorizes a municipality to designate any part of an area nearby, but outside its territorial jurisdiction, as an industrial district, and for industrial companies within the district to negotiate exemptions from property taxes on land, equipment, and machinery (National Association of State Development Agencies 1986, p. 610).

States and localities alike have spent substantial energies and considerable resources on attempting to attract firms. Often more is spent on subsidies to the firms than the firms were likely to return in tax revenue, employment, payroll, or business purchases. Jurisdictions continue to compete and permit businesses to play them off, one against the other.

But many jurisdictions are becoming more sophisticated in their recruitment activities. They are more selective in the companies that they recruit, at what cost, and for what benefit. More important, they recognize that the firms recruited may be far less important than those that are already there. As one economic developer noted, "We found that businesses were going out the back door faster than we could bring them in the front door." Most jurisdictions are now concerned with business retention as well as attraction and are attempting to facilitate new business starts and the expansion or modernization of existing businesses.

The tendency is to give increasing concern to each stage of the firm's life cycle and to consider the link among those stages. Pennsylvania's Ben Franklin Partnership, established in 1983 with a $1 million state seed grant, had grown by 1987 into a $350 million public-private partnership operating at four advanced technology centers located at major research universities throughout the state. The regional centers collectively involve 128 universities and more than 2,500 businesses in technology development and business start-ups and expansion (Thornburgh 1987, pp. 10–11).

Strategic Management. In its simplest form, strategic management means developing the ability to anticipate regularly the changes that will affect the jurisdiction wherever they may occur, to be flexible and proactive in adjusting policy to account for those changes, and to integrate related policies that bear on the economy.

Many local governments have planning offices, but most follow the historical pattern of municipal planning in the United States, focusing narrowly on land use and physical development to the neglect of economic and social factors. Although land use and growth management planning has become highly sophisticated in many local jurisdictions, it often overlooks important forces affecting the economy. For example, jurisdictions experiencing rapid growth have failed to anticipate and prepare to deal with increasing traffic from other jurisdictions. Those with declining populations and tax bases have failed to consider how these changes will affect their ability to maintain their capital stock and service levels in such critical functions as road maintenance, health clinics, and waste management.

Formal state planning is more sporadic than local planning. Virtually every state established a state planning board in the 1930s in response to federal grant programs but terminated them when federal support ended within the decade (Wise 1977, p. 11). A renewal of federal support for state planning in the fifties and sixties produced a new generation of state planning agencies, but they frequently lacked strong political or organizational support within state government.

Some states have established formal planning regimes that involve both the state and local governments. Oregon's 1973 land use laws required cities and counties to develop jurisdictionwide land use plans. Hawaii has a comparable law, Vermont has a major land use program, many states have coastal area regulations, and some states like Colorado and Florida have developed growth management plans (State Policy Reports 1987, p. 25).

The pattern of state planning today is mixed. In some states, the planning or policy development agency is a key player in economic strategy; in others, it has little economic or other policy role but is confined to a strictly land use, research, or technical role. As a whole, however, the state planning and policy agencies have been a key source of innovative thinking and expertise on economic strategy.[19]

Many, if not most, states have established formal economic planning bodies, some with permanent status and some with temporary tenure, to prepare a state strategy or plan. Such an approach was taken in the Mississippi Statewide Economic Development Planning Act of 1987.

Some jurisdictions have attempted to strengthen and expand their planning capability by adding economists and demographers to their planning staffs, creating offices of strategic planning, or establishing broadly based task forces on strategic planning and alternative futures. In general, there is a growing recognition of the need for a stronger capability to anticipate economic trends, understand their impact on the regional economy, and coordinate the numerous programs of government that affect economic performance.

Although most states and many local jurisdictions have undertaken some form of strategic planning effort to improve the economy, little is being done to link state and local planning efforts. In one such effort, the Washington State Economic Development Board held meetings in 12 cities to help local leaders set up economic development councils and various public and private organizations (Washington Economic Development Board 1987, p. 2). In Maryland, the governor established a task force in each of the six principal economic regions to develop region-specific strategies for state policy.

Political Choices. States and localities confront key political choices that affect their economic future. State and local officials can work at cross-purposes if they make contradictory choices.

One choice is whether to focus on short-run economic gain or to invest for the long run. The temptation to focus only on projects that will show results (or the appearance of results) at the next election can sacrifice the long-run interest in building a solid economic base. On the other hand, an exclusive concern with the long term or failure to act decisively to correct problems or seize opportunities in the short run can be just as costly.

A second political choice has to do with the extent to which a jurisdiction should focus its efforts on developing particular technologies, firms, industries, or sectors. Diversification reduces the vulnerability of dependency on any one industry and increases the likelihood of developing industries that will emerge as strong growth sectors. It may also spread resources too thinly, thereby risking the loss of competitiveness in any one industry. Focusing development, on the other hand, may enhance competitive advantage by targeting market niches that provide an edge. But it may also create dependency on a limited number of industries that will be vulnerable to superior competition or to changing consumer tastes or technologies.

A third choice has to do with the relationship between the quality of life and economic growth. A sound economy is the basis of a high quality of life. However, some types of economic growth can erode the quality of life by placing stress on public services (especially roads and schools), polluting the air and water, consuming recreational and environmentally important land, and driving up land values faster than income gains. Deterioration of the quality of life, in turn, can undermine the economy by driving away top-quality people and businesses.

A fourth political choice has to do with equity. What responsibility does a community (state or local) have to assure its poorest citizens of a minimal standard of living, and how can the chronically unemployed and the disadvantaged be brought into the mainstream economic development process?

State and local officials have a degree of latitude in making these decisions for their jurisdictions, but unless the choices at one level are in reasonable accord with the other level of government, they can cancel one another. A well-intentioned state program to concentrate educational and research efforts sufficiently to achieve impact can be diluted by political demands to spread resources around the state. For example, Ohio is moving toward establishment of 10 centers of excellence in higher education, and Maryland has four state-supported biotechnology centers (Plosila 1987, p. 33).

Regional Coordination and Synergy. In all the above roles, a major challenge to state and local governments is to coordinate policy and foster the synergy of economic factors within de facto economic regions.

Regional needs vary. Rural areas based on agricultural, mineral, and forest industries are losing population. Some states have assumed a major responsibility for dealing with the consequences of declining rural economies and are experimenting with ways to link their efforts with those of rural counties and towns.

The larger urban areas, meanwhile, are no longer the conventional metropolitan areas of common imagery with a central city and suburban periphery surrounded by rural countryside. The new urban agglomerations consist of multiple nodes of high-density commercial, industrial, and retail development in a vast and amorphous sea of low-density residential development and assorted other land uses. Some urban agglomerations now extend over 100 miles, and many overlap, creating the vast urban corridors of megalopolis envisioned by earlier urban planners. Simply providing basic urban services to these vast and complex areas is a major challenge for state and local governments. Traffic congestion in many is chronic. Assuring adequate water supply and waste management now requires not only far more interaction among local governments in the region but the active involvement of state governments as well.

But the equation of regional governance has an added economic dimension: regions have become the primary units of economic geography in the new global economy. In the past, southern California, southeast Michigan, and New England traded and competed with one another. Today, they and the other regions of the United States trade and compete with the rest of the world.

The close connection between new industrial organization and regional institutions is visible in the flexible manufacturing networks of Europe. For example, the Emilia-Romagna region of northern Italy, with a population of 4 million, has generated an estimated 325,000 small firms, 90,000 of them in manufacturing. These firms use advanced technology and service networks to provide the flexibility needed to perform complex manufacturing tasks that are competitive in the world economy. The service networks are supplied by a rich array of programs sponsored by trade associations, municipal and regional governments, trade unions, and technical schools and universities (Hatch 1987, pp. 4–5).

The effectiveness with which economic regions are governed is also a determinant of international economic competitiveness. And because, for all intents and purposes, the United States has no conscious national regional policy, current regional governnance is almost exclusively within the purview of state and local government.

THE STATE DIMENSION

Although both the state and local levels share powers in each of the five areas discussed above, both have their own unique responsibilities. This section describes the state's responsibilities.

Direct Impact. The economic foundations of regional economies and local jurisdictions throughout the state are affected by a broad range of statewide programs: transportation, education, agriculture, natural resources, licensing and regulation, commerce, and many others. Numerous quasi-public institutions, such as housing authorities, port authorities, public utilities, finance authorities, venture capital funds, and so on, are also economically important.

Statewide departments and policies dealing with education and transportation are likely to have more impact on the health of local economies than the actions of a state department of commerce or economic development. An adequate state transportation system in support of a local economy may require highways, ports, airports, waterways, and mass transit facilities, all of which are affected in myriad ways—planning, financing, building, operating, maintaining, and regulating—by the state. The same is true for water supply, waste disposal, job training, community development, agriculture, communications, energy, and housing. In these statewide programs, many of the important economic development decisions are made that affect local areas.

Effect on Local Capacity. States also affect local economies by determining the capacity of local governments to deal with their own economies. Local governments are the legal creatures of the state, from which they derive their basic legal, financial, and administrative powers. Many local governments are hampered by antiquated legal and administrative structures, inadequate revenue sources, and a maze of state laws and regulations that limit their ability to do their jobs properly. These deficiencies are well-known, but they generally have been categorized as failures of administration and local government service capacity. In today's competitive world economy, they now may also constitute deficiencies in local capacity for effective economic policy.

Most local governments advocate home rule, which would give them greater legal authority to adopt their own structure and process of government. A case can be made that such flexibility is now important not only to facilitate more effective government but to give local governments the authority they need to perform important economic responsibilities. They include flexibility to alter political boundaries in accordance with changing growth patterns; authority to enter into agreements with neighboring jurisdictions for joint service arrangements; authority to perform a full range of local services; adequate sources of revenue to finance programmatic responsibilities; and legal flexibility in planning, land use, and development to be able to undertake more innovative and complex arrangements involving the private sector.

Some states have explicitly recognized the importance of strengthening local capacity for economic development purposes. A relatively common approach is for the state development agency to establish standards for local economic development programs and to certify local governments when they have achieved the standards.

Some states recognize the fact that local capacity means more than improvements in distinct local jurisdictions, that it requires the strengthening of regional capacity as a whole. For example, the Pennsylvania Enterprise Development Program, initiated in the early 1980s, uses regional councils, comprised of member local governments, as an administering body for several of its programs. Among them are a revolving loan fund for small businesses, export promotion, family farm assistance, and labor-management cooperation (National Association of Regional Councils 1987, pp. 3–4).

Interstate Coordination. Because state boundaries frequently bisect economic regions, interstate coordination is required if state and local economic policies are to be complementary for any given multistate region. Local governments can achieve some degree of coordination with their neighboring counterpart local jurisdictions in other states, but their flexibility to do so depends in large measure on state law. Most interstate regional issues require the direct involvement of state governments themselves.

In recent years, such interstate institutions as the Southern Growth Policies Board have become increasingly influential. The northeastern, midwestern, Great Lakes, and western regions have all strengthened existing regional institutions or created new ones. The Center for the New West, for example, was established in 1986 (originally named the Western States Strategy Center) to bring together public and private leaders at the state and local levels throughout the West to mount more coordinated economic development efforts (Fosler 1988).

One interstate cooperative venture that explicitly recognizes the state-local connection is the Joined-by-a-River project undertaken by Illinois and Iowa to improve the regional economy of the Quad Cities area. The area is comprised of 14 communities (including Moline, Illinois, and Davenport, Iowa), forming a common economic region split by the Mississippi River, which also defines the state line. About half the area's 380,000 citizens live in each state. Each state appropriated $100,000 for a joint marketing effort that will include local entities as well as the state development agencies (*Economic and Industrial Development News* 1987).

THE LOCAL DIMENSION

The unique local responsibilities in the state-local economic partnership include direct impact, advocacy, and regional integration.

Direct Impact. As is true for states, local governments have the potential for direct impact in each of the five areas of economic responsibility discussed above.

The local economic development role varies widely by the type, size, form, and location of the local government. General purpose county and municipal governments are likely to have greater economic responsibilities than special districts, although the functions carried out by some special districts—in education, water supply, transportation, and other areas—have important economic content in their own right.

Advocacy. Local governments have an important role as advocates for sound economic policy at the state level. (Similarly, states, in combination with local governments, have an advocacy role to play at the federal level.)

Local governments serious about influencing state actions that affect their local economies know that the critical battles have to be fought in the major policy areas and agencies that are frequently outside the formal economic development agency: in the departments of transportation and education; in the offices of budget, finance, policy development, the attorney general, and the governor; and in the legislature. But most local governments limit their advocacy to programs or laws with specific impact in their jurisdictions, for example, road projects, training centers, and the like. Similarly, state associations of counties or municipalities tend to focus narrowly on state actions that affect local governments as a class.

Few local governments or their state associations have systematically thought through the way in which state government can strengthen the state economy as a whole. Consequently, few have a coordinated strategy for assuring that the state is performing its economic role effectively. In some states, local government representatives have participated in advisory boards or task forces formulating state economic strategy. And some local government officials are quicker than state officials to understand the new economic environment. For the most part, however, local officials are passive and aloof from broadly based state efforts, they approach state economic policy in a piecemeal fashion, or they have been put in a reactive posture by state initiatives. To date, they have not been a force for a more systematic and integrated approach to state economic policy.

Regional Integration. Local governments have a special role in developing the economic region of which they are a part. Just as states have a special role in interstate coordination, so do local governments in interlocal coordination within their regions.

A rich assortment of interlocal, regional institutions has evolved in the United States, from city-county consolidation to regional councils of government, interjurisdictional contracting, and joint service arrangements. These organizations and related regional forms of government have traditionally been considered in the context of service delivery and local government structure. In the new competitive environment, they are being viewed in terms of regional capacity for economic growth.

LINKING STATE AND LOCAL STRATEGIES

Under the conventional model, in which the economic roles of both states and local governments are perceived as limited to business recruitment, the relationship between state and local officials is comparatively simple. At both levels, responsibility for recruitment resides in a formally designated economic development agency. That agency might have one of a variety of names—commerce, industrial development, economic development—but whatever the name, its principal responsibility is to recruit business. The central intergovernmental question in such a relationship is whether officials in the state and local development agencies work together effectively to bring business to the state and to specific regions and jurisdictions within the state.

Even this relatively simple relationship is frequently strained. Local economic development specialists typically complain that the state program is essentially nonexistent; it is ineffective, ignores local efforts, or fails to coordinate with local efforts; and state recruitment is biased toward politically favored parts of the state.

Some states have eased such tensions by coordinating their recruitment activities with their local counterparts. Others have not. But these problems of economic policy coordination under the conventional model are miniscule compared to the challenge of harmonizing state and local efforts under the new model, which is concerned with economic foundations, process, and strategy for long-term economic growth.

The new economic responsibilities of state and local governments require the coordination of state and local economic strategies across a broad range of both traditional and new government programs. This interaction requires the formulation of compatible strategies in the first place. And it also requires coordination in the implementation of those strategies.

Formulation of Compatible Strategies. Formulating compatible state and local economic strategies is a challenging task—conceptually, administratively, and politically. If both state and local officials are still working under the old model, that is, a nearly exclusive preoccupation with business recruitment, coordinating policies may be comparatively easy, but the impact of the integrated state-local effort is not likely to be significant.

If officials at one level are working under the old recruitment model while those at the other level have moved on to the new model, then the chances of integrating state and local policies are slight. Officials at the two levels will not even be talking the same language.

Even if both state and local officials are attempting to formulate strategies that confront and try to take advantage of the new economic realities, their task, although "doable" and potentially highly rewarding, is nonetheless formidable. There must be a reasonable degree of agreement on the conceptual outlines of the new state-local economic role and on the division of responsibilities that role implies for each of the two levels of government. That division, moreover, will vary, depending on the size of the state and the local jurisdiction, the nature of the economic base, and nuances of the political culture of each.

For their strategies to be compatible, both the state and the local governments must have a strategy in the first place, one that can be communicated and negotiated with the other. Some jurisdictions have written strategies that can be read and compared. Others have evolved reasonably well-conceived strategies that, although not written, can be clearly articulated, understood, and negotiated. However, even in those rare instances when both states and local governments have relatively well-conceived strategies, seldom are there good institutional arrangements by which those strategies can be discussed and negotiated. The typical channels of state-local political communications—the legislature, state executive agencies, political parties, and the news media—are not the most felicitous for negotiating an economic strategy that involves new concepts and cuts across traditional programmatic and political turf. More productive channels are likely to be the offices of top legislative leaders and the governor, special task forces structured to include key state and local actors, and the "little ACIRs"—state-local commissions modeled after the federal Advisory Commission on Intergovernmental Relations.

The Florida State and Regional Planning Act of 1984 establishes a comprehensive and elaborate procedure for statewide planning that involves local governments and regional councils. The impetus for the Florida initiatives was more growth management than economic development, but farsighted Floridians see the two issues as inseparable; Florida's ability to manage its growth efficiently while preserving its quality of life will play a major role in determining its long-term economic performance (Florida Comprehensive Planning Committee 1987).

Some states and their local governments have attempted to work jointly toward the development of more specific strategies that focus on economic improvement in particular regions. For example, Ohio created the Ohio Riverfront Redevelopment Task Force (1987) to prepare a plan for the economic and environmental improvement of communities along the Ohio River over a 20-year period. The task force is comprised of the directors of the Ohio departments of development, health, transportation, natural resources, and environmental protection; one local official each from the cities of Cincinnati, Steubenville, Portsmouth, East Liverpool, and Marietta; three county commissioners; and representatives from business, civic, and labor groups.

Implementation of Compatible Strategies. Even successfully integrated economic strategies must be implemented in a coordinated fashion—through specific actions by specific institutions at specific times in specific places. Coordination is important to ensure that each strategy is internally consistent and regionally focused. For example, both state and local strategies may agree on the desirability of promoting the commercialization of technology. But putting research to work in commercially profitable ways requires a synergy among parts of various state and local economic programs: state-sponsored university research, technology institutes, business linkage programs, incubators, entrepreneurship training, financial and technical assistance, job training, and marketing assistance. Unless those programs are brought together and managed effectively at a given time and location, their impact is likely to be diffuse and ineffective.

Here again, as in the coordination of state and local strategy formulation, the institutional arrangements for assuring practical linkages in operation are weak at best.

Many of the state initiatives implicitly recognize the importance of geographical synergy. Enterprise zones and small business incubators, for example, are ways of mobilizing a combination of resources in specific places. But there is also a growing recognition of the need to involve more explicitly state and local actors in both the public and the private sectors in focusing programs and resources in specific regions.

Massachusetts was one of the first states to attempt consciously to direct development to distressed areas. It combined state programs and administrative directives to assist Lowell, Fitchburg, and other older industrial cities in the development of Heritage Parks and the conversion of old factories into new office and factory facilities (Ferguson and Ladd 1988).

Michigan, in the early 1980s, established the Community Growth Alliance Program to improve coordination among local economic development agencies (National Association of Regional Councils 1987, p. 9).

Iowa has established a network of regional coordinating councils to encourage local governments to work together on economic issues. Of particular concern in rural Iowa is the need to consolidate programs and facilities—such as schools, libraries, and health clinics—that individual local governments had operated independently but that strained tax bases can no longer support (Thoms interview 1987).

CONCLUSION

Changing economic and political circumstances have fundamentally altered the model of economic policy in the United States. The federal government no longer has a monopoly on economic policy, in part because of the changing global relationships and in part because state and local governments are better-suited to perform certain functions in the new economy. State and local government economic responsibilities have moved far beyond the narrow focus on business recruitment to include a broad concern with economic foundations, process, and strategy. These new circumstances no longer permit the neat distinction between state and local governments that has been customary during the past half-century of federal government predominance in the intergovernmental system.

The basic constitutional relationship between states and local governments has never been in doubt: local governments derive their legal powers from the state. But the pattern of de facto relationships established during the period of federal predominance found local governments increasingly viewing themselves as independent entities that often had stronger political and fiscal ties with Washington than with the statehouse. The states, meanwhile, seemed to atrophy in a system geared toward aggressive national policymaking that bypassed the state level and focused directly on local issues.

The inertia of these old habits does not fade easily, but fading it is. Many of the states have been among the leaders in the transition, taking the initiative to upgrade their overall capacity and experimenting with new approaches to public policy, including economic development. The state initiatives in economic policy have matured to the point at which it is apparent that local government efforts are critical to the success of state strategy. The state economy, after all, is comprised of the regional economies that fall entirely or partly within state boundaries. The strength of those economies is determined in part by the effectiveness of local governance.

Local governments, meanwhile, have discovered that their economic development efforts are increasingly defined by the actions of state government. Many state programs directly impact their local economy. Their legal, administrative, and fiscal capacity is determined by the state in the first instance. Their political boundaries typically cover no more than a small slice of the economic region of which they are a part, a region over which the state invariably has broader political coverage. And their individual economic programs—whether recruitment, export promotion, or education and training—can be enhanced or constrained by state programs in the same programmatic areas.

Consequently, the integral link between state and local governments and the inescapable wholeness of the state-local political-government system are slowly but inexorably reasserting themselves in the field of economic policy as in other state-local relationships. It is less than a perfect marriage. The political boundaries of states and their subdivisions are notoriously incongruous with the real contours of regional economies. Nonetheless, the formal boundaries, institutions of government, and political traditions that define the legal and political organization of subnational regions in the United States are centered in the states and their local subdivisions. And in an economic era that places so great a premium on effective action at the regional level, the ability of the state-local system to formulate and implement a coherent economic policy will be a key to regional—and ultimately to national—economic performance.

Notes

1. Numerous studies have surveyed state economic initiatives in recent years, including National Governors' Association. (NGA) 1987, 1986, 1983; NGA Center for Policy Research 1986; U.S. Congress 1984; President's Commission 1984; Clarke 1986; and Vaughn, Pollard, and Dyer 1986.

2. Total federal government receipts in 1986 were $769 billion. Total state and local 1986 receipts from their own sources (i.e., excluding federal grants, which totaled $104 billion) were $516 billion, equal to 67 percent of total federal receipts. If the $284 billion of federal social insurance receipts (principally Social Security) are excluded from federal receipts, the remaining $458 billion is less than total state and local government receipts (*Economic Report of the President* 1987).

3. Parts of the following sections were taken from Fosler 1987.

4. The announcement by Volkswagen that it would close its Stanton, Pennsylvania, plant is an indication that the competition resulting from overcapacity is affecting foreign as well as domestic manufacturers in the United States.

5. The net sum of these changes to date is that the United States currently has a

higher proportion of its population employed than any other industrial country and a lower unemployment rate than any country but Japan.

6. The growth in the volume of world trade began to slow in the 1970s, in part due to growing trade restrictions.

7. In essence, the United States has been consuming more than it has been producing, and making up the difference by importing from abroad. The nation financed both the national debt created by the budget deficits and the foreign debt created by the trade deficits by borrowing, and a substantial part of that borrowing has been from foreigners.

8. Fiscal policy (as conceived by Keynesians) essentially entails generating budget deficits during periods of recession in order to stimulate economic demand and building budget surpluses during periods of economic growth in order to keep the lid on inflation.

9. Just before the October 1987 stock market crash, the Federal Reserve had increased interest rates in order to curb inflation. But when the market crashed and the country found itself confronting a major financial crisis, the Fed promptly reversed its position and started pumping money into the financial system to prevent a liquidity crisis.

10. See Gilpin (1987) for a discussion of the radically changing international political economy and its implications for U.S. economic policy.

11. No doubt there will be promises of further assistance, as members of Congress attempt to demonstrate their concern with the pressing issues that confront state and local governments: education, day care, infrastructure, health, and so on. But state and local officials should be wary because the most likely form of such assistance would be negligible new funding accompanied by ponderous new regulatory requirements.

12. See Fosler (1988) for a discussion of economic policies in seven states.

13. The debate over what constitutes an appropriate economic climate is reflected in the contrasting approaches of different performance indices of the states. The Grant Thornton index uses "22 factors selected by manufacturers as important to business success," (Grant Thornton 1986). The Corporation for Enterprise Development (CfED) (1987) index uses broad measures in four areas: economic performance, business vitality, human resource and financial capacity, and government policies. Still another index ranks states according to their records on small business growth (INC Annual Report 1987).

14. The economic foundations are further defined in Committee for Economic Development (1986).

15. Much can be done to strengthen the management of county government. For example, the National Civic League is currently revising the Model County Charter and is also drafting model ordinances or local laws for noncharter counties to provide for professional management.

16. Although many economic development programs focus on job creation, others have turned to wealth creation (Vaughan, Pollard, and Dyer 1985).

17. The life cycle of the firm is also closely related to product cycles (Markusen 1985).

18. Although small and medium-size firms accounted for a large share of jobs and job growth, by 1980, "70 percent of all private economic activity was controlled and operated by eight hundred conglomerate firms while the remaining 30 percent was shared by 14 million firms" (Bergman and Goldstein 1986, p. 88).

19. The Council of State Planning and Policy Agencies, which is the national association of the various state agencies of the same name or purpose, is among the leading institutions in the country in forging the new state economic role.

References

Bergman, Edward M., and Harvey A. Goldstein. 1986. Dynamics, Structural Change, and Economic Development Paths. In *Local Economics in Transition: Policy Realities and Development Potential*, edited by Edward M. Bergman. Durham, N.C.: Duke University Press.

Birch, David L. 1987. The Booming Hidden Market. *INC Magazine* 9(11): 15.

———. 1979. The Job Generation Process. Cambridge, Mass.: MIT Program on Neighborhood and Regional Change. Photocopy.

Clarke, Marianne K. 1986. *Revitalizing State Economies: A Review of State Economic Development Policies and Programs.* Washington, D.C.: National Governors' Association.

Committee for Economic Development (CED). 1986. Leadership for Dynamic State Economies. New York: CED.

Corporation for Enterprise Development (CfED). 1987. *Making the Grade: The Development Report Card for the States.* Washington, D.C.: CfED.

Economic and Industrial Development News. 1987. 6(20).

———. 1987. 6(19): 2.

Ferguson, Ronald R., and Helen F. Ladd. 1988. Massachusetts. In *New Economic Role of American States*, edited by R. Scott Fosler. New York: Oxford University Press.

Florida Comprehensive Planning Committee. 1987. *Keys to Florida's Future: Winning in a Competitive World.*

Fosler, R. Scott. 1988. Economic Development: A Regional Challenge to the Nation's Heartland. *Economic Review* (Federal Reserve Bank of Kansas City) (May): 10–19.

———. 1987. *The Future Economic Role of Counties.* Washington, D.C.: National Association of Counties, Commission on the Future. Photocopy.

———, ed. 1988. *The New Economic Role of American States.* New York: Oxford University Press.

Gilpin, Robert. 1987. *The Political Economy of International Relations.* Princeton, N.J.: Princeton University Press.

Grant Thornton. 1986. *The Seventh Annual Study of General Manufacturing Climates of the Forty-eight Contiguous States of America.* Chicago: Grant Thornton.

INC Annual Report on the States. 1987. *INC Magazine* 9(11): 76–92.

Markusen, Anne R. 1985. *Product Cycles, Oligopoly and Regional Development.* Cambridge, Mass.: MIT Press.

National Governors' Association (NGA). 1987. *Making America Work.* Washington, D.C.: NGA.

———. 1986. *Time for Results: The Governors' 1991 Report on Education.*

———. 1983. *Technology & Growth: State Incentives in Technological Innovation.*

——. Center for Policy Research. 1986. *Revitalizing State Economies: A Report to the Committee on Economic Development and Technological Innovation.*

National Association of State Development Agencies. 1986. *Directory of Incentives for Business Investment and Development in the United States: A State-by-State Guide.* Second Edition. Washington, D.C.: Urban Institute Press.

Ohio Riverfront Redevelopment Task Force. 1987. Development of the Ohio Riverfront: A Twenty-Year Strategic Plan. Draft.

President's Commission on Industrial Competitiveness. 1984. *Innovations in Industrial Competitiveness at the State Level.* Menlo Park, Calif.: SRI International.

State Policy Reports. 1987. 5(12): 25.

Thoms, Allan T., Director, Iowa Department of Economic Development. 1987. Interview, 27 January.

Thornburgh, Dick. 1987. The State's Role in an Era of Economic Transition: The Pennsylvania Experience. Address to the Distinguished Lecture Series, School of Urban and Public Affairs, Carnegie-Mellon University, Pittsburgh, May.

U.S. Congress. Office of Technology Assessment. 1984. *Technology, Innovation, and Regional Economic Development.* Washington, D.C.

Vaughan, Robert J., Robert Pollard, and Barbara Dyer. 1985. *The Wealth of States: Policies for a Dynamic Economy.* Washington, D.C.: Council of State Planning Agencies.

Washington State Economic Development Board. 1987. *The Washington State Economy: An Assessment of its Strengths and Weaknesses.* Report to the Legislature, Volume II. (January).

Wise, Harold T. 1977. *History of State Planning.* Washington, D.C.: Council of State Planning Agencies.

Chapter Five

STRESS AND STALEMATE: ILLINOIS STATE-LOCAL RELATIONS IN THE 1980s

Charles J. Orlebeke

"What's in it for us?" This perennial question of representative democratic institutions was asked and answered in the spring of 1988 by State Senator James "Pate" Philip, minority leader in the Illinois legislature. "There is nothing in it for suburbanites or Downstaters. . . . Statewide tax increases benefit, generally speaking, the city [Chicago]. It doesn't help the suburbs" (*Chicago Tribune*, 27 April 1988, p. 2).

Philip, who represents some of Chicago's flourishing western suburbs, neatly captured what is probably the dominant theme in Illinois state-local relations, the three-way tension among Chicago, the communities that surround it, and "downstate" Illinois (all the rest of the state in any direction from Chicago, including north). In this case, Philip was reacting to a proposed increase in the state personal income tax being advocated by the mayor of Chicago, Eugene Sawyer, who had gone to the capital in Springfield to plead for more state support of Chicago's school system. Sawyer also called for an increase in the one-twelfth share of state income tax revenues returned to local governments on a straight population basis. Such a measure would obviously help Chicago, which contains more than one-fourth the state's population, but it would also spread the benefits around to the state's other 1,278 municipalities and 102 counties—and perhaps attract some vital political support in the state legislature.

None of these proposals was new; they have in fact been a staple of Illinois political debate throughout the 1980s, even earlier. If the past is any guide (and I believe it is), the debate in 1988 will result in a highly limited response to the most urgent pressures for state assistance, a response that disturbs prevailing political power arrangements as little as possible. To be sure, there have been limited and incremental shifts in these arrangements during the 1980s in response to either specific local programs or changes in fiscal or program policies handed down by the federal government. However, as Senator Philip's statement signals, reform (however defined) or substantial change in state-local relationships in Illinois seems an unlikely prospect.

This case study focuses on state-local relations in Illinois in the 1980s. It explores how many of the themes developed elsewhere in this book were played out in Illinois: the pressures of changing federal policies, troubled local economies, pressures to provide services despite shrinking budgets, complex systems of local government, tensions among regions and levels of government within a state, and the recent adoption of new revenue-raising mechanisms. This state presents a particularly lively story because Illinois politics tend to be outspoken and contentious, and Chicago politics have been especially volatile this decade. Responding to the challenges of the 1980s, Illinois's rival regions—Chicago, its surrounding suburbs, and downstate Illinois—have developed a few important new approaches to revenue raising and the provision of services. But Illinois has failed to adopt certain proposed overall measures, and some key issues of how localities are to deal with shrinking revenue bases remain unresolved, ready to flare up into crisis situations. To a greater extent than in most other states, stress and stalemate have been the major themes in state-local relations in Illinois throughout the decade.

THE BACKGROUND ON STATE-LOCAL
RELATIONS IN ILLINOIS

Illinois is a politically conservative state with a strong tradition of local control. "Ninety-five percent of what cities want from the state is to be left alone," a staff member of the Illinois Municipal League recently told me (Frang 1988). (The other 5 percent, it is reasonable to assume, would be money without strings.) Historically, Illinois state government has played the role of broker rather than leader, as the representatives of Chicago, its suburbs, and downstate Illinois have contended for shares of revenue raised at the state level.

These three areas, the city, its suburbs, and the rest of the state, divide the 11.3 million population of Illinois in roughly equal parts: Chicago has a population of 3 million, the suburbs have 4.1 million, and downstate Illinois has 4.3 million. Although Chicago does not dominate Illinois politics, it has been a powerful force historically

Stress and Stalemate: Illinois   113

because of its economic and cultural significance as well as its sheer size: it is 21 times larger than the next largest city, Rockford. During the two-decade-long mayoralty of Richard Daley (1955–76), Chicago was also a cohesive political force in the legislature. The city's claims on state resources had to be contended with, if not always satisfied, and the city expected the state to stay out of its internal political affairs.

Local governments have proliferated in Illinois, and a seeker of tidiness in state-local arrangements should probably bypass the state. It has 6,626 units of local government, far more than any other state and more than four times the national average per state. The total includes 102 counties, 1,279 municipalities, 1,434 townships, 2,782 special districts, and about 1,000 school districts. The total is inching downward, however, as the population decline forces school district consolidation in some rural areas.

The six-county Chicago metropolitan area, with a population of 7 million, includes 261 municipalities; however, separate units of government are typically responsible for libraries, parks, and education within or overlapping municipal boundaries. Within the city of Chicago, the homeowner pays property taxes to support Cook County, the Chicago Park District, the City Colleges of Chicago, the Board of Education, the Metropolitan Sanitary District of Greater Chicago, the Cook County Forest Preserve District, as well as the city government.

Three separate operating boards manage public transportation in the Chicago metropolitan area: the Chicago Transit Authority, which runs buses and trains within Chicago and a few nearby suburbs; PACE, a suburban bus system; and METRA, the commuter rail system operating between Chicago and suburbs. A fourth body, the Regional Transportation Authority, holds budget approval authority over the other three.

Despite Illinois's tradition of localism, a burst of state activism occurred in the early 1970s that did much to define state-local relations from then on. In 1970, the legislature passed a state income tax on individuals (2.5 percent) and corporations (4.0 percent)—a key event. The legislature took this step in response to a billion dollar deficit in the state budget and widespread opposition to further increases in local property taxes. Then-Governor Richard Ogilvie originally proposed that one-eighth of all income tax revenues would be redistributed to municipalities and counties; however, the legislature set the figure at one-twelfth. As already suggested, the local share of the state income tax became a persistent issue in state-local finance.

A second important event in 1970 was the approval of a new

constitution, which conferred automatic home rule status on all cities over 25,000 population and provided the home rule option to smaller communities, subject to local referendum. Home rule status provides broad powers to levy taxes and incur debt without seeking a local referendum, although the constitution [Art. 7, sect. 6(e)(2)] specifically ruled out local taxes on "income, occupation, or earnings." There has been a steady march of communities into home rule status—the number passed 100 in 1986—and a Northern Illinois University study (Banovetz and Ketty 1986) of Illinois home rule concluded that it "has been a critical component of the state's response to the economic crisis of the decade."

Also during the early 1970s, the state assumed control of the Aid to Families with Dependent Children (AFDC) and Medicaid programs; passed major bond issues to support construction of local water pollution treatment facilities, roads, mass transit, and airports; increased state school aid sharply; and created the Regional Transportation Authority in the Chicago area (subject to a referendum, which narrowly passed).

State initiatives in the 1970s coincided with a reasonably healthy economy for most of the decade as well as with a greatly increased flow of federal grants across the board: general fiscal support in the form of revenue sharing, increased funding of social service programs, and rising federal support for community development and public infrastructure.

But as Illinois entered the benchmark period in state-federal relations, the later Carter years, the picture quite suddenly darkened. At the federal level, President Carter took a reading of California's Proposition 13 and was born again as a fiscal conservative. Federal grants began the long slide that accelerated in the Reagan years.[1] Much more urgent were fiscal crises in two Chicago public agencies—the Board of Education and the Chicago Transit Authority (CTA). The Board of Education had suffered from years of mismanagement and thinly disguised deficit spending; the CTA was similarly a model of inefficiency, and it also refused to make unpopular fare increases to meet rising operating costs. Both agencies, as well as city political leaders, made the fundamental miscalculation that the state would somehow bail them out of the crisis. They were wrong. Instead, in the Board of Education case, the state created a new governmental entity, the Chicago School Finance Authority, and authorized it to issue $500 million in general obligation bonds guaranteed by a property tax increase. The state forced the CTA to raise fares, and again the legislature extended to Chicago area citizens the privilege of raising their own taxes, this time a sales tax increase of 1 percent in Cook County and 0.25 percent in the five "collar" cities.

STATE-LOCAL RELATIONS IN THE 1980s: AN OVERVIEW

The chief question for Illinois as it entered the 1980s was how to respond to a three-way squeeze: (1) the rising cost of public services, including education; (2) the waning ability of the state's revenue structure to generate money to support state service obligations in such areas as health care, corrections, higher education, and mental health; and (3) the highly likely prospect that the federal government under Ronald Reagan would not help with the first two problems.

Although the outlines of these problems were clearly discernible as the decade began, Illinois political leaders did not mount any systematic effort to deal with them. Politicians do not generally take the long view and Illinois was surely no exception. The state created no special commissions or task forces, neither the governor nor the legislature nor local government organizations made major policy pronouncements, and no statewide civic group or coalition specifically addressed broad questions of state-local relations or presented an agenda for change.

The decisions of the 1980s affecting state-local relations have tended to be ad hoc, reactive, and small in impact. When the state and local governments (particularly Chicago) confronted each other, the political rhetoric was unusually contentious and the political outcome not much beyond stalemate. For example, in a September 1981 radio interview, Governor James Thompson posed this rhetorical question: "Do you want me to bankrupt the state of Illinois because Chicago political leaders don't have the guts to solve their own problems?" The remark captured a number of themes in Illinois politics and also proved to be prophetic. Those themes included open conflict between the state and its largest city, the portrayal of Chicago political leaders as insatiable spenders and gutless to boot, and the assertion that Chicago's problems are its own to solve.

"Fend-for-yourself federalism," the term John Shannon (1987), former director of the Advisory Commission on Intergovernmental Relations (ACIR), applied to the national scene, applies to Illinois as well. As a fiscal partner in state-local finance, the state's role has barely held its own, largely because the governor and the legislature have been unable to agree on a permanent tax increase. Spending by local governments continues to rise, but Illinois localities are paying for those increases from their own sources. The state share of local school spending slid steadily from its high point (48 percent) in the mid-1970s down to about 40 percent. Few institutional change initiatives affecting state-local relations have occurred in the 1980s; state political leaders have simply been too preoccupied with the state's own precarious fiscal situation. In 1988, Governor Thompson acknowledged this point symbolically by combining his state of the state and budget messages: "This year the state of our state *is* the budget."

The state government has not been in complete retreat, however. In promoting economic development, Illinois has aggressively marketed its advantages nationally and internationally. Under the banner of Build Illinois, the state in 1985 committed itself to a $2.3 billion program to finance housing, economic development, and infrastructure improvements throughout the state over a five-year period. In education, the governor and the legislature bought into the national education reform movement, and in 1985 it "passed the most comprehensive package of school reform legislation in over a decade" (Bakalis 1986, p. 15). Both Build Illinois and education reform, however, have attracted criticism for falling far short of their rhetorical promise.

In state-local fiscal affairs in the 1980s, one would need to look hard for high drama. There has been stress and some progress. From the perspective of local officials, the legislature continued to indulge its penchant for complicating their lives without paying the price: the state raised homestead exemption for property taxes again in 1983, increased local employee pension obligations, and required home rule governments to engage in collective bargaining with their employees. Although 1981 legislation required the state to reimburse localities for such mandated expenses, the legislature has so far simply exempted each new obligation from the State Mandates Act.

On the more positive side, the legislature in 1983 did agree to restructure the Regional Transportation Authority, providing for a much more stable revenue base, including a state subsidy. In a direct response to the demise of general revenue sharing, the legislature empowered counties to levy a 0.25 percent sales tax on the entire county tax base, not just the unincorporated areas. Nor had the city of Chicago and the state lost the ability to cut deals on specific matters, such as financing mechanisms for professional sports stadiums and for expansion of the city's huge McCormick Place exposition center. And in an exquisitely ironic bargain between Governor

Thompson and the late Mayor Harold Washington, the state police agreed to take over traffic patrol of Chicago's interstate expressways in exchange for permission to open state lottery sales outlets at Chicago's O'Hare Airport.

In assessing the state role in the Chicago metropolitan areas, the Regional Partnership, a coalition of civic and business organizations, concluded in its 1987 State of the Region report (p. viii):

Without ignoring the significant improvements that have occurred in economic development funding, reorganization of the Regional Transportation Authority, infrastructure programs and the like, it is impossible to assess the state of the region without concluding that adequate state response is missing in issue after issue.

The State of the Region specified education funding, health care for the indigent, low-income housing, and social services as areas in which the state was falling short. The report went on to say that "the state has not picked up its piece of the New Federalism equation." In the narrow sense, this last criticism is not completely fair because Illinois did take over programmatic responsibilities devolved from the federal government—such as the new block grants and the Job Training Partnership Act—in a reasonably effective and straightforward way. But in the broader sense, the political stalemate that resulted from state fiscal problems has effectively blunted state initiative along a larger front of state-local relations.

State Finances in the 1980s

Illinois state finances in the 1980s could be characterized as an extended exercise in crisis management. In the late 1970s, there was little turbulence on the surface, but underneath the trends were ominous. After the close of the 1982 fiscal year, the state comptroller (1983, p. 1) reported that the state's fiscal health, "while appearing to be on a par with the previous fiscal years was unfortunately in a somewhat precarious position." Sales tax revenues, hit by recession, had come in $333 million below estimate—the largest contributor to a $538 million shortfall. In addition, about $500 million in fiscal year 1982 obligations, including a school aid payment, were juggled into fiscal year 1983. A tax increase was inevitable.

In 1983, Governor Thompson adopted a strategy of presenting a doomsday budget for state fiscal year 1983–84, which called for decreases in state school aid, elimination of state revenue sharing of the income tax, elimination of the general assistance (welfare) program, and sharp cutbacks in social services. He followed this with a $1.6 billion proposal for new revenues, including an increase in the personal income tax from 2.5 percent to 4 percent. On the eve of the new fiscal year, the legislature passed a much smaller package, $963 million, built around an 18-month temporary increase (expiring June 30, 1984) in the income tax to only 3 percent, a one-cent increase in the state sales tax to 5 percent, and a five-and-one-half-cent-per-gallon increase in the state gasoline tax. The revenue package included an $85 million subsidy to the regional transportation authority. Doomsday had been averted, but state school aid had increased only 1 percent, and the state comptroller (1984, p. 5) reported at the end of the fiscal year 1984 that "the fiscal position of the General Fund was not dramatically improved."

State spending has continued to rise gradually since 1984, with the help of a brisker economy and the permanent sales and gas tax increases passed in 1983. A brief respite from fiscal crisis emboldened the governor and legislature in 1985 to pass and sign the "Build Illinois" capital improvement program and increase school aid $400 million, including about $100 million to fund an educational reform package. But in early 1987, shortly after being easily reelected to an unprecedented fourth term, Governor Thompson again proposed an increase in the state income tax. The legislature refused. Using his broad amendatory veto power, the governor reluctantly cut back on school aid, higher education, and other services to prevent fiscal collapse. Throughout the 1988 fiscal year, the state had to resort to such stopgaps as short-term borrowing and stretching out payments to hospitals and other Medicaid vendors. Medicaid payments were suspended entirely in April until the new fiscal year began on July 1.

Governor Thompson adopted a different strategy in presenting a fiscal year 1989 budget proposal. This budget is essentially a stand-still spending plan, based on current revenue sources. The governor has urged a modest but unspecified increase in the state income tax, choosing to join rather than lead a push for more revenues.

The persistence of fiscal stress at the state level in the 1980s has created a chilly climate for state initiatives that would assist local governments. The extent to which state assistance has been maintained is more the result of duress and indirect forces than deliberate policy. For example, the 1970 constitution abolished the local corporate personal property tax which was difficult to administer and poorly enforced. The constitution mandated the legislature to levy a replacement revenue source by 1979. The legislature avoided the replacement issue throughout the 1970s until the state Supreme Court

Table 5.1 SOURCES OF REVENUE FOR ILLINOIS LOCAL GOVERNMENTS
(EXCLUDING SCHOOL DISTRICTS), 1978–86 (THOUSAND DOLLARS)

Fiscal year	Federal	State	Own source	Total
1978	$ 825,900	$ 664,900	$3,247,100	$ 4,955,500
1979	1,089,400	730,200	3,721,100	5,766,000
1980	1,233,300	853,700	4,109,600	6,539,200
1981	1,439,300	992,200	4,729,700	7,613,700
1982	1,342,900	1,024,100	5,313,700	8,113,900
1983	1,385,200	970,800	5,864,400	8,685,200
1984	1,308,000	1,034,700	6,324,400	9,123,800
1985	1,145,399	1,214,200	6,816,800	9,649,900
1986	1,068,397	1,388,087	7,270,080	10,201,624

Source: U.S. Bureau of the Census, 1987.

ordered local governments to stop collecting the tax whether the legislature did or did not act. The legislature finally responded by adopting an additional tax on corporate income, partnerships, and utility capital investments. Under the distribution scheme adopted by the legislature, local governments, including school districts, have received as much and more from the replacement tax, and about $500 million annually has been shifted from the "own source" side of the ledger to the "state aid" side. The 1983 increase in the state gasoline tax also helped local governments because under a complicated distribution formula, fixed shares of this revenue source are returned to municipalities, counties, and township and county road districts. Chicago's income from the state gas tax, for example, increased about $10 million annually (from $43 million to $53 million) following the 1983 tax rise. Similarly, the temporary income tax increase in 1983 caused a favorable blip in local revenue levels because of the automatic one-twelfth revenue share feature. Despite these small gains in state support, the dominant message from Springfield to local governments has been: "You're on your own."

Revenue Trends in Illinois Local Governments

Trends in local finance in the 1980s reflect the patterns of state and national politics. Total general revenues received from all sources by Illinois local government (excluding school districts) approximately doubled in current dollars between 1978 and 1986, from $5 billion to $10.2 billion. (See table 5.1.) The rate of year-to-year revenue increasing, however, slowed down as the state moved further into the 1980s. A clear breakpoint occurred in the 1982 fiscal year,

Table 5.2 SOURCES OF REVENUE FOR ILLINOIS LOCAL GOVERNMENTS
(EXCLUDING SCHOOL DISTRICTS) AS PERCENTAGES OF THE TOTAL
GENERAL REVENUES, 1979–86

Fiscal year	Federal	State	Total	Own source		
				Property tax	Other taxes	Charges and miscellaneous
1979	18.89%	12.66%	64.54%	28.10%	16.73%	19.70%
1980	18.86	13.06	62.85	26.34	15.77	20.70
1981	18.90	13.03	62.12	23.76	17.66	20.70
1982	16.55	12.62	65.49	24.26	18.69	22.50
1983	15.95	11.18	67.52	25.11	19.35	23.10
1984	14.34	11.34	69.32	26.91	19.06	23.40
1985	11.87	12.58	70.64	26.87	19.80	23.96
1986	10.47	13.61	71.26	26.45	20.09	24.73

Source: U.S. Bureau of the Census, 1987.

when total revenues increased only 6.6 percent over 1981, whereas the jump in 1981 over 1980 was 16.4 percent. Over the eight years, of the total $5.2 billion increase in revenues, half was added in the first three years (1979–81), and half was added in the following five years (1982–86), and on an increasingly larger base.

Many factors contributed to this pattern of slower revenue growth, but the most obvious one was the leveling off of federal aid in the early 1980s, followed by actual declines in 1985 and 1986. As indicated in table 5.1, federal aid crossed the billion dollar mark in 1979, remained in the $1.3–1.4 billion range in 1981–84, then fell back in 1985 and 1986 to a level just below the $1.1 billion 1979 figure.

Although the dollar amount of federal aid held up through 1984, the percentage share of federal aid in total local revenues peaked in 1981 at 18.9 percent and dropped rapidly to only 10.5 percent in 1986. (See table 5.2.) In contrast to lagging federal contributions in the 1980s, the state aid share of local revenues has held relatively constant in the 13 percent range, with the exception of dips below 12 percent in 1983 and 1984.

In general, Illinois local governments have opted to increase spending at a slower rate in the 1980s, and in doing so have been forced to replace federal dollars with local own source dollars. As table 5.2 shows, the peak year of federal aid (1981) coincided with the low point in "own source" revenues as a percentage (62.1) of total revenue. Since 1981, the local share has moved up steadily and in 1986 stood at 71.3 percent. Within the broad own source category, the

Table 5.3 SOURCES OF REVENUE FOR ILLINOIS MUNICIPALITIES AS
PERCENTAGES OF THE TOTAL GENERAL REVENUES, 1979–86

Fiscal year	Federal	State	Total	Own source		
				Property tax	Other taxes	Charges and miscellaneous
1979	17.89%	11.93%	69.46%	23.56%	28.62%	17.27%
1980	19.49	13.10	66.75	21.20	26.78	18.77
1981	17.45	13.12	68.70	21.58	25.98	21.14
1982	15.83	13.68	69.87	20.93	27.03	21.91
1983	15.30	12.16	71.95	21.11	28.57	22.26
1984	12.92	12.53	73.65	21.48	29.04	23.13
1985	10.08	13.32	75.72	20.39	30.60	24.73
1986	9.30	13.37	76.84	19.58	30.15	27.11

Source: U.S. Bureau of the Census, 1987.

property tax has maintained its position as the single largest revenue source, but it has lost ground relatively as local governments have turned increasingly to other taxes and to various fees and charges. By 1986, the property tax contributed 26.5 percent of total revenue, other taxes 20.1 percent, and charges and miscellaneous 24.7 percent. The property tax had accounted for almost one-third of local revenues as recently as 1975.

Total local government general revenues in Illinois are divided among the four categories of government as follows, based on 1986 figures: municipalities accounted for 49.5 percent, counties for 18.9 percent, townships for 3.4 percent, and special districts for 23.2 percent. Each type of government tends to draw from a somewhat different mix of revenue sources, and a few key trends are worth highlighting. The most striking change in the mix since the 1970s has occurred in municipalities, where the property tax share of local resources moved steadily downward, falling below 20 percent in 1986, and the other two categories of revenues have increased their shares. (See table 5.3.) "Other taxes" showed a moderate increase, rising to about 30 percent in 1985 and 1986; however, "charges and miscellaneous" showed a sharp rise, moving from only about 17 percent in 1979 to over 27 percent in 1986. Among the four types of government, municipalities therefore have the lowest relative reliance on the property tax and the highest reliance on charges. The reason is probably quite straightforward: municipal politicians, who are usually the most visible political leaders in an area, have tried to avoid unpopular property tax increases and have turned to other taxes on service users that voters perceive as fairer.

OTHER ASPECTS OF ILLINOIS STATE-LOCAL RELATIONS

Several aspects of state-local relations in Illinois deserve closer scrutiny. They include the position of Chicago, recent events in education reform and financing, Governor Thompson's economic revitalizing program dubbed "Build Illinois," and the effect of the end of federal General Revenue Sharing (GRS) on the state and its localities.

The Case of Chicago

Chicago has traditionally been a major force in Illinois politics, actively pursuing its own interests and resisting state interference. Although it has not typically joined forces with other local governments on a state-local agenda, Chicago's successful claims on state government rub off on other local governments as suburban and downstate legislators bargain for financial shares or other trade-offs. Therefore, the drift that has taken place in state-local relations in the 1980s can be partly attributed to the weakening of Chicago's leverage in state politics following the sudden death of Mayor Daley in 1976.

Daley's death introduced a succession of four mayors, none of whom was able to approach Daley's ability to lead and deal effectively, either within Chicago or outside on the state and national scenes. The initial leadership transition was apparently smooth: the city council chose Alderman Michael J. Bilandic, a respected if colorless council leader known for his grasp of city finances. However, in the 1979 Democratic mayoral primary election, Jane Byrne, a former consumer affairs commissioner under Daley, upset Bilandic after a snow removal fiasco obliterated Bilandic's image of competence. An instant folk heroine, Byrne rolled over token Republican opposition.

Byrne's style of leadership was combative and unpredictable; her administration quickly came to resemble a revolving door as aides and department heads came into and fell out of favor at high speed. She sought reelection, but her political vulnerability attracted two strong challengers in the 1983 primary: Richard M. Daley, the late mayor's son and Cook County State's Attorney, and Harold Washington, a congressman and leader of Chicago's black community. Washington won a close victory in the three-way primary and an even closer victory over his Republican opponent (State Senator Bernard Epton) in a nasty, racially charged campaign.

Washington's election began a tumultuous three-year period known as "council wars," in which white aldermen, led by Edward Vrdolyak, controlled the city council 29–21 and frustrated Washington's reform agenda at many points. In 1986, a court-ordered redistricting of aldermanic boundaries triggered a special election that produced a 25–25 split, with the mayor holding the crucial tie-breaker council vote. In April 1987, Washington consolidated his position, defeating Vrdolyak, who was running under a third party label, and Republican Don Haider. Soon after, Vrdolyak, who had been chairman of the Cook County Democratic party organization, announced his switch to the Republican party. Vrdolyak was succeeded by Washington ally George Dunne, who is also the elected chief executive of the Cook County Board of Supervisors.

Washington's sudden death seven months later shocked the city and ended the promise of stability in Chicago politics. In a bitter succession struggle, two of Washington's allies in the city council, Aldermen Eugene Sawyer and Timothy Evans, sought the mayor's job. Sawyer prevailed, but his winning bloc consisted of Washington's old enemies in the council and only 5 out of 19 black aldermen. Evans continues to claim that he is the rightful heir to the Washington legacy and will probably challenge Sawyer in the next election— whether in 1991 or sooner, depending on the outcome of legal maneuvering still going on at this writing.

On the wider stage of Illinois politics, the political drama played out in Chicago in the 1980s has been engrossing theatre, complete with comedy, tragedy, and stunning plot twists. But Chicago's lack of sustained political leadership has weakened its leverage in state government: the clear signals sent to the legislature in the Daley years have often become scrambled by local dissent. In addition, the turbulence in city government provides a rationale for anti-Chicago forces to withhold state assistance until Chicago can get its act together. The result has been to force the city to raise additional revenues from its own sources: a city sales tax for general revenue, another state-authorized 1 percent sales tax for mass transit, a five-cent-per-gallon tax on gasoline and jet fuel, other smaller-yield taxes, and most important, property tax increases. But a spin-off of Chicago's going it alone is that other local governments are not receiving any help from the state either.

Education Reform

The 1980s brought significant reforms to that key area of state-local cooperation, public education. Under the 1970 Illinois constitution, the state has "primary responsibility for financing public elementary and secondary education" (Art. 10, sect. 1). The definition of primary is much debated: local public school leaders assert that the state should provide at least half of local school operating budgets in the aggregate. The state actually did approach that milestone in the mid-1970s; however, with school aid accounting for roughly one-quarter of the state general fund budget, there is no way that school aid could have escaped the effects of fiscal stress on the state budget as a whole. By 1983, the state share dropped to only 38 percent as school aid was cut over $100 million in one year. State spending for education went up in the 1984–87 period, increasing the share to 42 percent, but a $131 million cut in fiscal year 1988 has reduced the state share again to an estimated 40 percent (Illinois Comptroller's Office 1987). As state support has wavered from year to year in the 1980s, local school boards have had to go to the property tax to make ends meet.

The political and fiscal environment in Illinois in the mid-1980s seemed hardly conducive to a bipartisan substantive initiative focusing on the quality of education. Nevertheless, to the surprise of nearly everyone, that is what happened in 1985, with the passage of the Illinois Education Reform Act. This act grew out the work of the Commission on the Improvement of Elementary and Secondary Education, a body established by the legislature in 1983 and co-chaired by a state senator and a state representative. The commission, working with a new state school superintendent (Ted Sanders) and the governor, "provided a forum for ideas that had been wallowing in legislative indifference" for years (Sevener 1985, p. 29.) The recommendations that emerged "called for a substantial alteration in the form or character of the state's relationship with local schools" in areas in which "one finds the likelihood of long-term and pervasive change" (Sanders 1986, p. 18).

Following the commission's recommendations closely, the legislature's reform package required the state board of education to adopt "state goals for learning" in six disciplines; required local districts to adopt their own objectives consistent with the state's and assess student performance regularly in a public report card, raised teacher certification requirements to include passing a basic skills test, and mandated more rigorous evaluation of existing teachers and school administrators. The package also included new programs in reading skills, support for special summer school programs, a preschool program for at-risk children, and several programs for teacher and staff development. About $100 million in categorical grant funds was appropriated for the new programs.

The 1985 legislation also took on the volatile school district consolidation issue, requiring districts falling below minimum enrollment targets to begin moving toward reorganization with neighboring districts. A political uproar ensued in the affected districts, and in the spring of 1986, an election year, the governor and legislature agreed to delete the deadlines in the law. Gradual attrition in the number of school districts will no doubt continue in Illinois, but not under a state-aimed gun.

Other major educational issues were either deferred or side-stepped completely in the reform package. School aid formula revision—that perpetually rancorous issue in almost every state—was postponed until 1987 and then postponed again. No action occurred on a minimum pay standard for teachers. Most mandated course requirements for high school graduation were left intact. Also largely unaddressed were the agonies of the Chicago public schools, where teachers mounted their longest strike in history in the fall of 1987 and where civic and parent groups have been demanding a greater voice in educational policy and personnel decisions. The 1985 legislation did require each Chicago school to establish a school improvement council with a limited advisory role on budget, curriculum, and personnel. However, it is likely that any future improvement in state aid for Chicago will be tied to a much more extensive decentralization plan of the sort being advocated by Chicago civic groups— shrinkage of the central bureaucracy, more autonomy for school principals, and increased accountability throughout the system.

In sum, one can conclude with some reservations that education was the area of the state's most concerted activism in state-local relations. It seems likely, also, that the legislature will continue to be assertive. As a former state superintendent put it, "The role of the legislature in educational matters has now become paramount. We may have technically created a State Board of Education in 1975; by 1985 that board had effectively become the General Assembly" (Bakalis 1986, p. 17).

THE BUILD ILLINOIS PROGRAM

Governor Thompson presented his "Build Illinois" program in 1985— a flagship effort to instill vitality into the state's struggling economy. An ambitious and multifaceted program, Nora Newman Jurgens (1986a, p. 15) characterized it as:

An all encompassing attempt to deal with the state's crumbling infrastructure, disappearing jobs and shrinking tax base. It is an attempt to turn the state around after ten years of slow growth and neglect. It is also a response to the "New Federalism."

Build Illinois was pitched as an economic development and infrastructure initiative, and its potential for directly influencing state-local relations was limited. It might have signaled a new assertion of state leadership in program areas in which local governments stand to benefit; however, as implemented, Build Illinois became a slush fund for random projects identified through legislative trading.

As originally presented, Build Illinois was to allocate $1.3 billion in economic development, transportation, environmental, and university building projects over five years. The entire program was to be financed mainly by Build Illinois limited obligation bonds, backed by a 2.2 percent sales tax diversion that in turn was to be offset by a new tax on the private sale of used cars.

The unraveling of Build Illinois is a complex tale that will not be told here in detail. The political price for legislative approval was that the legislature demanded that first-year bond proceeds be divided between the governor's projects and the legislature's projects. The various legislative blocs carved up the available money with special preference to legislators facing reelection in 1986.

Because the number of projects approved for funding far exceeded the appropriation, there was further discord between the governor and the legislature about which projects would actually go forward. The wrangling continued into the second year of the program, with the legislature increasing its control of the program (Jurgens 1986b, pp. 44–45).

In 1987, Governor Thompson proposed a $700 million expansion in Build Illinois along with increases in the income and gas taxes. The entire proposal stalled in the legislature, and since then, Build Illinois has consisted of working through the grab bag of projects approved in the first two years. The Build Illinois slogan does not appear in the governor's 1988 budget/state of the state message.

A casualty of Build Illinois's demise has been a weakening of the state role in funding wastewater treatment facilities. Wastewater management is a key local government issue in more than 200 communities, including 103 municipalities and sewer districts in Cook County that are still out of compliance with federal clean water standards. Throughout the 1970s the state environmental protection agency funneled money on a 70–30 match basis to local governments, drawing on both a state 1970 antipollution bond issue and federal grants. Now the bond money is gone and federal grants have been sharply cut back, leaving Illinois communities out of compliance and staring at an apparently firm federal deadline of 1 July 1988.

Governor Thompson's 1987 Build Illinois proposal included almost $300 million for wastewater treatment, including a $70 million revolving fund required as a condition for receiving federal revolving loan funds. He got nothing. Scolding the legislature in his 1988 message, Thompson (p. 6) said that 200 communities face "coercive penalties" and will "pay a terrible price":

For the lack of a $70 million match, $350 million in federal revolving loan funds will be taken from Illinois and given to other, smarter states. I hear complaints in this and other chambers about the low return of federal dollars to Illinois. Small wonder when—by inaction—we're kicking them out the front door.

The funding sources proposed by Thompson in 1987 were taxes on computer software and nonprescription drugs. In repeating his proposal in 1988 for the $370 million wastewater treatment program, Thompson omitted mention of a way to pay for it. Although the new taxes proposed in 1987 were again introduced in 1988, they are not given much chance of passage (Winnetka Talk 1988, p. 7).

EFFECT OF THE END OF GENERAL REVENUE SHARING

In federal fiscal year 1986, the Department of Treasury sent $182.5 million in GRS funds to more than 1,800 eligible Illinois municipalities, counties, and townships. Chicago's allocation was $59.4 million and Cook County's was $21.1 million, about 44 percent of the state's total allocation. Rockwood Village in Randolph County received a check for $222, one of 164 jurisdictions whose share was less than $1000. In the aggregate, GRS accounted for about 2.5 percent of total general revenues of all general purpose governments. Illinois's share of GRS had not changed much since enactment, but its relative contribution had of course declined: in 1975, 7 percent of total general revenues came from that federal program (Illinois Commission on Intergovernmental Cooperation 1986, p. 6).

Although the loss of GRS had less than a seismic effect on the structure of Illinois's local finances, some jurisdictions had come to depend on the program for a substantial part of their budgets. Even so, the adjustment was not necessarily painful. For example, New Trier Township in northern Cook County lost $180,000, or 30 percent of its general fund budget—funds that had been used to support nonprofit organizations providing social services such as a senior center, youth counseling, and a battered women's shelter. To replace this revenue, the township boards simply nudged its property tax levy up about $10 on a $200,000 house (to $53) and proclaimed that "township services are still a real bargain to the taxpayer and a valuable asset to the community at large" (New Trier Courier 1988, p. 7).

At the other extreme from affluent New Trier Township is the city of East Saint Louis, a profoundly impoverished city of 55,000, "where politics have long been less than a civics textbook example" (Chicago Tribune, 3 May 1988, p. 20.) East Saint Louis's GRS allocation was $1.2 million, about 18 percent of its $6.8 million budget, and its loss represents "a main source of the city's financial woes," according to the city comptroller (p. 20). East Saint Louis lost municipal garbage service in late 1987, when it fell behind in payments to its private trash collection firm, and the city made plans in May 1988 to lay off 80 out of 300 employees to keep meeting its payroll. Intensifying the fiscal crisis was a $3.4 million judgment against the city awarded to a man beaten up in jail by another inmate in 1984. With a median household income of less than $8,000, an official unemployment rate of 14.3 percent, and massive blight throughout the city, East Saint Louis needed more than federal GRS to offer even a basic level of services to its citizens (p. 20). What the loss of this program did was to intensify the level of desperation by several notches.

For county governments (except Cook County), the legislature offered a way to recover lost GRS funds (and then some) by enacting a 0.25 percent sales tax. A significant feature of this new authority was that counties could collect the levy on a countywide tax base, whereas its existing authority to levy a 1 percent sales tax was limited to unincorporated areas—a shrinking base in suburban areas where municipal incorporation and annexations continue at a steady pace. The Taxpayers' Federation of Illinois (1986) estimated that the new sales tax could produce about $73 million in revenue for Illinois counties, more than three times the $22.3 million flowing to the eligible 101 counties from the expired GRS program. Eighty-five counties have jumped at the chance.

The big winners in the GRS/sales tax trade-off are the most urbanized counties, particularly those in the Chicago area. DuPage County, in the rapidly developing western suburbs, for example, was estimated to collect more than $13 million in sales tax compared to its GRS allocation of less than $2 million. Several other counties could look forward to tripling or quadrupling their previous GRS allocations.

In approving the county sales tax option, the legislature also streamlined "county government's almost incomprehensible tax structure": 19 previously separate property tax funds were consolidated into a single operating fund with one maximum tax rate (Knoepfle 1986, p. 22). The maximum property tax rate was to be cut 3 percent upon enactment of the sales tax; however, few counties were at the limit, so this property tax relief feature was largely a phantom.

STATE-LOCAL RELATIONS IN ILLINOIS: THE OUTLOOK FOR THE FUTURE

The 1980s in Illinois state-local relations have so far been years of stress and stalemate. The main sources of stress are the decline in federal grants, the rising cost of public services, and the inability of political leadership to fashion a consensus around a course of action for the state as a whole. As the decade winds down, the elements of persistent stalemate seem securely in place: a shrewd and durable Republican governor—first elected in 1976—jousts with a legislature organized in both houses by Democrats, Chicago has an acting mayor with doubtful prospects for restoring the city's leverage in state politics, and downstate and suburban interests exert a strong conservative pressure against an activist state posture, but they vigorously bargain for shares of any new resources.

When stress escalates to crisis, the state has demonstrated the capacity to patch together a response that eases the crisis and leaves the climate of stress unchanged. The process is untidy, characterized by procrastination, occasional rancor, and unpredictable outcomes. But it is also a condition that Illinois citizens seem ready, if not content, to live with.

Notes

Mary Edwards, a doctoral student in public policy analysis, University of Illinois at Chicago, provided valuable assistance in researching this chapter.

1. For an analysis of the effects of federal grants on Illinois, see Orlebeke 1987, pp. 303–331.

References

Bakalis, Michael J. 1986. Illinois School Reform: After the Cheering Stopped. *Illinois Issues* (May), 15.

Banovetz, James M., and Thomas W. Kelty. 1986. Home Rule: Renewing Trust in Local Government. *Illinois Issues* (May), 9.

Chicago Tribune, 27 April and 3 May 1988.

Frang, Larry, Director of Fiscal Programs, Illinois Municipal League. 1988. Telephone interview, 15 April.

Illinois Commission on Intergovernmental Cooperation (CIC). 1986. *A Review of Local Government Resources in Illinois*. Springfield, Ill.: CIC.

Illinois Comptroller's Office. 1987. *State of Illinois Fiscal Condition Report*. Springfield, Ill., 31 December.

———. 1986. *State of Illinois Fiscal Condition Report*. Springfield, Ill., 23 July.

———. 1984. *State of Illinois Fiscal Condition Report*. Springfield, Ill., 27 July.

Illinois Constitution, Article 7, Section 6(e)(2); Article 10, Section 1.

Jurgens, Nora Newman. 1986a. Build Illinois: The Plan and the Master Plan. *Illinois Issues* (January), 15.

———. 1986b. Build Illinois: Round 2. Illinois Issues (August/September): 44–45.

Knoepfle, Margaret S. 1986. Counties and Township Face Life ARS (After Revenue Sharing). *Illinois Issues* (December), 22.

New Trier Courier. 1988. 5(1), 7.

Orlebeke, Charles J. 1987. Illinois. In Richard P. Nathan, Fred Doolittle, and Associates, *Reagan and the States*. Princeton, N.J.: Princeton University Press.

Regional Partnership. 1987. *The State of the Region*. Wilmette, Ill.: Pioneer Press.

Sanders, Ted. 1986. Illinois Educational Reform: A Thoughtful Response to Crisis. *Illinois Issues* (May), 18.

Sevener, Donald. 1985. Education Reform: The Outcome. Illinois Issues (August/September), 29.

Shannon, John. 1987. The Return to Fend-for-Yourself Federalism: The Reagan Mark. *Intergovernmental Perspective* (Summer/Fall).

Taxpayers' Federation of Illinois. 1986. *Tax Facts* (April).

Thompson, James R. 1988a. State of the State/Budget Message. Springfield, Ill., 25 February.

———. 1988b. State of the State/Budget Message. Springfield, Ill., 25 February, 1. Press release.

——. 1981. Statement Made During Taping of WBBM "At Issue" Program, quoted in *Chicago Tribune*, 5 September.

U.S. Bureau of the Census. 1987. *Governmental Finances*. Washington, D.C.: Government Printing Office.

Winnetka Talk, 5 May 1988, 7.

Chapter Six

STATE-LOCAL RELATIONS IN ARIZONA: CHANGE, WITHIN LIMITS

John Stuart Hall

State-local relations in Arizona, like those in all states, are the result of formal constitutional-legal arrangements and informal factors affecting the relative power and management of the state's public institutions. Among the latter factors are the personalities and skills of public officials in various organizations and resources—financial and other—available to and mobilized by different entities. Paramount questions, particularly during recent discussions of retrenchment and devolution, include: How, and to what degree, do these forces relate? Will major changes in one set of factors result in major shifts in the other set and in overall state-local relations? Have recent national domestic policy changes brought about important shifts in the state's formal intergovernmental arrangements and informal balance of political power? How have state-local relations in Arizona changed during the 1980s?[1]

Recent research on Arizona intergovernmental affairs underscores the relative nature of these questions and the consequent difficulty of providing complete answers.

ARIZONA STATE-LOCAL RELATIONS, BEGINNING WITH THE FUNDAMENTALS

At the heart of state-local relations are formal matters: the rules of the game and official players. As elsewhere, local governments in Arizona are legal creatures of the state. The state creates local units, defines their scope and authority, restricts their finances, dictates the possible form of government they may adopt, limits the nature and extent of their intergovernmental activities, and possibly even abolishes them (Berman forthcoming). Table 6.1 shows the number and kinds of local government in Arizona.

Table 6.1 TYPES OF GOVERNMENT IN ARIZONA

Type	1977	1986
Counties	14	15
Cities and towns	70	81
School districts	230	227
Special districts	106	253
Total	421	577

Aside from special districts, Arizona has few units of local government compared to other states. Many of these units, the cities and towns, have relatively broad powers and functions and can respond to citizen demands for services in all the traditional areas of local government. Arizona counties, on the other hand, are primarily administrative arms of the state. County boards of supervisors are elected policymakers who must compete with other elected county officials—row officers such as the county sheriff, assessor, and attorney—to govern.

Special districts are limited purpose governmental units generally responsible for only one function, such as fire protection, irrigation, flood control, and so on. The increase in special districts between 1977 and 1986 is largely a function-changing classification of small districts. They may be created by either the legislature or county supervisors acting in accordance with state law. School districts are a form of special districts that are autonomous.

Because all local governments are ultimately creatures of the state and many functions of local government are monitored, mandated, and controlled by the state, it would be easy to conclude that state-local relationships in Arizona are somewhat one-sided. But closer examination suggests that local units are far from powerless, that current events are not likely to lead to their demise, and that, in fact, some of these events have enhanced the power of local government.

To understand this delicate balance of power requires that we begin by acknowledging that the state is really many separate entities, sometimes working at cross-purposes. The roots of fragmentation of state government are structural.

Adopted in 1912, the Arizona constitution reflects Jacksonian democratic frontier values. It provides for multiple executives (independently elected state officials), short terms of office and minimal qualifications for elected officials, and a plethora of boards and commissions with both legislative and executive powers. The constitution also allows for direct legislation by the people through the referendum and initiative processes as well as popular control of elected officials by recall. Since 1912, a few constitutional amendments and governmental reorganizations have affected these arrangements, but in essence, state government still "reflects the spirit of democratic control through the dispersion of power" (Sackton 1980, p. 17).

Arizona's bicameral legislature has been a dominant voice in state policy making over the years although it was traditionally the model of a part-time, amateur legislature. That situation changed somewhat in recent years as the legislature increased its professional staff. It was not many years ago that junior members of the legislature had neither office space nor clerical-secretarial assistance. Now they have, and standing committees have expanded their staffs, as have the Joint Legislative Budget Committee, the Legislative Council, the Internship Program, and other units that assist the legislature.

The populist spirit was also institutionalized in the executive branch. Although the governor has important powers of appointment and veto, including item veto power over appropriation bills, the powers are constrained constitutionally. One such constraint is the many commissions and boards that are created by statute and accordingly are responsive to the legislature, not the governor. In effect, the more than 150 boards, commissions, councils, and offices represent a fourth branch of government. Although they are frequently shown on an organization chart as part of the executive branch, they have quasi-legislative and judicial powers and are responsible to the governor only informally.

Despite these and other structural forces of fragmentation, the governor's office and certain key state agencies have played an important part in intergovernmental affairs and policies. Much of the potential power of the governor's office is personal and is tied to the governor's ability to work with the legislature, key state agencies, the media, and national and local units of government.

Arizona's last two governors illustrate how personal skills and styles influence the scope and power of that office. In many respects, including their desire to envision and implement intergovernmental change in Arizona, there could be no greater contrast than Bruce Babbitt and Evan Mecham.

Governor Babbitt (who served from 1978 to 1987) was an activist in intergovernmental matters and he was particularly interested in re-sorting national, state, and local government functions. He was an active member of the Advisory Commission on Intergovernmental

Relations and was the Democratic governor cited by President Reagan in his 1982 State of the Union "New Federalism" speech as favoring a new division of federal and state functions. Although Babbitt disagreed with some specifics, he was a strong advocate of the need to sort and swap. As he said in an article (*Arizona Republic* 1982) following the New Federalism speech:

It's time for a real revolution to get the federal government out of the neighborhood library, out of matching funds, out of issuing mandates about the funding of a local park. We really ought to pull this mess apart and reassign the functions and responsibilities.

But at least in Arizona, the models of functional intergovernmental change promoted by President Reagan and Governor Babbitt were not to be.[2] These large-scale changes were blocked by political and economic realities that overwhelmed personal powers of persuasion of the president even when he was joined by other respected elected officials like Governor Babbitt.

For the Arizona story, it is important to understand that Babbitt knew a lot about intergovernmental matters, had a vision of functional reconstruction that often served as context for discussion of state-local divisions of responsibility and overall balance of power within the state, and was well aware of changes in U.S. federalism and the meaning of those changes for Arizona politics and policy.[3]

It was no surprise, given Babbitt's interest, experience, and knowledge of federalism, and given the state legislature's historic reluctance to examine federally financed programs, that he moved quickly in 1982 to capture for executive agencies, and develop, a new distribution process for the nine new block grants of the Reagan domestic program. This move worked to enhance both executive (as opposed to legislative) and state (as opposed to federal) power.

The short and stormy reign of Governor Evan Mecham was, in almost all ways, a sharp departure from the trend toward gradual centralization of authority and strengthening of the governor's office that was most apparent under Babbitt. Mecham lasted little more than one year before being simultaneously impeached, indicted, and subjected to recall, thereby clearly winning "the Triple Crown of political malfeasance".[5]

This is not the place for the Evan Mecham story, but the problems with his administration were so severe that it was hard to tell who, if anyone, was in power. The Mecham controversy virtually paralyzed state government. Particularly toward the end of his stay (January to April 1988), proponents and opponents tended to focus on him at the expense of public policy. Aside from an early but aborted attempt to beef up county law enforcement at the expense of existing state Department of Public Safety programs, Mecham did little that directly affected the state-local relationship. His larger problems seemed, however, to dilute state authority and confidence in government in general and, most specifically, left the executive branch powerless.

At the level of political symbolism and policy leadership, the year and one-half of Mecham's tenure reinforced existing beliefs of many in Arizona that government in general and state government in particular are ineffective. Although these dynamics probably did nothing to enhance state-local relations, it would be unfair to say that the governor's direct interactions with local units were much more than the tip of the iceberg of daily state-local interactions and decisions during that time. Much of the real-world policy interaction between state and local units continued despite the mutual preoccupation of the governor and the legislature with each other. It did so because most of the state-local interaction is between 577 units of local government and approximately 35 state agencies. Among these agencies, those that work most closely with local governments are shown in table 6.2.

From the early 1970s to the present, the budgets, structures, and routines of state-local relations in Arizona have changed substantially. Public programs delivered by the agencies listed in table 6.2 have grown in cost and coverage, and state responsibilities have increased in keeping with the budget growth. How and why have these major departments developed so rapidly in a state known for its conservative philosophy—and during a time of widespread proclaimed allegiance in Arizona to tax and spending limits, Reagan domestic budget cuts, and state tax reductions? The short answer to that question is *growth*. From 1970 through 1987, the population almost doubled (from 1,795 million to 3,405 million), and its major urban areas grew even faster. For example, the Phoenix metropolitan area grew from 980,000 in 1970 to 1,970,000 in 1987 (Melnic 1988, table 1).

Arizona's dramatic growth and immigration created demand for new and expanded public services. The state agencies and their local government and nonprofit organization partners are charged with responding to these demands.

Major organizational and resource changes affected many areas of state government, including those that were the focal points of state-local interaction during the 1970s and early 1980s. These major changes

Table 6.2 TOTAL BUDGETS OF ARIZONA STATE AGENCIES CLOSELY
ASSOCIATED WITH ARIZONA LOCAL GOVERNMENTS, FY 1988
(MILLIONS DOLLARS)

Department	Year Created	Appropriated Funds	Nonappropriated Funds
Education	1970	$1,030.0	$ 194.6
Transportation	1974	312.7	257.6
Economic Security	1972	231.5	411.3
Arizona Health Care Cost Containment System	1983	187.2	112.0
Health Service	1974	99.9	42.5
Environmental Quality	1987	15.5	25.9
Commerce, (formerly Office of Economic Planning and Development)	1985 (1973)	3.8	14.0
State Totals		$3,321.0	$1,785.0

Source: Arizona Joint Legislative Budget Committee (1988, p. iv).
Note: Amounts shown as total spending authority include appropriations from past
sessions, and some carry forward balances. Appropriated amounts are primarily
state general fund appropriations for the year indicated. Nonappropriated amounts
are primarily federal funds.

were usually initiated by the legislature. But it was often responding
to needs and demands articulated earlier and elsewhere in the political system. For example, the Department of Economic Security
(DES), the equivalent of the Department of Health and Human Services (HHS) at the national level, was created by the legislature in
1972. DES was an organizational response to fragmented human
service delivery by several smaller agencies. Problems associated
with this fragmentation became clear during the War on Poverty and
were the subject of many discussions, including a statewide Arizona
Town Hall. Although DES was a reform initiated by the legislature,
it was also a response to the pressures of national domestic policy
and internal state dialogue.

Similarly, multiple pressures external to the state, such as changing federal aid programs, national economic shifts, and U.S. court
cases, were processed through constituents and legislators to contribute to legislative problem solving in the state-local arena. In most
cases, within-state pressures also contributed to setting the legislature on the road to reform. Legislative action in other states, court
decisions and the threat of further litigation, and financial woes of
independent local school districts all stimulated the large increase
in state funding for public schools that took place during the 1970s.

In the same way, national policy and local public finance combined to provide the tension for legislative development of the indigent health program, the Arizona Health Care Cost Containment System (AHCCCS). Arizona began the 1980s as the only state not participating in Medicaid. After much discussion and debate during the late 1970s, the legislature finally adopted AHCCCS, which was approved by HHS as a Title XIX demonstration project and began operations in 1983. Until then, Arizona's indigent health needs were the responsibility of county governments and were typically met by county public hospitals. The result was uneven care and severe financial difficulties in some counties.

Legislative decisions affecting state structure and capacity in the other departments listed in table 6.2 were also responses to the twin forces of national change and local capacity. But the big wave that pushed most of this change through Kindgon's (1984) "policy opportunity window" is growth and related demand for public services.

New programs and resources from both national and state sources were brought into the state government sphere during the past 15 years. The period was marked by a steady increase in state government budgets, personnel, and activities. By these measures, the power of state government is greater now than it was in 1970. But how much? Many Arizona local governments were also expanding. To assess state-local power requires further specification of the intergovernmental changes and examination of the net effects of that evolution. Who wins and who loses?

BIG TICKET CHANGES IN THE ARIZONA STATE-LOCAL SYSTEM

From the mid-1970s to the present, major changes in Arizona finance, agency organization, and public programs directly affected state-local relations. Table 6.3 helps place these changes in context.

The items and actors listed in the table are certainly not exhaustive. The list is derived from interviews and analyses of reports that focus on intergovernmental policy making within Arizona. These are the types of items most frequently mentioned in response to probes concerning what important actions changed state-local relations in fundamental ways. It is no surprise that the changes cited tend to center on money and power. Important for our analysis, key fiscal changes and arrangements initiated by state actors, for the most part, occurred

Table 6.3 MAJOR CHANGES AFFECTING ARIZONA STATE-LOCAL RELATIONS

Major change	Agent	Year
Changes in finance and taxation		
State tax sharing	voters, legislature, League of Arizona Cities and Towns	
Gas tax		1921
Sales tax		1933
Income tax		1933
School finance reform	legislature, state and federal courts	1974, 1979
Property tax and spending limits	legislature, voters	1921, 1978, 1980
Creation/reorganization of major state agencies dealing with local issues	legislature, League of Arizona Cities and Towns, governor, Arizona Academy	
Department of Economic Security		1972
Department of Health Services		1974
Office of Economic Planning and Development/ Department of Commerce		1973/1985
Transportation		1974
Environmental quality		1987
Major policy changes		
Nixon-Ford block grants	president/congress	1973–75
Groundwater Management Act	governor, legislature, League of Arizona Cities and Towns	1980
Reagan block grants	president/congress	1981
Indigent health care (Arizona Health Care Containment System)	legislature, governor, U.S. Dept. of Health and Human Services	1983
Cancellation of General Revenue Sharing	congress/president	1986

prior to major fiscal and policy shifts of the 1980s. Similarly, most major organizational changes preceded new federalism initiatives. Yet the items listed in table 6.3 result from the interplay of intergovernmental forces that provides context for understanding state-local responses to financial, institutional, and organizational challenges of the 1980s.

CHANGES IN REVENUE, 1980–88

The state's revenue is relatively balanced, diverse, and elastic. All major forms of state taxes are used in Arizona. As table 6.4 demonstrates, sales and income taxes account for more than three-quarters of the state's general fund revenue, with sales tax providing almost one-half the total funds needed to run the state.

From the perspective of many other state political systems, this revenue structure has several enviable characteristics. Most obvious, it allows for public sector growth without initiating political battles over major new taxes. At least over the past 30 years, heavy use of the sales tax has allowed state and local governments to respond quickly to the service demands generated by the region's prodigious growth.

The Local Tax Base

The state's basic revenue structure has served state and local governments well over recent decades. Major provisions for state-local *sharing* of the state's responsive tax base are locked in place. Local units, including cities, towns, and counties, can count on population-based formula shares of important revenues. Incorporated cities automatically receive a population-based share of 15 percent of total state income taxes. Each city's share is deposited directly to its general fund. A portion of the state's 5 percent sales tax is also automatically returned to cities, towns, and counties following population criteria.

State gasoline taxes are split among the state Department of Transportation (50 percent), counties (20 percent), and cities (30 percent). Again, local government shares are allocated by population.

Table 6.4 ARIZONA GENERAL FUND REVENUES, BY SOURCE, FY 1986–87

Revenue	Percentage
Sales tax	49%
Income tax	36
Property tax	3
Sin taxes	3
Other	9
Total	100%

Source: Berman, N.d., p. 147.
Note: The total tax revenue was $2,317,531,000.

The lottery is a newer, important source of shared revenue. Created in 1981, 75 percent of proceeds (approximately $23 million in 1987) is distributed to Arizona's cities and towns for transportation. Approximately 25 percent of lottery profits are returned to counties to help them carry out mandated but—from the county perspective— underfunded services such as health care and law enforcement.

Because all these revenues are distributed on a population basis, they reinforce Arizona's major industry: growth. Local governments that increase in population automatically increase their share of these revenues without taking political risks associated with creating new or raising old taxes.

Perhaps more important for Arizona's municipalities are local options, including decisions that affect both the sales tax rate and base. Although the state sales tax is 5 percent, individual cities and towns may choose to increase that tax within their boundaries up to 7 percent and may choose to exempt certain categories of sales from the tax.

As a consequence of this revenue system's structure, state and local units in Arizona rely much less heavily on property taxes than elsewhere. Although not perfect because of population shifts that are sometimes difficult to forecast, revenue sharing by formula within the state gives state and local officials an extra measure of stability in revenue projections.

But this relatively efficient and politically palatable distribution of revenues has largely been a function of the state's constant growth and development—the ever-expanding economic pie. Herein lies the potential bad news.

Limits

Continued growth, particularly at rates that many in Arizona have become accustomed to, is not guaranteed. A change in natural economic forces would limit public sector growth. But this eventuality is problematic and would likely be placed in the gloom-and-doom category by those who forecast continued economic buoyancy.

Even if the economy continues to expand, self-imposed revenue limits will constrain public finance. In keeping with the dominant philosophy of fiscal constraint, state and local spending has been limited for most of Arizona's history. The state's first spending limit was enacted in 1921. This limit on local government budget and tax growth was relatively liberal and was easy enough for local units to live with because of many exemptions and loopholes and because of the state's ever-expanding tax rolls. However, Arizona's tradition of placing limits on public finance put the state well ahead of the fiscal constraint wave that hit many other states in the late 1970s. Nevertheless, the legislators were leery of increased voter sentiment to reduce taxes and accordingly took special measures in the late 1970s to limit public taxing and spending further. They placed more stringent limits on state and local government spending by limiting state revenue appropriation increases to no more than 7 percent of the state's estimated total personal income for that year. In addition, the legislature reformed education finance by increasing state funds and decreasing local property taxes for that purpose. The legislature also sponsored and voters approved general property tax limitations and elimination of some of the loopholes that had allowed local governments to circumvent the earlier 10 percent limitation on budget growth.[6]

These formal constitutional and legislative changes were accompanied by other legislative actions that effectively limited state revenues. Some of these actions seemed merely to represent additional nervous reactions to presumed tax limit fever, the taxpayers' revolt, or whatever the malady that seemed to be driving many politicians at the time. For example, it was during the early 1980s that the state repealed the sales tax on food and took over teacher retirement costs from local school districts. Those two actions together account for an estimated current loss of about $290 million from the general fund. In addition, the state continues to be locked into a homeowners' (property-tax) rebate that costs about $170 million in 1988. Other smaller exemptions were a part of the legislature's response to the perceived demand for tax decreases. These actions add up. In 1988, Arizona attempted to deal with a $350 million deficit—out of a total budget of $2.9 billion.

Additional limits on state revenues are a part of both the financial system's basic construction and recent state policy decisions to increase reliance on *formulas* to distribute state resources. Public education, indigent health care (AHCCCS, the state's version of Medicaid), and prison construction account for most current state spending, and all are open-ended, formula-driven programs. As one legislator (Hill 1988) concluded, "It just grows like topsy."

These decisions to fund education, indigent health care, prison construction, and a number of smaller programs on the basis of formulas that rely heavily on population growth, combined with formal expenditure and tax limits, in effect set state priorities automatically. Aid to local governments is also a state priority. In fact, it is a priority that comes off the top because fixed percentages of major revenues are automatically distributed to local units. In addition, large sums that are earmarked for most of the programs just mentioned go to or at least pass through local units responsible for policy implementation. In Arizona, school districts were taken off the hook by school finance reform, and counties—formerly responsible for indigent health care—are greatly assisted by state and federal funds for AHCCCS.

Despite these financial arrangements, local officials remain concerned about important issues such as the costs, as opposed to the formula-related benefits, of growth. In addition, many are concerned about how to meet pressing human service needs in the wake of programmatic cuts as a result of President Reagan's domestic policies and constraints imposed by the Gramm-Rudman-Hollings cap. Longer-term concerns that tend to set jaws rigid involve political power.

Human Services

Resource changes within the state were greatest for certain categories of human services during the 1980s. At the time, significant reductions in government spending for many human services combined with dramatic increases in need. Both trends are well-documented. For example, an Urban Institute study (Musselwhite et al. 1987, p.i) of the nonprofit sector's response to retrenchment found that, excluding health care and the AHCCCS program, the inflation-adjusted value of human services spending in 1984 was 16 percent below that for 1981 in Maricopa County (the Phoenix metropolitan area) and 11 percent lower in rural Pinal County. This change was the result of federal cuts that were not restored at the state and local levels. These reductions in areas such as housing, employment and training, various social services, and community development have either persisted or deepened in recent years as a part of Gramm-Rudman-Hollings Act provisions.

Increasing social service needs of the state, particularly its metropolitan areas, are also well documented. A recent (1988) report of a Maricopa County needs assessment takes several hundred pages of documentation to explain unmet needs by categories of human services.

Organizations trying to meet these needs are hard pressed. The Urban Institute study (Musselwhite et al. 1987) demonstrated the viability of the public-private partnership in response to human service needs. But it also showed that nonprofit providers of many human services depended far more on public funds than most would guess. In 1982, for example, the nonprofit sector spent about 37 percent of the $679 million of total public spending for human services in Maricopa County. Public funds of this magnitude represented almost 50 percent of the total revenues of nonprofit service providers during the early to mid-1980s.

Naturally, federal withdrawal increased pressure on state and local government units and private sector organizations involved in the delivery of many human services. Yet in Arizona there is little in the way of state or local supplementation of federal human service cuts. There is some evidence of private increases in terms of both the number of nonprofit service providers and user fees to balance nonprofit budgets (Hall et al. 1985; Salamon, De Vita, and Altschuler 1987). But these increases are small compared to state budget investments and increases for collaborative state and local programs such as indigent health care and public education during the 1980s.

THE DIRECTION OF STATE FUNDING AND POWER

Recent state general fund investments in public education and indigent health care cost several hundred million dollars annually. These resources and the program architecture that accompanies them have purchased some increase in state control. But how much? And at what price?

New State Initiatives

Indigent health care is now provided by the state's unique mix of public and private local providers. Prior to AHCCCS, indigent health care was the financial responsibility of counties (small ad hoc state financial bailouts aside). After AHCCCS (and after a brief and unsuccessful experiment with a private firm hired to manage the program), county financial and program responsibility for indigent health care and the medically categorical needy was greatly reduced. According to the AHCCCS model, and to some degree its reality, counties became but one of many potential entities that could compete to provide these health services. Private physicians' groups, nonprofit community health centers, and counties all compete to provide these services that are funded by federal, state, and county revenues. Federal funds for this purpose have grown from zero in 1982 (Arizona was the only state with no Medicaid program) to $87.1 million in

FY 1987 and a projected expenditure of $109.8 million in FY 1988. The annual growth of federal funds since 1983 has been accompanied by a proportionate growth in total program costs; so that total state appropriations for the program in FY 1988 will be approximately $376 million (11.3 percent of the total $3,320.6 billion appropriated). Program growth means a projected appropriated funds total of $643.0 million for FY 1989, the equivalent of 16.1 percent of state spending authority ($3,948.2 billion).

Because it captured less than 1 percent of state appropriations prior to 1983, indigent health care in the 1980s represents a major shift in state government emphasis. Not only did funding increase, but the new AHCCCS redefined public indigent health care responsibilities and procedures.

In public education (kindergarten through grade 12, K–12), the state also moved from a modest to a major financial position in a policy partnership with local school districts. The shift from predominant reliance on local property taxes to state general fund support, begun earlier, was the largest change in Arizona's state and local fiscal history. Prior to the 1974 special legislative session on school finance, the state contributed approximately $231 million for public K–12 education—only 29 percent of total local school district expenditures. Following two special sessions on educational finance and tax reform (the second in 1979), the state share of total revenues for public K–12 education in FY 1988 rose to $1,020,478,000, over 60 percent of total spending for local schools.

A well-cited proposition, particularly in the school finance literature, is that major state finance increases result in increased state control. The rhetoric usually centers on state power and local control, and it can become quite emotional, as it did recently (Jersey City 1988, p. A8), when the state of New Jersey took over formal control of Jersey City schools:

Thomas A. Shannon, executive director of the National School Boards Association, likened the new state role to that of a doctor deciding to become an attorney general. It transforms the state, he said, "from a supportive diagnostician and healer to a relentless, icy-blooded prosecutor, more concerned with documenting the case for takeover than curing the ills upon which the takeover is based."

Some policymakers and analysts observed a connection between increased state funding and increased control over public education in Arizona during the past decade. As policy analyst Harold Hodgkinson (1988, p. 9) put it: "The Golden Rule is still in operation— he who has the gold makes the rule."

Inquiries about the specifics of state control and power in Arizona's public education system, like questions about operational difficulties brought on by that old local government villain, red tape, tend to elicit emotion among local officials that is out of proportion to actual transfer of power. For example, new state guidelines and rules concerning curriculum matters are seen by many locals as unwarranted intrusions. Many similar issues, important to the school community, are points of conflict among state legislators, Department of Education leaders, and local school district officials and their constituents. But at the policy level, the fact remains that more than 200 *independent and autonomous* school districts, with substantial differences in the number of students and the quality of their education, are operating. Accordingly, even those who give lip service to the funding-control increase proposition should give some consideration to the conclusion that any significant change in "state policies will have to be mediated through some series of local filters" (Hodgkinson 1988, p. 9).

Public education and indigent health care are state-local policy areas that have been greatly changed by state action during the past 15 years. Undoubtedly, these major fiscal and programmatic additions were accompanied by increased state involvement and, particularly for indigent health, increased control. In this sense, state power was enhanced at the expense of local control. But it is also clear from the budget increases observed in the development of these programs that the costs of state entry into and expansion of these policy arenas were high.

National Withdrawal and State Assumption

State assumption of much greater regulatory and policy-making authority from certain federal programs, particularly the 1981 block grants, seemed, on the face of it, much less costly to the states than they were in fact. Beginning in 1981, federal funds went directly to the states to support block grants for social services, health services, small cities community development, elementary and secondary education, and so on. These large grants incorporated many smaller aid programs that previously went directly from federal agencies to local governments. As a major part of the Reagan administration's devolution package, the 1981 block grants enhanced state power in those areas with little required state investment except in program development and management.

As reported in the Princeton University (Hall and Eribes 1987) and

Urban Institute (Musselwhite et al. 1987) studies of devolution of national domestic programs, the Arizona government did little to replace national domestic budget cuts in most program areas. The operating budgets of most social and human service programs have been eroded significantly. Revenue limits described earlier, coupled with major new state investments for public education, indigent health care, prisons, and mass transit, have left little space for supplementation of national reductions in most social and human services. At this time, Arizona evidences neither the political will nor the fiscal ability to add large sums to such programs.

Despite federal cutbacks, many social and human service programs remain, funded largely by federal block grants *to the states.* State agencies have taken over the management of many activities previously administered by federal departments. In Arizona, these activities are still funded primarily by federal funds that overall have more than doubled during the 1980s. Table 6.5 shows a fairly stable federal aid pattern for FYs 1987–89.

Table 6.5 demonstrates the close relationship between state and local governments that was forged to provide services in the activities receiving state and local grants. This table does not control for inflation and masks some lasting cuts that occured in the early 1980s in job training, social services and community development block grants, maternal and child health care, and other human services. Yet it is clear that many programs survived and some prospered through state-local collaboration and state management of many federally funded programs.

Arrangements and resources portrayed in table 6.5 suggest a shift from focusing on the financial plight of particular human service activities and needs to real politics. How are state agencies using this new power? Are they taking control?

Particularly from a state-local relations perspective, the answers to these questions must be qualified. In areas like community development and housing, employment and training, transportation, and to some extent, behavioral health, the state's role has certainly expanded. Local officials with responsibilities in these policy areas during the 1980s have learned about dealing with state agencies.

Cooperation or conflict vary significantly among agencies and among local jurisdictions. Some agencies, such as Commerce or Education, simply have more experience than others with local governments. Similarly, rural Arizona communities have had more interaction with state agencies, programs, and officials than have the metropolitan regions of Phoenix and Tucson. Until the onset of the 1981 block

Table 6.5 STATE-LOCAL DISTRIBUTION OF FEDERAL FUNDS, BY FUNCTION, FEDERAL FY, 1987–89 (MILLION DOLLARS)

Service	Type of grant		FFY 87	FFY 88	FFY 89
	State	Local			
Education					
Educationally deprived	x	x	42.0	45.4	49.9
Head Start		x	23.9	25.7	27.6
Impact aid		x	61.7	56.3	56.3
Handicapped	x		19.6	20.5	22.5
Vocational rehabilitation	x		16.2	17.8	18.6
Other education	x	x	29.3	29.9	30.8
Subtotal			192.6	195.7	205.7
Employment and training					
Employment services	x		27.3	27.8	28.0
Job training		x	30.9	34.6	36.5
Other employment and training	x		4.3	5.4	5.6
Subtotal			62.4	67.8	70.0
Health services					
Arizona Health Care Cost Containment System	x		97.5	112.5	272.2
Other health services	x	x	19.8	19.9	20.1
Subtotal			117.2	132.4	292.3
Nutrition					
Child nutrition	x		51.3	56.0	59.8
Women, infants, children	x		30.2	32.9	35.4
Other nutrition	x		2.5	2.6	2.7
Subtotal			84.0	91.5	97.9

(continued)

Table 6.5 STATE-LOCAL DISTRIBUTION OF FEDERAL FUNDS, BY FUNCTION, FEDERAL FY, 1987–89 (MILLION DOLLARS)

Service	Type of grant		FFY 87	FFY 88	FFY 89
	State	Local			
Social services					
Aid to Families with Dependent Children/child support	x		68.1	69.5	69.6
Social services block grants	x		34.7	35.8	36.5
State Legalization Impact Assistance Grant	x	x	0	18.1	13.2
Other community services	x	x	23.1	23.6	25.0
Food stamp administration	x		20.5	21.2	22.1
Low income energy	x		8.4	6.4	6.6
Social security disability administration	x		6.3	6.5	6.8
Criminal/juvenile justice services	x		4.1	2.1	3.9
Homeless services	x	x	1.0	1.0	0.6
Subtotal			166.3	184.3	184.3
Infrastructure					
Airports	x	x	11.8	13.6	14.4
Community Development Block Grants	x	x	28.4	27.3	25.7
Economic development	x	x	1.1	1.1	1.1
Highway aid	x		203.0	208.5	208.5[a]
Urban Development Act Grants		x	0	2.7	1.9
Urban mass transit	x	x	13.1	19.5	22.4
Other transportation	x	x	2.3	2.2	2.2
Industrial safety	x		1.1	1.1	1.1
Subtotal			260.8	276.0	277.1

Service	Type of grant		FFY 87	FFY 88	FFY 89
	State	Local			
Natural resources					
Agriculture livestock	x	x	3.4	4.0	3.3
Environmental Protection Agency wastewater		x	12.2	14.5	15.2
Pollution control	x		3.7	3.5	3.5
Recreation/environment	x		9.3	9.4	10.2
Emergency affairs	x		1.5	1.5	1.5
Energy conservation	x		0.8	0.8	0.8
Oil price settlement	x		1.6	0	0
Subtotal			32.4	33.6	34.7
General assistance					
Revenue sharing		x	0	0	0
Interior payments in lieu of taxes		x	8.5	8.5	8.5
Subtotal			8.5	8.5	8.5
SUBTOTALS					
State only			642.7	676.4	852.6
Local only			106.3	107.7	109.5
Combined state and local			175.3	205.7	208.4
State and combination			818.0	882.1	1,061.1
Total grants			924.2	989.9	1,170.5

Source: Fiscal Planning Services, Inc. (1988).
Note: Totals may not add due to rounding.
a. Some estimates place FFY 1989 formula grants as low as $131 million. However, subsequent discretionary funding could significantly increase highway aid. The FFY 1989 figure is, therefore, the FFY 1988 sum of formula and discretionary funds.

grants, urban officials dealt directly with their federal counterparts and viewed the state as "at best not involved in their program and at worst an obstructionist jurisdiction" (Hall and Eribes 1987, p. 286).

Rural Arizona jurisdictions, on the other hand, had been involved with state agencies as partners in employment and training (CETA), areawide economic planning and development, and many technical assistance activities. And despite reapportionment effects of increased urban representation in the statehouse, rural jurisdictions have maintained a strong and often united front in the legislature.

Long-term perceptions and perspectives surrounded the state assumption of control of such programs as Community Development Block Grants and the Job Training Partnership Act. In general, representatives of rural Arizona have been more supportive of the devolution of dollars and power to the state than have urban officials and interest groups that have large stakes in federal programs in Phoenix and Tucson.

Awareness of potential criticism of the state's operational assumption of power in these and other areas has no doubt played a large part in the cautious approach of agencies to the allocation of funds and creation of rules surrounding the block grant programs. For the most part, state agencies have allocated these revenues using population-based formulas adjusted for the state's political geography. This approach follows the legislature's example with state revenue-sharing formulas. Thus it is in many ways the politically safe bet. One expert on state intergovernmental matters called this "the peanut-butter approach to allocation: spread it around !"[7]

For the most part, state officials have not assumed policy leadership through program architecture. Local jurisdictions are generally given plenty of latitude to develop programs within broad guidelines. The same observer described state oversight of the block grant programs, "state agencies are now playing federal cops to some extent but not developing their own programs."

Much of the current criticism of state agency lack of leadership and partial paralysis is both unfair and reminiscent of attitudes expressed by local officials about federal agencies during the boom days of federal aid to local governments. These charges are unfair because state agencies today, like their federal counterparts during the mid-1970s, are developing policy, albeit slowly, incrementally, and unevenly. Local officials really would not have it any other way, as their state counterparts know, which is why it works that way. But, of course, the system also operates under an iron law of intergovernmental relations that requires each layer of government to be critical of governments above them for telling them what to do and to chastise those below them for not doing what they are told.

These dynamics, perhaps more than any other factor, account for general criticism of state agencies. Specific charges vary by issue and agency, but all major state agencies experience some degree of discomfort in their role as middlemen between local and federal governments. Perhaps the best current examples are the Departments of Environmental Quality (DEQ) and Transportation (ADOT). As the state's newest major department, DEQ is supposed to broker federal air and water quality mandates and state and local responses. Arizona, particularly the Phoenix metropolitan area, faces severe air quality problems. Until recently, there has been little state and local government response to this problem compared to the blame for delays in response. Not surprisingly, given the iron law, many local officials contend that major delays are the result of squabbling between the Environmental Protection Agency (EPA) and DEQ over how to deal with the problem. Although there is little latent love for EPA among Arizona local governments, one official put it this way: "I would rather deal with EPA directly and get rid of the DEQ middleman."

Similarly, ADOT is attempting to play catch-up with a transportation system that is totally inadequate for the state's current and projected urban growth. Transportation funds account for about 15 percent of the state's $1.2 billion in federal aid projected for FY 1989 (table 6.5), and they represent a large share of the federal funds increase from $677.9 million in FY 1983 to $1.1 billion in FY 1987 (Arizona 1989, p. 6).

Relations between ADOT and local units have been somewhat better in recent years even though that agency has been actively developing new regulations and criteria for evaluating local projects and applications. These rules may have been easier to take because of money—there has been more of it for highways in Arizona during the 1980s—and because of ADOT's experience in dealing with local governments through an established in-state regional arrangement.

But growth-related demands are straining ADOT and local governments when federal funds for transportation are increasingly difficult to acquire. EPA contends that federal funds will be even more difficult to acquire if the state does not make significant progress on its air quality. Air pollution, transportation, and related problems are particularly acute in the Phoenix metropolitan area, which not only contains more than one-half the state's population but is one of the fastest growing metropolitan regions in the country.

These pressures of finance and transportation needs led Phoenix area voters in 1986 to pass a one-half-cent increase in the sales tax to add 231 miles of freeways over the next 20 years. This move was remarkable in an area known for its reluctance to increase taxes and for fragmentation of public and private leadership. Leaders from the legislature, cities and towns, chambers of commerce, and assorted civic organizations joined forces in developing the plan and promoting voter acceptance. In this case, necessity was the mother of both invention and intergovernmental cooperation.

Tucson, the other major metropolitan area, faces a similar quality-of-life conundrum, as have other fast growing but smaller areas. Thus far, voters in Tucson have turned down tax increases for transportation. They—as well as the voters in other growth areas of the state—are likely to be looking to the sales tax and other options in the near future.

SUMMARY: THE STATE-LOCAL BALANCE IN THE 1980s

The Arizona state-local intergovernmental system is doing more and costing more in 1989 than it was in 1980. State general fund revenues more than doubled, as did total federal revenues received. The state government took on some new programs and expanded others. To some extent, power shifted from the national government to the state capital. The devolution decade enhanced this evolution and growth of Arizona state government and many of its local jurisdictions. Yet certain qualifications need to be added to the general conclusion that national devolution left the state as the big winner of recent intergovernmental power shifts:

□ The relationship between formal structural intergovernmental arrangements and informal dimensions, such as personal political power, is complex and dynamic.

□ The most significant structural changes in Arizona's state-local relations occurred *prior* to President Reagan's initiatives and related politics of devolution in the 1980s.

□ Viewed in total, recent federal aid changes are relatively modest and appear to have stabilized. Yet severe cuts for particular human service programs have not been replaced, resulting in major service changes for effected programs and people.

□ With new programs and authority, the state has acquired significant new responsibilities. Those attempting to provide state leadership to solve many problems may have increased resources, but they consider themselves as winners only of headaches previously shared by national and local actors.

□ State arrangements for sharing tax revenues, passing along block grants to local units and generally using local government and organizations for much service delivery, provided for the automatic dispersal of major resources and responsibilities to the local level. The state-local partnership shared at least some of the spoils of devolution.

Overall, the Arizona intergovernmental story of the devolution decade implies some tension between institutional arrangements that tend to endure despite significant growth and change associated with informal dimensions of governmental affairs. If significant institutional reform were possible in the U.S. political system, one would think it would occur in a new, vibrant, and dynamic place like Arizona during a time of national devolution and retrenchment of domestic programs, like the 1980s. Some change in rules, regulations, and legislation affecting state-local arrangements was naturally ongoing; some was the direct result of recent national domestic policy changes. But a most interesting aspect of this story seems to be the modest and incremental nature of Arizona's response to the promise of devolution and to its growth-related needs.

Arizona's immediate intergovernmental future is likely to be reactive and *needs driven*, responding to demographic, economic, and political forces already in progress. These realities, far more than changing federal policies, will structure further change in state-local relations. Major specific needs that will at times perpetuate tension, but at times result in cooperative problem solving, center on state leadership changes and the drive for local self-determination.

In the wake of the Mecham administration and significant recent changes in the state's national and state legislative leadership, there is an understandable urge to do something about state government. Many would say that the current Arizona leadership situation leaves nowhere to go but up. Any pendulum that swings in the direction of new and improved state level leadership is likely to carry corollary swings toward state government reform and some centralization.

On the other hand, there is a natural negative reaction in Arizona to state-imposed solutions of local problems; the iron law applies. Local governments are interested in continued revenue sharing with the state; they would like the state to continue to manage and deliver some of the tougher human and social services, but they are adamant about the need to retain local control. To deal with some of the immediate problems that are seen as most severe in the metropolitan areas, local governments stress self-determination, self-help, and local option, not assistance.

A series of recent newspaper articles, research reports, studies, town hall meetings, and legislative inquiries provide compelling descriptions and diagnoses of metropolitan problems that seem intractable in the face of current state-local efforts (Peirce 1987; Hall 1987; Melnick 1988).

Most improvements under discussion could be accomplished only with strong state-local cooperation and implementation of a level seldom seen in Arizona. Some of these changes are far more politically feasible than others. All would affect Arizona's state-local capacity. Examples include:

□ county home rule
□ school district consolidation
□ horizontal tax base sharing (jurisdictions within a metropolitan area would share sales tax revenues of prosperous shopping centers and other regional facilities)
□ joint use (multijurisdictional use of costly facilities and programs to achieve economies of scale)
□ new civic organizations, such as the Valley Civic League (recently established with objectives like those of the Minneapolis-St. Paul Civic League), and
□ growth limits or boundaries for metropolitan services.

CONCLUSIONS AND IMPLICATIONS

What will happen to future state-local relations in Arizona is a function of past precedent, new politics, and changing federalism. This mix of old ways and new needs may merit different and somewhat uncertain solutions. But whatever they are, those solutions will have to meet the test of U.S. politics. Any significant solution needs to preserve the vision—the illusion?—of the ever-expanding pie.

Zero-sum solutions, such as those offered in the early days of the Reagan administration and, ironically, in the last Mondale campaign, do not work because they run counter to this driving force of U.S.

politics. Poll after poll shows that people want better services, and book after book declares the power of special interests in prodding policy.[8]

State and local governments in Arizona, as in other states, must at least appear to respond to public demands for more and better services while holding off on tax increases to survive. This tension for Arizona governments may be a little greater than elsewhere for two reasons.

First, state and local officials are constantly playing catch-up to growth-related needs. Further, because of relatively recent additions to the state's public policy system, there is a lack of experience in many aspects of public policy that could help in the catch-up process. There are, of course, some advantages to being young and growing—particularly given the state's revenue sharing practices—that have helped local governments attempting to keep pace with these challenges.

A second major challenge to state and local government responsiveness is derived from the prevailing political culture. Many in Arizona consider limited government the best kind. This is Goldwater country, long written off by Democratic presidential candidates and well known for its conservative tradition.

Many in Arizona are quick to arouse with "mad-as-hell-sloganeering" when the target is government. Accordingly, national movements like the taxpayers' revolt and the Reagan revolution were popular in Arizona. During the late 1970s and early 1980s, it was particularly important for elected officials to talk about limited or limiting government, even though Arizona governments were by all measures growing rapidly. Budgets, personnel, highways, prisons, indigent health programs, education, wastewater treatment facilities, and much more blossomed in the desert during this period. Many Arizona voters may be simultaneously angry with and demanding of state and local government for the same reasons that Arthur Schlesinger, Jr. (1988), cites to explain the failure of the Reagan revolution:

Sometimes government intervenes too much. Its regulations become pointlessly intrusive. Its programs miscarry. Exasperations accumulate. The Reagan counter-revolution may well have been a bracing experience for the American Government. But Reaganism, while tapping the inflaming and accumulated exasperations, has quite failed to transform them into a revolution against the affirmative state.

Many of Arizona's local political leaders have pondered this dilemma: how to increase services and still win elections in a conservative political culture. The frequent answer is: *use the intergovernmental system*. From the national-state perspective, local governments are useful employees who can do the work when they are properly instructed.

It is in the best political interest of all units in our complicated federal system to work together to maximize response and credit and to minimize responsibility for finance and failure. It is also in the best interest of the partners to keep the system complicated. That is because, when seen clearly and in total, both costs and responses are far greater than many people would imagine and are easy pickings for new politicians at all levels.

It is the obscure, shadowy—some would go so far as to say hidden—aspects of U.S. federalism that gall some reformers. Yet intergovernmental arrangements often succeed because they are not tested by full democratic review.

So it is as sometimes silent partners that Arizona governments have grown, prospered, and provided public services in a climate of limited government. These partners will continue to work with each other and with the national government and nonprofit organizations to meet demands for increased services.

All partners will, of course, continue to negotiate profits and losses (credit and blame, responsibilities, and revenues), but the U.S. federalism corporation is large, has immense latent power, is slow to change, and is in business for the long term.

Notes

The author is grateful to Richard Nathan of Princeton University and Lester Salamon of the Johns Hopkins University for intellectual and financial support for the line of inquiry that is continued in this paper. Helpful comments on a draft of were made by Louis Weschler of Arizona State University and Blaine Liner of The Urban Institute.

1. For recent articles that summarize findings and conclusions on Arizona, see Hall and Eribes (1987, pp. 280–302); Hall (1986, pp. 185–207; Musselwhite et al. (1987); and Maricopa Association of Governments (1987).

2. For a detailed, excellent, if somewhat understandably biased account of these realities, see Williamson (forthcoming) on U.S. federalism.

3. The state legislature devotes most of its time to taxing and spending *state* funds, but it has never had the power of appropriating federal funds. The issue of federal fund appropriation has been debated many times, was defeated by state voters when it was referred to them in 1984, and when resurrected by the state Senate in 1987, died in the House.

4. For a full description of the Arizona adoption of these block grants, see Hall and Eribes (1987, pp. 287–8); for more details on the 1981 changes and the nine block grants, see Nathan, Dolittle, and Associates (1987, chs. 2 and 3).

5. The title was bestowed by Claudia Dreifus (1988). See McClain (1988) for the best chronology of Mecham's decline and fall.

6. All this action took place between 1978 and 1980. For a more complete discription of these measures, see Hall and Eribes (1987, pp. 281–3).

7. This is a loose translation of observations made by Jack DeBolske, Director of the Arizona League of Cities and Towns and the state's foremost expert on state intergovernmental affairs during an interview coverning state-local relations, June 1988.

8. Stockman (1986) is the best evidence, if not the best book, to document this proposition.

References

Arizona. *Statement of Federal Funds: Fiscal Year 1989.* Phoenix: State of Arizona.

Arizona Joint Legislative Budget Committee. 1988. Appropriations Report.

Babbitt, Bruce. 1982. *Arizona Republic*, 19 February.

Berman, David R. N.d. Growth Management: Problems of Pursuit, Control and Adaptation. In *Urban Growth in Arizona: A Policy Analysis*, edited by Rob Melnick. Tempe, Ariz.: Arizona State University, Morrison Institute for Public Policy.

Dreifus, Claudia. 1988. The Belles of Recall. *Ms.* (June): 44–51.

Fiscal Planning Services, Inc. 1988. FEDFACTS III: Final Appropriation FY 1988. In Arizona Joint Legislative Budget Committee (JLBC). *Fiscal 1988 Federal Funds Update.* Phoenix: JLBC.

Hall, John Stuart. 1986. Retrenchment in Phoenix, Arizona. In *Reagan and the Cities*, edited by George E. Peterson and Carol W. Lewis. Washington, D.C.: Urban Institute Press.

——, ed. 1987. *Valley Growth: United or Fragmented?* Tempe, Ariz.: Arizona State University, School of Public Affairs.

Hall, John Stuart, and Richard A. Eribes. 1987. In Richard P. Nathan, Fred C. Doolittle, and Associates. *Reagan and the States.* Princeton, N.J.: Princeton University Press.

Hall, John S., et al. 1985. *Government Spending and the Nonprofit Sector in Two Arizona Communities: Phoenix/Maricopa County and Pinal County.* Washington, D.C.: Urban Institute Press.

Hill, Jeff. 1988. Quoted in *Arizona Republic*, May 22.

Hodgkinson, Harold L. 1988. *Arizona: The State and its Educational System.* Washington, D.C.: Institute for Educational Leadership.

Jersey City Declared Academically Bankrupt. 1988. *Washington Post*, 29 May.

Kingdon, John W. 1984. *Agendas, Alternatives and Public Policy.* Boston: Little Brown.

Maricopa Association of Governments. 1987. *1988–1989 Human Services Plan for Maricopa County.* November. Maricopa, Arizona.

Maricopa County Needs Assessment Project. 1988. Maricopa County, Ariz. Computer printout.

McClain, Paula D. 1988. Arizona "High Noon": The Recall and Impeachment of Governor Evan Mecham. *PS: Political Science and Politics* (Summer): 628-38.

Melnick, Rob, ed. N.d. *Urban Growth in Arizona: A Policy Analysis.* Tempe, Ariz.: Arizona State University, Morrison Institute for Public Policy.

Musselwhite, James C., Jr., et al. 1987. *Human Services Spending in Phoenix and Pinal County: The Changing Roles of Government and Private Funders.* Washington, D.C.: Urban Institute Press.

Peirce, Neal. 1988. Urban Challenges: A Vision for the Future. In *The Arizona Republic and Phoenix Gazette,* 1988.

Sacton, Frank J. 1980. *Arizona Government in the National Context.* Tempe, Ariz.: Arizona State University, Center for Public Affairs.

Salamon, Lester M., Carol J. De Vita, and David M. Altschuler. 1987. *Phoenix Nonprofit Organization: The Challenge of Retrenchment.* Washington, D.C.: Urban Institute Press.

Schlesinger, Jr., Arthur. 1988. *Washington Post,* 1 May.

Stockman, David. 1986. *The Triumph of Politics.* New York: Harper and Row.

Williamson, Richard A. N.d. *Federalism: Reagan's Efforts to Decentralize Government:* Lanham, Md.: University Press of America.

Part Two

FRAMEWORK FOR ALIGNMENT OF ROLES AND JURISDICTION

Chapter Seven

ANALYTIC APPROACHES TO STATE-LOCAL RELATIONS

Harold A. Hovey

Is there something wrong with state-local relations in the United States today? Most readers would probably answer "yes." Certainly, the level of dissatisfaction is high. Organizations of local officials in nearly every state have an agenda for changes in state policies regarding the functions and taxing authority of local government. Legislators too have many criticisms—local governments are too small or too large to perform effectively, they spend too much and/or serve too little, they fail to educate children properly, and more. At the local level, there are frequent campaigns to alter the structure of local government through changes in governing arrangements, or in the scope of government by means of school district consolidations or break-ups, mergers of cities and counties, annexations, and creation and abolition of special districts. These criticisms were explored in more detail in chapter 3.

With all of this smoke, it is reasonable to assume there is fire someplace. The question is where. State-local relations is one place to look—but not the only one. Sometimes critics say that the wrong level of government is making a decision when what they really mean is they do not like a particular decision and think it would be made more in their favor by some other level of government. For understanding possible changes in intergovernmental relations, it is important to recognize that a serious criticism involves two elements: defining the facts of the situation and judging the situation as right or wrong by certain chosen criteria.

This chapter is an attempt to put the criteria for determining the appropriate level of decision making on the table. There they can be analyzed independently of the policy decisions.

SEPARATING SERVICE PROVISION, CONTROL, AND FINANCE

Defining the Locus of Decision Making

In the hurly-burly world of state and local politics, there is a tendency to consider together some decisions that are not inherently linked conceptually. They are: who provides a service, who supervises and controls the provision of a service, and who pays for the service. Experience shows that they can be separated in reality. There are nine possible combinations of the three factors. This chapter focuses on the four combinations that are possible from the viewpoint of a government unit that is providing a service.

Provision Yes, Control No, Payment No. There is no reason why the party actually providing a service must either pay for it or control the conditions under which the service is provided. Everyone who hires someone to mow the lawn and feed the dog understands this point. The service provider does the work, but how the work will be done is prescribed by the buyer and the costs are paid by the buyer. There are many noncontroversial examples in government in which government buys services from private suppliers, including doctors, home health care workers, and waste disposal companies. Governments also buy services from each other—local governments from other local governments, states from counties, and so on. A good example is the purchase of state and local administrative services by the federal government in making field disability determinations for the Social Security program. The federal government sets the policy, and state and local officials carry it out and are reimbursed for their services.

Provision Yes, Control Yes, Payment No. Sometimes governments provide a service and control how it is provided but do not pay for the service. For example, the federal government and some states make in-lieu-of-tax payments that are conceptually related to municipal services such as police and fire protection.

Provision Yes, Control No, Payment Yes. This case is included because it is a theoretical possibility. But the handles for control are payment and provision, so examples are rare. An example is the temporary detailing of an employee to another organization. The donor organization provides the employee's service and pays him or her, but the donor controls who receives the services.

Sometimes a local or state government provides a service and pays the full costs of providing the service, but another government controls and supervises what is provided. Federal mandates governing the removal of architectural barriers for the handicapped and federal court mandates on jail and prison conditions are examples. So too are state mandates that schools offer certain curricula, such as state history classes, unaccompanied by state funding.

Provision Yes, Control Yes, Payment Yes. One government controlling, providing, and paying is a standard pattern, more honored in the breach than the observance. Street cleaning, public higher education, and local parks are examples.

Other Situations. With one exception, all other possible combinations of provision, control, and payment are covered above. State and local government provision of disability determinations illustrates provision without control or payment to local and state government, but it also illustrates payment and control without provision by the federal government. The exception is the null set—no provision, no control, and no payment. This arrangement describes how local government relates to national defense, for example. These situations can be ignored.

Practical Applications of the Concepts

The conceptual ability to separate considerations of the provision of services from those related to control and funding is important to understanding specific issues in state-local relations. Yet these considerations are so often mixed in practice that they are often confused in practical discussions, so meaningful options often are ignored.

Local professional fire protection provides an example. To perform this function requires some minimum level of capacity—say, a full-time crew of four, a truck, and a dispatcher. With three crews required for 24-hour, 7-days-a-week coverage and some provision for absences, perhaps 14 people are required. This number (or something like it) is inherent in the technology of fire protection. *That technology is totally independent of whether fire protection is provided by municipalities, counties, the state, or the private sector.*

Fire protection is typically public because each of us has a vested interest in our neighbors' level of fire protection, for a neighbor's uncontrolled fire could easily spread to our residence or business. Therefore we will not allow a system in which people have the option of not contracting for fire protection. We do not want our neighbors to get a free ride by avoiding paying for fire protection, so we require fire coverage of everyone. By historical accident, we effect this requirement through taxes and a fire department that provides services at no incremental cost to anyone who must use it. But we also have a vested interest in assuring that anyone who damages our bodies and autos on the highways is able to pay for the resulting damages. To meet this end, we do not provide public insurance; we require insurance coverage as a condition of driving, with private companies supplying the market. Fire coverage could be provided in the same way.

The costs of fire protection are not proportional to the property taxes traditionally used to pay for this service. A house on a brush-filled, fire-prone hillside of Los Angeles or a run-down wooden attached structure in downtown Los Angeles costs more to protect than a detached single-family home with hydrants nearby or a commercial building with a sprinkler system and standpipes. These differences are not reflected in fire protection taxes in Los Angeles. But they are reflected in the differences among fire protection costs in Los Angeles, Pasadena, and La Crescenta—all separate municipalities in one area.

The issues of how much fire protection is mandated, how much differential is charged for differing risk, and how the costs are otherwise allocated among persons are *all* independent of whether fire protection is provided by: the three separate municipalities; the Los Angeles department for Los Angeles and, by contract, the other two; the county; the state; a special fire protection district; or one or more private companies under regulation of one or more of these entities. The diversity of municipal service arrangements in California shows the range of possibilities for fire and police protection, waste disposal, and other functions.

Criteria for the Appropriate Level of Service Provision

The issue of the appropriate level of government to provide a service is relatively straightforward compared with issues of control and financing. Resolution of the provision issue is a function of the technology of production of the service, specifically whether there are economies or diseconomies of scale, and the jurisdictional question. Is the scope of responsibility needed to perform a function consistent with the jurisdiction of the government attempting to perform it?

Economies of Scale. For every service provided by government, there is a technology for providing the service and costs associated with production inputs (such as wages and salaries, equipment, and consumable supplies).

Local schools provide an example. It is widely (though not universally) agreed that a decent high school provides college preparation (e.g., math through calculus, physics, chemistry, and at least one foreign language) by teachers qualified to teach in these disciplines and that class sizes of up to 25–30 are educationally acceptable in these subjects. A wealthy family could hire tutors for each of these subjects, but such an arrangement is out of reach for most. Costs decline sharply as more students are involved. Per student, tutors for two cost about half of tutors for one, and per student, tutors for 100 cost something like one one-hundredth of per-student costs for one. But per-pupil costs stop declining when the student population reaches 1,000 or so—the point at which additional math and foreign language instructors are hired.

The conventional wisdom in education is that bad things happen when a single high school serves 2,000 or 3,000 students. Time is lost moving from distant class to distant class, opportunities to excel on the single football team and yearbook are confined to a lower percentage of students, and students feel lost in the crowd.

As a district grows from one high school to 100, there are essentially no economies of scale. But a few higher degrees of specialization are permitted. For example, one specialized psychologist may now handle 100 gifted children and another 100 educably mentally retarded rather than one general psychologist handling 50 in each group. But there are also bureaucratic costs. The principal who used to report to a board now reports to a superintendent. The physics instructors now have a physics curriculum coordinator. These changes make it unlikely that a system with 100 high schools is inherently cheaper or more expensive to run or is better or worse educationally than one with two high schools.

As this discussion suggests, economies of scale often give *absolutely no* indication about who should pay for services, who should control the provision of the service, or what tax or user charge base should stand behind it. A 1,000 to 2,000-pupil high school can be run with no tax base at all; put another way, each household voluntarily becomes the tax base. Private high schools work this way. Another possibility is to have (or create by consolidation) a school district covering kindergarten through grade 12 (K–12,) with enough 9–12 or 8–12 students to maintain such a high school and another district purchasing high school spaces from it. Western states have a similar arrangement for specialized graduate programs. Still another possibility is used in Illinois, where some school districts handle K–8 only. The taxpayers of these districts are also taxpayers of another district that runs the high school.

Other possibilities are suggested on the large end of the continuum. Because values other than economies of scale may be lost by large school districts, New York City has experimented with, in effect, dividing the city into smaller school districts, each with its own local board. A similar move is being considered in Chicago.

A Scale Appropriate to the Dimensions of the Problem. Some services are provided on a place-specific basis whereby governments of widely varying sizes perform the service. Examples are local road maintenance, schools, fire and police protection, and water supplies from wells. The situation changes, particularly for regulation, when what needs to be done covers a geographic area that is not within any current or likely future government boundaries, for example:

□ The regulation of the flow, withdrawal of water, pollution runoff, and pollution control of a river basin obviously requires control over all parties affecting pollution or taking water from the basin. This need is met by a combination of national pollution control regulations and regional compacts established for the management of resources like the Colorado River.

□ The regulation of groundwater withdrawal, ocean fisheries, migrating waterfowl and fish, and oil and gas pools spanning more than one jurisdiction presents a common-pool problem. All the players, including regulators, have an incentive to allow withdrawals from the pool that will maximize the returns of its citizen-taxpayers. But following that incentive will, in conjunction with comparable action by other players, deplete the pool at an uneconomical rate. The results will be a fishery that is fished out, water tables that are too low for economical extraction, and oil and gas in the ground that cannot be removed because pressure has dropped too precipitously. These situations are handled in various ways—ranging from no action to interstate compacts to federal regulation.

□ The economic development of regions spans political boundaries. Examples are the Ozark Mountain area, Appalachia, and the southern delta country. This consideration was partly handled at one time by federally sponsored regional commissions, but only Appalachia now has a formal federal economic development mechanism.

□ The regulation of the purity of foods produced at one location and consumed in another now depends on the kind of food and the relationship between the importer (e.g., foreign country or interstate) and the place to which the food is being imported. Meat and poultry and some other products are sometimes handled by a joint federal-state program. Drugs and cosmetics are handled by federal regulation.

Scope of control is frequently an issue in limitations on local government powers. Technology makes it difficult to supply water without control of a watershed, to supply an airport without owning land outside central cities, and to handle garbage without a landfill in rural areas. To deal with these situations, many local governments have extraterritorial powers, including the right to own and control land. Other mechanisms operate when they do not—cooperative agreements, state control, and regional authorities.

Criteria for the Appropriate Location of Control

Externalities. A socially appropriate decision is one that involves weighing the advantages and disadvantages of alternatives for those affected. Put another way, such a decision involves assessing costs and benefits for those affected. Each formulation relies on those affected. Problems arise when the decision-making government does not include in its definition all those affected by the decision.

To simplify, Town A can avoid an annual cost of $10 million for building a secondary sewage treatment facility rather than discharging waste after only primary treatment, but it costs Town B, downstream, $15 million more to clean up the river to supply water than it would have if Town A had provided secondary treatment. Clearly, in the interests of the welfare of all, Town A's secondary treatment facility should be built. But if the decision is to be made solely by the voters and/or elected representatives in Town A, the decision is likely to be not to build. The costs of construction and operation are internal to A's taxpayers, but the benefits are external. Put another way, the cost of A's not treating the waste is felt by B—what economists call a negative externality.

The interests of both Town A and Town B in the decision making can be considered in a variety of ways. A decision made by a higher level of government or special district encompassing both towns will achieve this result, as will some sort of subsidy for Town A's construction costs or a mandate from a higher level of government.

In practice, there are substantial difficulties in defining externalities. It is, for example, not clear how much stake a New York resident has in the elementary education standards for a Texas child. It is even less clear what the values might be to New York residents in knowing that mental health patients are treated humanely in New Mexico.

The Values of Uniformity and Costs of Diversity. Imagine three people entering an ice cream store where cones cost $1. The three have different tastes for ice cream. Individual A likes butter pecan and would pay $1.20 if the seller charged that much, but A does not like strawberry at all and would prefer nothing to a strawberry cone; A would even pay $.20 to avoid having it. Any other flavor would be worth $.95 to A. B would pay $1.20 for strawberry and $1 for any other flavor offered. C wants chocolate, also worth $1.20, but would pay $1.10 for strawberry and $1 for any other flavor. In the normal course of ice cream buying, each would select a favorite, the store would collect $3, and the consumers would receive a total of $.60 in benefits they would have paid for but the store could not figure out how to collect from them (consumers' surplus, as economists call it).

Now suppose that a rule is imposed on the three that they must all order the same flavor. The benefits stack up this way:

Consumer	Strawberry	Chocolate	Butter Pecan
A	$ −.20	$ .95	$1.20
B	1.20	1.00	1.00
C	1.10	1.20	1.00
Total	$2.10	$3.15	$3.20

If the group calculated its decision on the basis of total benefits, it would pick butter pecan. But in a majority rule system without logrolling (swapping votes on one issue about which strong feelings prevail for votes on another about which indifference prevails), B and C will both vote for strawberry and net benefits of the majority's decision will be $2.10. No matter how anyone votes, the three can never produce by majority rule the benefits they could achieve if each pursued separate choices in the marketplace.

Much the same situation prevails in the real world. Parents of young children are likely to favor extensive spending on public schools, playgrounds, zoos, parks, and other publicly provided amenities that they see as considerably cheaper if provided by government than if purchased in the private sector. Affluent individuals are likely to be willing to spend more on the roads, fire and police protection, and the arts than less affluent people. Those who are just making ends meet generally would opt for lower taxes and a lower level of public services. Young adults may opt primarily for publicly provided tennis and swimming but retired persons may prefer golf courses, walking trails, and senior citizen centers. Anytime decisions about these kinds of issues are made centrally, there are bound to be losers.

The advantages of diversity have combined with the relative freedom that citizens had in establishing new municipalities during the nineteenth and much of the twentieth century to create service differentiation among jurisdictions in many metropolitan areas. Some suburbs have high levels of public service and relatively high taxes. Others attract new families with a reputation for good public schools and low costs for other services. Metropolitan area residents demanding high service levels and wanting to avoid high taxes frequently settle in unincorporated areas around major cities.

Preferences aside, there are significant differences in circumstances among geographic areas. Uniformity has its costs in that situation as well. One example is air pollution standards for automobiles, which apparently do not work well in cities, such as Denver, during the winter. Another is nationally uniform standards for interstate highways regarding the steepness of grades and the radius of curves. The costs of these standards in most parts of the country are relatively low and the benefits high because of the large number of vehicles served. But when applied to infrequently traveled interstates in the mountainous West, some of these standards are not optimal from the perspective of highway engineering economics.

Absent any other considerations, and there are substantial other considerations, the diverse interests of individual citizens would suggest that any government decision making be made at the lowest level possible. For this reason, U.S. policies are to be preferred over worldwide ones; state decisions are to be preferred over national ones; large county ones, and so on. The "and so on" is key because the logic does not stop at any size, no matter how small the government. The greatest deference is paid to the choice of individual households when the household is the decision-making unit, no decisions are imposed by the public, and no taxes are levied.

Overriding Policy Imperatives. Some people's feelings are so strong about an issue that they tend to favor control by the level of government that will do what they want and oppose control by any level of government that will not. For example, if capital punishment is bad, the best result is a national mandate against its being used by any authority—federal, state, or local. Next best is a national policy that permits abolition of capital punishment by any subnational government choosing not to use it. Worst is a national mandate that capital punishment must be used. If abortion is bad, the best result is a national prohibition. The second best result is a decision that states are free to opt for a policy of their choosing.

There is no obvious line to be drawn between one individual's policy preferences and another's. One line that has been drawn in national debates is that fundamental civil rights are an issue of over-riding national interest. But the application of this rule is at issue. Does it, for example, obviously dictate a one man, one vote rule at the state and local levels with a different rule applied to represen-tation in the U.S. Senate? Does it dictate a particular electoral system, such as plurality decisions versus runoffs and single-member versus multimember districts, or affirmative action in hiring?

The same issues arise at the state level. In many state courts, the issue of state constitutional guarantees inherent in state constitu-tional provisions assigning the state the responsibility of providing for public education is being debated.

Diversity of control has inherent limitations when citizens have the option of choosing to subject themselves to control of more than one government. In litigation, the phenomenon is known as forum shopping—finding the jurisdiction with the legal precedents and justices most likely to favor one's case. The diversity appears as well in preemption issues, in which the question is whether a higher level of government has eliminated the possibility of diverse policies in the lower level of governments.

Criteria for Allocation of Financing Responsibility

Inability to Ration Services and the Free Rider Problem. In the nature of things, some services cannot be enjoyed by some at their expense while others who do not pay are denied the benefits. The most ob-vious example is national defense. It is inherent in the nature of defense tech. ologies and doctrine that any systems that defend Chi-cago also defe d Peoria and any systems that defend Peoria also defend Chicago. Left to their own devices, the citizens of Peoria might well decide to let the citizens of Chicago pay the entire bill. To prevent this situation, the costs of defense are spread among tax-payers of the whole nation. A less extreme example is regulation to avoid adulterated food and drugs and air and water pollution. A free market system for such governmental services simply would be un-workable because free riders would predominate.

As a practical matter, this problem appears in a slightly different fashion in the public sector, in which people can be excluded from benefits in theory but cannot be excluded in practice. Two examples are parks and mass transit. The number of persons seeking to use these services on any given day varies in ways that cannot be predicted far in advance. When it snows, people do not use the parks much, but the staffing remains the same. They do flock to mass transit, however. A balmy day in the spring or fall will raise park usage and cut into mass transit usage as people opt for driving to work or going to parks instead. The theoretical solution to this situation could be one of the following:

□ A demand and capacity charge as used by electric and gas companies for industrial users. Customers pay one charge to buy the right to consume at times of their own choosing; they pay it whether they choose many or no times at all. They pay a second charge based on their actual use. Golf clubs work in this way. An initiation and/or membership fee pays for availability of the course and a greens fee pays for its use, including the costs of the grounds staff and other operating costs.

□ Peak hour charges, often used by restaurants and in theater ticket prices. Prime times (e.g., Friday and Saturday evenings) cost more and weeknights and matinees cost less.

Although such charges have been advocated for mass transit, for allocating space on highways during rush hours, and for other public services, U.S. public policy favors a single uniform charge for many public services, giving a partial free ride to those who use mass transit only when the weather is bad.

The free rider problem often has a spatial dimension, which arises when a public service is available to the population of a wide geographic area at no or a low user charge but is paid for by the central city or central county. Examples are central city parks, zoos, cultural and convention centers, and full-scale mass transit systems accessed by out-of-system commuters by car and remote parking or benefiting such commuters by reducing congestion on roads they use in commuting to central cities. One major criterion is that governments are large enough to encompass potential free riders.

Although financing by a high level of government is an option for dealing with externalities and free riders, it is by no means the only option. The previous example of Town A's decision to build a sewage treatment plant primarily benefiting Town B is an example. A higher level of government can reduce the cost to Town A through aid—

one purpose of the federal wastewater treatment program. But the higher level of government can drop the financing and rely primarily on regulation—the way in which federal policy is developing.

The previous discussion describes considerations relevant to allocation of functions among governments. It relies upon the preferences of households as they might be expressed through the mechanism of voting and elections and in the marketplace. As most economic discussions do, it tacitly assumes that the distribution of voting power and economic power is morally acceptable. In classic formulations of the problem in public finance, the previous sections deal with the allocation functions of government. Those functions have as their objective the maximization of welfare, as economists define welfare.

Consequences of Economic Power Allocation. Government has another function. That is to redistribute wealth and income among the citizens. This function is inherent in any tax system. So long as there is any government at all—say, just courts to enforce private rights and courts and legislatures to renew a decision that the least government is the best government—there must be taxes to sustain the government. Anytime there is a tax system of any kind, some decision is involved about who must contribute how much to pay for it.

This concept is best illustrated by a three-household society with one rich family, one poor family, and one average family. The tax scheme to support its government's legal framework and defense could be shared equally or, arguably, allocated in proportion to benefits. In those cases, the three families would pay equal amounts and the tax would take a larger percentage of the poor family's income than the rich family's. Another approach is to collect taxes in proportion to income, in which case taxes will be higher per family for the richest family. Another approach is to excuse the poor family from tax burdens on the grounds that they cannot pay and spread the burden between the middle-income and rich family, with the rich family paying more.

These approaches are respectively known as regressive, proportional, and progressive taxes.

But there is more to taxation. Income, however defined, is not an unambiguous guide to the ability of households to pay. Wealth does not bear a totally proportionate relationship to income. So any tax scheme based on wealth, such as property taxes, will not appear equitable in relation to income, and any tax scheme based on income will not appear appropriate in relation to wealth. Consumption is another characteristic of the household that is not totally proportional to either wealth or income.

In addition, our economy harbors major entities other than families or households that may be asked to pay a share of taxes. Those entities include business corporations, religious orders, nonprofit corporations, trusts, partnerships, and estates. There are continuing arguments about whether and how such entities should be taxed and how taxes levied on them affect the standard of living of households of various income classes.

The story does not end there. Government spending is not neutral but can be focused deliberately on regions with concentrations of high- or low-income populations, government employment can be allocated on other than a marketplace basis, and government procurement can be explicitly or implicitly set aside to favor certain groups.

Economists view this as the distribution branch of government, conducting an activity different from merely seeking to allocate resources optimally to achieve the maximization of income for the total citizenry.

Because people have unequal access to inherited wealth and unequal earning capacity, their resources available to purchase public or private goods and services will differ. Thus some will be able to purchase adequate food, adequate housing, and polo ponies. Others will be able to purchase adequate food and housing but not polo ponies; still others will be able to get enough to eat but will not be able to afford adequate housing, much less polo ponies. Still others, left to their own devices, will not even be able to feed themselves and their children.

If all poor and rich live in the same jurisdiction, government can clearly influence consumption patterns by influencing ability to pay. This influence can be effected by taxing the rich to turn money over to the poor—the effect of welfare cash assistance. It can also be done by subsidizing consumption from general taxes with some sort of a means test applied to recipients; food stamps, general assistance, Medicaid, low-income energy assistance, higher education tuition grants, and some other policies do so. The tax system also has more subtle impacts in reducing the costs of some goods and services and increasing the costs of others. For example, the property used for a grocery store serving the poor is normally taxed, but the property used for polo fields often is not or is taxed at lower rates than those applicable to grocery stores.

The issue of what and who should be subsidized and taxed cannot be resolved by the application of logic and analysis because the preferred outcome is, in part, a question of individual ethical standards. Fortunately, this issue need not be resolved in dealing with state-local relations. Instead, its existence must be recognized, but its magnitude and exact dimensions need not be described so long as it is recognized that many people will not be satisfied with the status quo, and many would not be satisfied with any possible revision of the status quo.

The Entanglement of Economic Power and Intergovernmental Selection. Once the existence of subnational governments is recognized, the question of government organization and finance is no longer separable from the question of income distribution. Subdividing government means that each jurisdiction will have differing characteristics, including ability to pay (however measured), difficulties in providing public services, and voter taste for public services. *If local tax decisions are allowed to have any impact whatsoever on levels of spending and taxes, the choice of geographic coverage of the subdivisions will affect the distribution of resources among citizens of the nation and any state within it.* No public policy that allows any autonomy in taxes and spending among political subdivisions can ever eliminate this linkage.

But the choice of an optimal distribution of purchasing power is a matter of ethics, to which there is no right answer. It follows, therefore, that no scheme of subdivisions can be prescribed as offering a single correct answer. The best that experts can be expected to do is to show the consequences of various decisions on the subnational division of labor.

Approaches to Income Assistance for the Needy. Suppose we begin with a nation that has per capita income of $10,000 a year and also has people who are not capable of earning any income. All readers are likely to recognize that there are some such people: perhaps those who are disabled or mentally incompetent. As a nation, this society is willing to make cash transfers for a family of three of $400 a month. Now we decide to divide this nation into units—say one called Connecticut and one called Mississippi. The lines are drawn for this subdivision so that per capita income in Connecticut is $15,000 a year and Mississippi's is $7,500. The two states have the same population, but Mississippi is given two-thirds of the poor. No policy is set by the nation on what to do about the poor.

Given these facts, the ability to pay through a proportional tax system in Connecticut will be twice that of Mississippi. If a progressive tax scheme is preferred, Connecticut's ability to pay will be more than twice that of Mississippi. Mississippi's need for cash assistance will be twice that of Connecticut. The broad public policy options are now these:

□ Equal tax effort: If the tax rates and bases of the two jurisdictions are identical, Connecticut will raise twice as much as Mississippi but will be able to spread the welfare budget over half as many recipients, so its benefits will be four times higher than in Mississippi.

□ Equal benefits levels: If both governments provide equal benefits, regardless of the level chosen, Mississippi's taxes will be four times higher than those in Connecticut.

□ Compromise outcomes: Both these solutions are likely to be unacceptable in the real world. The expected outcome is that welfare payment levels will be higher in Connecticut and tax rates lower while welfare benefits will be lower in Mississippi and tax rates higher.

In the compromise solution, the poor in Mississippi are adversely affected in two ways, compared to the situation in which the national government sets the policy and collects the taxes. First, Mississippi welfare recipients receive less. Second, any tax scheme is likely to take away more of their purchasing power. The situation is reversed for the poor in Connecticut.

The mathematics of this situation provides more and more extreme examples when the unit of government becomes smaller because the smaller areas incorporate more homogeneous populations—concentrations of rich and poor. The examples become even more impressive when the flexibility in choice of tax bases is limited. Some extreme examples are available in the United States today. Among school districts, a few fortunate industrial enclaves have a tax base consisting of large industrial concentrations or several nuclear power plants but very few students. Such districts can afford gold-plated education, paid for with a tax rate that is minuscule by national standards. School districts serving lower middle-class bedroom communities have large numbers of pupils but low-value residential property and, in some areas, essentially no industrial or commercial property in the tax base.

Among municipalities, some have high concentrations of poor persons and low-value residential property while others also benefit from commercial and industrial property and have residents with few service needs.

Among counties, where the topic of aid to the poor is real in states that leave the general assistance function to counties, central counties may have relatively low tax bases but a concentration of the poor eligible for such programs.

Failure of Aid from Higher-Level Governments to Erase These Problems. As is shown more rigorously in the following chapter's discussion of distribution formulae for aid programs, no amount of aid from a higher level of government to a lower level can solve these distribution problems. Aid can ameliorate these problems, but not solve them. For example, national aid of $400 per welfare family financed by taxes that fall more heavily on Connecticut residents (per capita) will equalize both tax effort and welfare payments in Mississippi and Connecticut to the $400 level. But Connecticut will have the resources to finance a somewhat higher benefit than the nationally subsidized benefit, and the four-to-one Connecticut advantage over Mississippi will reappear. To avoid this situation, the national government can power equalize, so that a dollar of tax effort in Mississippi raises three national dollars for each Mississippi dollar. But as shown, such a policy would lead to national spending in excess of what national policy would call for if there were no political subdivisions. The other alternative is to subsidize totally the $400 minimum and bar state action to raise the benefit over $400. This choice could be called an aid program, but the selection is of semantic interest only. All money spent is raised by the national government, and the national government sets uniform benefit levels in all subdivisions. This policy may have the appearance of a federal system, but it is economically identical to a national system.

Voting and Its Defects in Allocating Power. Although voting and arrangements for turning votes into representatives and, ultimately, public policy are taken for granted in the U.S. system, the voting process itself has defects in representing popular will, and all arrangements for selecting representatives and their voting suffer from conceptual defects. This fact does not mean they are wrong or less than the best available, but it does mean there are faults. These faults are sometimes attributed to state and local governments; to do so is erroneous because they are inherent in any voting system and appear at the federal level as well.

The first problem with voting is that those ineligible to vote are not represented. Suppose, for example, the national policy issue were whether to finance government spending on a pay-as-you-go basis or use national deficits on the order of 2–4 percent of gross national product. The impact of those deficits would be to saddle future taxpayers with the interest costs associated with the enjoyment of present taxpayers of their level of national defense, Social Security, and other programs. Such a debt-oriented policy would be economically favorable to the retired and those near the end of their working lives but most unfavorable to those under 18. The voting scheme used to decide this policy issue accords no votes to those under 18 or to unborn children.

The second problem is that voting disproportionately provides power to the groups that are more likely to register than not, and among registered voters, to those more likely to vote than not. Responsive government in a voting context means responsive to those who vote, who are, disproportionately, white rather than black, high income rather than low income, highly educated rather than less educated, and older rather than younger.

The third problem is that the logic developed for representation inherently creates problems because several different logics can be viewed as more representative than others. Suppose Group A has 55 percent of the electorate and Group B has 45 percent. If all representatives are elected at large, Group A has the decisive votes on 100 percent of the representatives. If proportional representatives are used, Group A will have 55 percent of the representatives. If single-member districts are used, Group A will likely have substantially less than 100 percent of the representatives, depending on the extent to which Group B clusters in certain neighborhoods and thus holds a majority in some of the single-member districts. This imbalance is not a problem of any particular ethnic group. Most of the court cases have developed in settings where Group B is black and single-member districts are the preferred alternative, but cases are now being brought when Group B is white. The mathematics of vote dilution mechanisms that turn minority voting into majority control does not change regardless of whether the majority group is black or white, Democratic or Republican, Federalist or anti-Federalist.

These problems of representation are not unique to local and state governments in the United States. In fact, the U.S. government has two flaws not found in the voting systems of either state or local governments: a significant portion of the electorate of the District of Columbia (and as many territories and possessions as particular readers may choose to count) are disenfranchised entirely, and the allocation of two Senate seats per state gives disproportionate power to residents of states with smaller-than-average populations.

Competition as a Constraining Factor

The theoretical discussion of voting and the economics of deciding on tax and spending levels and distribution assumes that the decisions of each government are made in isolation from the decisions of others. This situation is emphatically not the case within the United States. In fact, competitive forces which pit state against state, local governments in one state against the state-local policy of other states and communities, and local governments in the same state against each other. This competition can have powerful impacts on taxing and spending policies. Arguments for avoiding such competition are one of the strongest forces for centralization of government power.

CONCLUSIONS

Many criticisms are made of the policies of local and state governments in the United States. This book focuses on criticisms that involve questions of whether the system of intergovernmental relations is functioning well. No criticism of this system is involved if it is agreed that the right level of government has full control over the decision, and its processes for decision making conform to democratic norms.

The key question is how to define the right level of government to be making decisions in light of reasonably objective criteria. Dealing with this question requires understanding of three different kinds of involvement any level of government can have with any particular public service: delivering it, controlling its provision, and financing it. Each of these decisions can be separated from the others, as many practical examples show—although it is often to the advantage of persons arguing a particular case to assume that they are linked.

Just about any entity—private or public—can deliver services. The scope of the delivery system should be at about the point at which economies of scale cannot be reaped by more size and higher unit costs would be experienced if the size were decreased.

Selecting the locus of control of collective decision making involves recognition that some values are lost when any locus of control exceeds the basic decision–making units such as individuals or households. Collective action of any kind inevitably dilutes individual choices while opening possibilities for group achievement of ends that might not be achievable by any combination of individuals acting independently. A key factor in setting the appropriate level of control is avoiding externalities—situations in which the group of decisionmakers does not reap all the benefits or bear all the costs of their decisions.

As a practical matter, many advocates of public policies forum shop. That is, they seek to focus power in the level of government they feel is most likely to choose policies they prefer.

Deciding on the level of government to assume responsibility for financing services is closely related to the scope of benefits provided, specifically, whether free riders can be avoided.

All considerations of the appropriate locus of control—ranging from the free market to full governmental control—assume the legitimacy of economic power, voting power, or some combination of the two. But there are many reasons to believe the allocation of both kinds of power are ethically imperfect, although there is no objective way to determine what, if anything, should be done. The existence of subnational units inevitably creates disparities among their citizens because each jurisdiction will have service needs and fiscal capacity differing from those of the others. As a result, identical programs will require tax differences, and tax uniformity will produce differing program levels. These problems can be solved only by full takeover by a higher level of government, although they can be mitigated by intergovernmental aid programs.

In recent years, many functions have been shifted gradually from local government to the states and from the states to the federal government, often with the concurrence of the officials of the lower levels of government. Much of the motivation of these changes has been to reach the appropriate level of financing. But control may have unnecessarily, even inappropriately, migrated upward with financing. Further, actual provision of service may also have moved to higher levels even though no economies of scale and some loss of voter control may have been involved.

Conversely, the desire to maintain certain aspects of local control may have prevented certain service activities from rising to levels where economies of scale may exist. Waste disposal provides an example. A central disposal facility may offer economies of scale, but this factor is no reason why collection schedules must be uniform among governments sending waste to a central collection point.

When the questions of providing service, control, and financing are separated in this manner, it is by no means evident that current state-local-federal allocations of responsibility represent the right answers.

The following two chapters further explore these questions of allocation of responsibilities among the three levels of government. Chapter 8 assesses the current patterns of control in the main functional areas of government, and chapter 9 provides terms of analysis to help the reader better understand the impact of state funding decisions on different types of localities.

Chapter Eight

ALTERNATIVES FOR FUNCTIONS

Harold A. Hovey

The patterns now found in state-local relations nationwide are not the result of a single theory of federalism being applied to specific functions such as transportation and education. Instead, patterns of state-local relations have developed in each functional area—from education to transportation, from law enforcement to park management. Cross-cutting areas such as land use, infrastructure, and economic development have also developed in response to pressures of their own.

Those pressures and influences nationally include federal aid and regulatory policy, demographic patterns of need and resources, the professional doctrines of various fields, policy decisions of past years, and the technological environment in which services are provided. This chapter examines each major field of state and local activity, discussing such aspects as current patterns of control of the activity, current funding patterns, and the intergovernmental issues that currently draw the most attention.

ASSESSMENT OF FUNCTIONAL AREAS

Elementary and Secondary Education

The strong tradition in the United States is for education to be delivered by local government, what the U.S. Department of Education calls local education agencies. Throughout most of the country, the local education agency is an independent school district with its own boundaries, which often follow but may be separate from county and municipal boundaries; its own elected board; and its own taxing power. In some areas, particularly the Northeast, the school district is dependent—that is, it receives funds from a parent government, such as a New England town or a Virginia county, and has its policies controlled to varying degrees by the officials that provide the funding.

The private sector provides for the elementary and secondary schooiing of about 10 percent of the school-attending population. The majority of private schools are religiously oriented, mostly Catholic, with a residual of private elementary and secondary education in the South resulting from desegregation and white flight from the public schools and limited private education nationwide supported by parents who are willing to pay more for education in the expectation of results superior to those that can be obtained from the public schools. There is little public support of private elementary and secondary education, primarily because of constitutional restrictions dealing with the separation of church and state. Governments can, and often do, provide secular services such as textbooks and school transportation. Two states, Iowa and Minnesota, allow tax deductions for limited portions of the expenses of parents who send children to private schools.

Local education agencies rely heavily—in some states exclusively—on property taxes as their local revenue source. Particularly in states with many districts, there are sharp disparities in the tax capacity of districts per pupil. As a result, equal taxes produce unequal educational spending among districts. There is a widespread presumption that educational opportunity is unequal as a result. Most states have responded to this situation with state aid programs designed, in effect, to equalize the tax base among districts and with state aid covering one- to two-thirds of school costs. Hawaii organizes the entire state as a single school district. States provide about half the combined state and local costs of local schools, a percentage that has been increasing over the past several decades.

State aid has brought a measure of state control consistent with the concept of a minimum program being supported with state aid. The minimums concern such matters as class size, types of electives offered in high school, number of days of school per year, maximum distance students should be required to walk to school, and much more. The education quality movement of the early 1980s has brought further state control over such matters as graduation requirements; student testing; teacher pay plans, including versions of merit pay; and required subjects. States traditionally have controlled the definition of who is qualified to teach.

The federal government has never provided general support for local schools. Instead, it maintains a major education research program, provides funding for students with a tie to the federal government (such as Indians living on reservations and children of military personnel), and supports particular programmatic initiatives, of which those in special education and for disadvantaged children are the most important. The federal government has also experimented with narrow categorical programs (e.g., audiovisual instruction), but they have been folded into block grants, and the degree of federal control over state and local decisions has been reduced.

The major current issue in elementary and secondary education control does not challenge the basic concept that local boards will control the administration of the function; instead, it concerns the extent to which state standards will govern the exercise of that control. The current trend is toward increased control over such matters as teacher salaries, class size, teacher reward systems, academic eligibility standards for athletics, and the definition of basic skills necessary for graduation. One extreme of increased control is being proposed in many states—and was recently enacted in New Jersey—allowing states to put school districts in receivership to raise education standards. A countervailing control movement is occurring in some states by relaxing procedural controls for school districts that meet or exceed state performance standards for student achievement.

State-local funding issues are perennial. The underlying issue is the extent to which the state will reach a standard whereby the same tax rate in each district will produce the same revenue per pupil in each district. Although the U.S. Supreme Court has declined to define such a standard for states as being required by the Constitution, some state courts have found a version of such a standard to be dictated by state constitutions. Litigation on this subject continues in New Jersey and elsewhere.

School consolidation is a major issue in the states that have many small school districts. Consolidation permits districts to meet standards, such as those providing certain minimum numbers of subjects in high schools, more easily. Consolidation inevitably reduces local identity associated with athletics and the use of school buildings for local functions. It also usually produces a situation in which the tax rate of one of the consolidating districts is likely to be increased. Furthermore, there is little evidence that consolidated districts provide better educational opportunities than nonconsolidated ones, and they often produce longer travel times for students, which is the reason that the consolidation issue constantly comes up in Nebraska, for example.

Higher Education

Higher education in the United States began as a strictly private function. In the nineteenth century, public higher education was given a major boost by land grants associated with the establishment of state universities in the territories being newly settled, Ohio and Michigan, for example. This tradition was continued with the settlement of the West. States also responded to the need to train teachers with the establishment of regionally oriented teacher colleges (the so-called normal schools). The influx of students after World War II resulted in a sharp expansion of state university systems that included: the conversion of the former regional institutions to full-fledged universities, often with graduate and professional programs; the establishment of community colleges and university branches in smaller population centers; and the establishment of new universities in major population centers. Currently, private institutions account for about one-fourth of higher education students seeking degrees.

The typical state college and university system is governed by systems of boards. Details vary among states, with some boards performing more than one function. Basically a board governs each major campus or, in some states, a system of campuses. A board, often a second one, provides for overall coordination of the higher education system. Officials of such boards are state officials. Historically, some local governments provided higher educational institutions, but they were generally de facto, and often de jure, absorbed into the state systems.

The costs of public higher education are divided between student fees and tuition and state subsidies. Nationally, the state subsidies account for about two-thirds of state higher education instructional funding. Some states distribute the subsidies on a per student basis; the allocation systems in others more closely resemble the budgeting process for state agencies. The federal government provides limited funding of institutions, with a concentration on special situations such as professional training, historically black institutions, and sponsored research.

The student charge component of university budgets, public and private, is indirectly supported by state and federal scholarship and loan programs and grants. The federal grants are oriented toward disadvantaged students, and loans are more widely available to middle- and lower-income students. States participate in the federal student loan program and have grant, loan, and work study programs of their own—many administered by the higher educational institutions.

Most higher education is clearly a state function with no local involvement. An area of continuing controversy in some states concerns community (junior) colleges and vocational education programs providing for grades 13 and 14. Many of these programs developed as local programs, but state support has expanded a version of career-oriented vocational education to preparation for grades 15 and 16 to be undertaken at state universities. State control and funding of these institutions has been expanding gradually, but local tax effort still provides substantial support for many of them.

Income Maintenance

The major means-tested cash assistance program in the United States is Aid to Families with Dependent Children (AFDC). The federal government funds more than half this program with matching state and, in some states, local funds. The federal government sets eligibility conditions and has detailed rules determining the administration of the means test. States have considerable discretion in some matters, including whether intact families are eligible and how much the monthly payment is. Since the 1970s, the federal government has taken full responsibility for the Supplemental Security Income (SSI) program for the aged, blind, and disabled. Some states supplement the federal assistance by transferring cash to the federal government for distribution, some states distribute their own supplements, and some states do not supplement federal assistance at all. The federal government pays the full costs of food stamps, excepting a portion of administrative costs, and provides limited income support in the form of food distribution and low-income energy assistance. Medical costs for recipients of cash assistance are subsidized in the Medicaid program, generally using the same cost sharing applicable to AFDC. States have discretion in determining the services that will be covered by the program and whether certain poor persons not receiving cash assistance will be covered.

Although the federal government maintains broad controls over these programs, all but SSI are administered by state welfare agencies and, in many states, local welfare offices operating under state direction with major state funding. For persons not eligible for cash assistance from federal programs, state and local governments maintain general assistance programs. Control and funding for these programs are statewide in some states, but there are major elements of local funding and control in others.

New commitments to low-income housing with substantial subsidy take place through a variety of federal programs, with states involved in administration along with local quasi-governmental public housing authorities. States also provide a financial intermediary function through state housing authorities, and some states devote their resources to low-income housing as well. But much of the low-income housing in the United States is provided by the public housing authorities with federal subsidy.

Social service programs (e.g., programs for the aged, foster care, child abuse prevention) are provided by state and local governments, with federal support from a variety of programs and federal controls that are relatively limited compared to the income support programs.

The major issue in income-tested programs has been the same for decades—the level of government that should assume responsibility for funding these programs and the associated issue of control, eligibility standards, and payment levels provided. There is an enormous mismatch of resources and need for service from these programs. At the state level, this difference appears in the contrast between states with less-than-average fiscal capacity and higher-than-average potential recipients, such as many southeastern states and states with more fiscal capacity and less need for funds for income-tested programs. At the local level, the problem appears primarily between central cities and urban counties, with limited fiscal capacity and higher-than-average need, and suburban and rural areas.

As a result of these factors, many state officials have long urged a federal takeover of income maintenance programs, perhaps with the exception of the administrative responsibilities. Responding to the same factors, many local officials have urged both state takeover of local responsibilities for federally supported programs in the states that have not already made this move and state responsibility for general assistance. Movement toward greater centralization involves many issues. One is the choice between lowering benefits in some areas or raising spending for the central government to bring statewide or nationwide standards up to the highest standard in any jurisdiction. Another concern, particularly affecting federal takeover of welfare, is that the federal government would then be covering the costs of cash assistance, but state and local governments would maintain control over the programs (e.g., public health, education, employment, and training) offering the greatest potential for welfare prevention and diverting persons from welfare to work.

Discussions of federal takeover of welfare generally assume that local offices would continue to perform functions such as intake, counseling, eligibility determination, and payments administration. However, there is occasional, mostly academic, discussion of integrating the eligibility and payments function with federal income tax administration.

Health

The primary financing of major provider charges for health care (hospital costs and the types of costs covered by major medical policies) comes from: the federal Medicare program for those over 65; the federal-state Medicaid program for low-income persons not covered by Medicare; private health insurance; and the private resources of those receiving care.

Medicare is basically a federal program. States affect Medicare costs through any regulatory control they may exert over health care provider charges and terms of service. For those eligible for Medicare and Medicaid, the states pay the Medicare Part B premium for major medical and thus move those covered into the Medicare system. There is little sentiment for change in any major aspects of the division of labor among levels of government associated with Medicare.

Private payment for health care is influenced by the federal government through tax policy, but the primary responsibilities rest with the state and the private sector. With past federal encouragement, some states have attempted to regulate aspects of health care, including construction of major new facilities and certain charges, although not all states have participated in these activities as they relate to private-pay patients.

In most states, indigent care not covered by other programs is paid for by the health care providers. They recoup their costs primarily from charges to paying patients. There has been some interest in state programs to pick up some of these costs. Some states maintain indigent care funds that, in effect, formalize the subsidy of indigent care from taxes on services provided to paying patients. A few states, such as Hawaii and Rhode Island, have other indigent care programs, and Massachusetts has adopted an extensive comprehensive health plan.

State and local governments also appear in the health care market as providers, particularly through state university teaching hospitals and county hospital facilities. With exceptions, these entities are treated for reimbursement purposes in a fashion similar to commercial and nonprofit providers without connections to government. The division of responsibility in public health is relatively clear. The federal government is the primary source of research in disease prevention and control, with minor amounts provided by a few states. Local governments are the primary mechanism for traditional public health functions such as restaurant inspection, immunization, and epidemic control. States have supervisory responsibility over local authorities, and some states provide some public health services directly.

The primary federalism issue in health care concerns responsibility for the health care of the indigent in Medicaid and other programs. State roles in regulating health care charges are ambiguous in their interaction with federal policies on Medicare reimbursement policies and with federal policies affecting the ability of states to mandate employer-provided benefits such as health insurance. The state-local relationship in public health functions is stable, but there is agitation for state takeover of Medicaid costs in the states where there is still some local responsibility for them.

Transportation

In air transportation, the primary concern is financing the air traffic control system and the airports that serve major air carriers. General aviation is served by a combination of the major airports and smaller local airports. Many of them are private. Others are run by governments with a major portion of costs defrayed by user charges. Some states subsidize construction of general aviation airports. The federal government handles air traffic control with essentially no state or local involvement. Airports are typically bond financed by the local, and occasionally state, independent authorities that run them. Debt service for the bonds comes from: federal aid based on federally collected user charges and allocated primarily according to the needs of individual airports, landing fees, and concession fees for retail establishments in the airport lounge areas, parking, and the like. Situations vary so widely across the country that little can be said generally about state-local relations in air transportation.

Rail transportation regulation is a field that has largely been preempted by the federal government. States have assumed some roles in subsidizing passenger service and in maintaining abandoned lines, but the state role is limited, and there is no local role in intercity rail.

The situation in highways and mass transit exhibits a variety of overlapping federal, state, and local roles, with considerable agitation for more precise definitions of relative roles. With minor exceptions, such as roads on federal lands, the federal government does not use general fund monies to support highway and road construction and maintenance. The federal government collects a gasoline tax and other highway user charges, which are dedicated to a trust fund and are eventually disbursed in support of road programs, primarily construction and major renovation carried out by state and local governments. The federal assistance is provided through a collection of categorical programs targeted by the type of road—interstate highways, bridges, and so on.

The dominant factor in state-local relations in highways is the classification system in each state. Certain roads are designated as part of the state system. Construction and maintenance responsibilities for those roads are the state's, although it sometimes enters into agreements for local participation in those activities and the road patrol and safety function. The classification system continues through local governments with a hierarchy of county roads and municipal and township roads in most states and special local road districts in some states.

A few states allow local governments access to the tax base associated with motor vehicle registrations; drivers' licensing; and purchases of vehicles, parts, and fuel. But the common pattern is for the states to administer all these user charges and share the revenues with local governments, predominantly on the basis of where the revenue is raised. These funds typically do not defray all expenses; local property taxes make up most of the difference.

There has been considerable discussion of sorting out the functions of the federal government and state and local governments relative to highways and roads. All the proposals have significant implications for the resulting relationship between state and local governments. The proposals have in common the shucking of federal responsibility for roads and highways of primarily local rather than national significance. They differ in what roads would be covered and whether access to the federal tax base would accompany the shift of responsibility. They also differ in the treatment of the local-federal link in highway transportation. Many of the proposals would terminate the link.

There are continuing issues between local and state governments in highway transportation. They frequently arise in connection with the problem that motor fuel taxes, levied at fixed rates, do not raise enough money to cover past patterns of maintenance and construction because inflation affects the costs but not the revenues, and economies in fuel consumption have been reducing highway revenues per vehicle mile traveled in the absence of rate increases. Because this financial problem affects local road agencies as well as state highway departments, local officials have been clamoring for at least their share of any increased state taxes. States often follow this pattern, although there is some emphasis on a greater state retention of funds, primarily to finance road projects tied to economic development opportunities considered of statewide significance.

Uncertain federal policy makes the field of mass transit considerably more volatile than highways. Federal aid has provided a major share of the capital outlays of mass transit systems and a relatively deep subsidy for their operating costs. These programs are under attack in the budget process and are potentially to be devolved to state and local governments under transportation sorting-out proposals.

At the state and local levels, the predominant configuration for mass transit is a system or systems encompassing a central city and many of its suburbs. These systems typically do not cover even the nonfederal portion of their operating and capital costs. The general view that the responsibility for subsidies should correspond to the reach of the transit system has generated regional transportation authorities in many urban states. In some cases, such as New York and New Jersey, they are state entities. In others, they are regional bodies with separate taxing authority. In still others, they are regional bodies without taxing authority. Often state governments contribute to operating and/or capital costs. There is considerable continuing debate over the level of subsidies to be provided, which governments should provide them, and the organization and control of agencies financing transit.

Parks and Recreation

With the exception of a period during which the federal government subsidized park acquisition and construction, the pattern of responsibilities for recreation and park activities is one of consistent division of federal, state, and local responsibilities. The federal government maintains federally owned wilderness areas and the National Park System, which comprises those parks having an appeal to a national constituency. The costs of these parks are paid by general federal revenues and user charges.

States maintain state park systems consisting primarily of parks that draw from an area broader than a single local subdivision. These costs are also covered by a combination of general funds and user charges. Local governments, including some regional park authorities, maintain another level of parks, with user charge participation confined primarily to golf courses and other more expensive facilities.

There is little agitation for changes in these arrangements.

Law Enforcement and Corrections

Much of the concern over potential changes in law enforcement and correction matters now lodges at the state and local levels. The federal role includes leadership in research, development, and statistics gathering and certain unique federal law enforcement functions relating to federally defined crimes. The overlaps between federal and state crimes (e.g., drug dealing and bank robbery) are handled, with some tensions, through cooperative arrangements. Federal law enforcement officials also handle information exchanges (e.g., on wanted felons) that are inherently national in scope.

At the state and local levels, criminal law and jurisdiction clearly overlap. But as a practical matter, states tend to confine themselves to patrol of state highways, maintaining a central clearinghouse for statistics, data on vehicles (including stolen ones), and criminal information files. Special state task forces on organized crime, drugs, and other subjects overlap federal and local responsibilities, also generally handled by cooperative arrangements. In some states, state police have authority to administer state law off the highways, but funding constraints at the state level have minimized conflicts arising from this role. Local law enforcement officials handle the rest, with overlapping jurisdictions often a problem between municipal police officials and county sheriffs.

In many states, there have been attempts to rationalize the court system's dual hierarchy of locally oriented courts and state courts of first jurisdiction. Gradual movement toward a state-funded and state-controlled system is the pattern; New York provides the latest example. If a recent state court decision is implemented, Pennsylvania will soon follow.

Local jails and state corrections facilities have persistent overlapping responsibilities. Jails typically perform two separate functions; they act as temporary holding facilities for those awaiting trial and permanent facilities for those serving sentences of less than a year or so. Both local jail administrators and state prison administrators are being pressed by federal courts to provide more space and better facilities for prisoners. The increasing number of prisoners and these standards have strained capacity. This situation encouraged state officials to make more use of local jails, sometimes purchasing substantial amounts of space, as in Louisiana, and occasionally forcing local jailers to keep prisoners rather than transfer them to state custody when state facilities have reached capacity. Local officials have argued with state officials over reimbursement for these prisoners, and there have been successful attempts to encourage states to participate in the capital costs of expanding jail facilities.

Employment and Training

For decades there have been state, local, federal, and private programs oriented toward employment and training. They are often free-standing programs run separately through higher education, elementary and secondary education, workers' compensation, unemployment compensation, and rehabilitation-training programs associated with addicts, welfare recipients, inmates, those requiring vocational rehabilitation, and other special groups. The problems of possible conflicts, overlaps, and people falling in the gaps of various programs are numerous. As a result, many of the federally funded efforts have had a strong component of coordination and control mechanisms, as currently exemplified by private industry councils.

The resources available directly through employment and training programs are dwarfed by the resources devoted to essentially the same subject matter by private worker training, education (including adult and vocational education), the placement and eligibility determination operations of state employment services, and other special programs. Generally, the affected federal, state, and local agencies administering these other programs, as well as private employers, are willing to cooperate in planning and coordination mechanisms and to contract their services to employment and training agencies. But little integration of the services has been provided.

Water Supplies and Sewage Treatment

The provision of domestic water is typically a function of the private sector (e.g., domestic wells, industrial water intakes) and local government, including regional water authorities. Until recently, the primary federal role was in connection with federal multipurpose river basin development activities, primarily in the West. As this activity has declined, the federal role has expanded, principally through regulation of public drinking water safety.

The federal role in wastewater treatment is more extensive. The initial federal approach was to create a separate regulatory framework for municipal sewage collection and treatment and to fund part of the costs of the local investment required to meet those regulatory standards. However, the massive costs of federal participation and other federal priorities led to attempts to reduce the federal role through lower federal cost sharing and tighter eligibility requirements, attempts to involve state governments in funding, and ceilings on federal appropriations.

The state role in wastewater treatment reflects diverse patterns of response to federal regulation, federal funding, and local needs. Many states provide at least loan financing for wastewater treatment investments at the local level, and some states substantially subsidize these efforts. In instances of pollution sources from many local governments affecting a key resource—such as Puget Sound, Boston Harbor, and the Chesapeake Bay—state leadership and multistate cooperation are more intensive.

Nonetheless, the primary source of funding for municipal water supplies and waste treatment continues to be local government. Much of the financing of capital outlays and essentially all the operating costs are paid through user fees.

With gradual federal withdrawal from funding in this field, the key state-local question is: what is the extent of state participation in financing wastewater treatment investments? In some parts of the country, another key state role concerns decision making on regional authorities to finance and manage the delivery of water and the collection and treatment of sewage.

CROSS-CUTTING ISSUES INVOLVING SEVERAL FUNCTIONS

Many issues involving such diverse topics as corrections and water supplies, highways, and schools have been treated at least in part through programs and regulations that cut across these individual functional fields.

Land Use

In most states, fundamental decisions about land use remain in local hands, although there is room for considerable difference of opinion over control of land use decisions among county governments, municipalities, and townships. This difference is particularly a problem where decisions can be affected by changes in municipal boundaries. Some states have chosen to take somewhat more aggressive roles in certain land use decisions through regulation and/or tax policy. Vermont and Oregon provide examples of overall development strategy. Many of the states with fragile coastal areas have, often with federal stimulus, taken a special interest in their regulation and control. Examples are California and, increasingly, Florida and New Jersey. Other states have adopted policies for the preservation of certain types of land, such as open space, farmland, and marshland. Examples are Massachusetts and Rhode Island.

In all these instances, there is a tension between state and local regulatory roles.

Infrastructure

From one perspective, capital outlays, like operating costs, reflect an integral part of planning and budgeting for any function. For example, provision of elementary and secondary education includes provision of consumable supplies, such as paper, wages and salaries; depreciable property, such as school buses and computers; and real property, such as school buildings. From another perspective, it is possible to separate out an infrastructure component, typically defined as the real property component of capital outlays.

This approach has been more the subject of studies made, speeches given, and bills introduced than of bills passed, funding provided, and actions taken. At the federal level, there are proposals for an infrastructure bank that would capitalize comparable efforts in each of the 50 states to provide funding for public and, in some versions, private infrastructure. There are counterpart proposals, such as the New Jersey Infrastructure Bank and MassBank, but none has achieved legislative approval, and many are not being actively pressed by their sponsors.

Many state and federal policies, however, have separated capital outlays from operating costs and treated capital outlays more favorably in funding decisions. For example, the federal government provides a large share of the capital costs of major highway investments but no operating costs. It has funded much of the cost of new mass transit capital investments but a much lower share of operating costs. Its sewage treatment programs are limited to capital outlays. At the state level, states often provide 100 percent of the costs of higher education construction, but they share operating cost responsibility with students and, in the case of community colleges in some states, local governments. State programs also provide loan or grant assistance for school construction, local jails, and other public investments at the local level.

Local agitation for an increasing state role in financing local infrastructure has been considerable. Much of it is simply part of a general desire for state rather than local taxpayers to fund local projects. But some initiatives reflect a perspective that capital cost needs are distributed differently from operating cost needs. For example, a rapidly growing area will experience disparate needs for new road and school construction and new public buildings. An extreme case of this situation is the public facility need associated with new military installations, massive energy investments, and large new factories. States have developed a variety of arrangements for special infrastructure assistance in these situations.

Economic Development

State officials work closely with local governments and private economic development groups in such fields as community readiness for development and industrial recruiting. But the big money in economic development relates to infrastructure investments that are integral to plant location decisions (e.g., water and rail connections to a plant site) and infrastructure investments—such as four-lane highways in rural areas—made in the expectation that they will lead to future development.

The federal government contributes to public facility investments associated with development through the Farmers Home Administration, Economic Development Administration, Appalachian Regional Commission, and other programs. The Reagan administration attacked funding but succeeded only in reducing it. Further cuts appear likely. These reductions and the many possibilities, some involving states, for bond financing mean that many local development projects in both the private and the public sectors must be packaged by combining state, federal, local, and private sources of funds.

SUMMARY

This overview of functional division of responsibilities and the alternatives for change in each function will not come as news for most readers. Many of the arrangements are of long standing, and changes in functional roles tend to evolve slowly.

Evolution has not normally occurred in line with any overall thinking about the roles of the different levels of government. For example, state governments have entered the field of local sewage treatment primarily because a federal program tended to draw them into that role. State governments have not assumed a comparable role in water supply and solid waste disposal because they lack an incentive from either local pressures or federal programs.

As a practical matter, most issues that will affect the future of state-local relations and of state-local-national relations will continue to be decided in these individual functional contexts. Many of the pressures on legislatures and governors, for example, are concentrated on the specifics of dealing with disparate subjects, such as education and highways. The local consideration of these issues is influenced by local division of labor, such as school districts independent of general purpose government, that encourages dealing with one subject in isolation from the others. State legislative committee organization and division of responsibility among state agencies encourage this same approach.

Even so, some overriding principles of state-local relations do influence the overall resolution of many of these specific functional issues. Whether readers approve of the impact that the Reagan administration has had on federalism over the 1980s, the changes in policy regarding federal responsibilities and state-local control of policies have had some, although imperfect, consistency. State and local governments have been assuming a larger share of the costs of most domestic government activity, particularly in transportation, education, and social services. Most of the time, control over service decisions has devolved along with financial responsibility. As a result, which level of government is responsible for what decisions has become somewhat clearer.

There are examples at the state level of the same sorting out of intergovernmental roles. Minnesota and other states are dealing with proposals not necessarily near enactment. But in other states, some deliberate sorting-out policy has appeared. In New York and Michigan, many key decisionmakers have worked more than a decade to reduce the local role and increase the state role in financing (and controlling) functions that frequently had greater local government involvement in the past. New York has taken higher education to the state level and is making the same moves with its court system. Michigan, among other activities, has broadened the base of support for the arts and cultural programs of Detroit.

Chapter Nine

FINANCING STATE AND LOCAL SERVICES

Harold A. Hovey

Many complexities of state-local relations arise from the fact that the same state policy may impact quite differently on different communities. This chapter deals with subtle but important aspects of state financing of services delivered by local government. To many state and local officials, these issues seem so complex and specialized as to be appropriately left to the experts. But as this chapter shows, state aid decisions determine the extent to which funds must be raised locally. This decision, in turn, determines the tax competitiveness and service levels of individual local governments and, ultimately, the prosperity of these governments and their corporate and household citizens. Therefore these issues are of general interest and concern.

Actually, state officials can decide on state-local fiscal issues in only a few ways. Matters become complex when these basic approaches are combined, are subjected to limits and hold harmless provisions, or are applied to distributions made to hundreds of local governments in extensive computer calculations.

Reflecting the underlying simplicity of the concepts involved, this chapter concentrates on two basic themes: need and fiscal capacity.

The term *need* is used as a proxy for what should be spent for a given function by a given local government. These proxies take on many forms in current state financing formulas. For schools, the fundamental unit of need is pupils, suggesting that the more pupils a district has, the more it needs to spend. Another proxy is vehicle registrations for road funding; others are population for public health programs and aged population for programs for the elderly.

Fiscal capacity simply measures the capacity of individual districts to meet needs from local resources. This factor can be defined in a variety of ways. One common way is to look at the tax base that state laws allow a district to use in meeting a particular need, such as the valuation of taxable property to meet school needs.

Need can be measured in extremely complex ways. For example, the unit of a pupil can be defined either as a pupil who is enrolled, regardless of whether he or she attends on any given day, or as the average attendance. Pupils can be elaborated as a measurement concept by counting extra fractions of pupils for special characteristics of the pupil (e.g., in high school, needing special education) or by considering the types of program provided (e.g., college students in high-cost medical schools). None of these elaborations of need changes the basic concepts involved.

Likewise, the measurement of fiscal capacity can be made more complex by shifting from the base of a particular tax to some broader concept of economic capacity. This is frequently done in federal programs, in which state per capita income is often found in formulas that allocate federal aid among states. Many states have experimented with comparable formulas, using a variety of indicators of local fiscal capacity.

The same distribution approaches on the part of the state will have a different impact on communities with different fiscal capacities. This chapter examines four basic types of jurisdictions:

□ *Enclave* is blessed with large valuations from industrial property and few residents, so its fiscal capacity is large and its needs small compared to other jurisdictions.
□ *Average* has both an average fiscal capacity and average needs. In most states, average would be typified by a county seat with some industrial and commercial activity and a diverse citizenry in terms of both income levels and needs for government services.
□ *Poor* has a fiscal capacity that is well below average, but its high percentage of poor families indicates a high need for government services. Poor is typified by rural counties in the South and by urban concentrations such as East Cleveland and East Saint Louis.
□ *Aspiring Poor* has a below-average fiscal capacity and average needs, but it seeks a relatively high level of government services, so it levies somewhat higher taxes than average.

In considering the examples in the discussion that follows, the reader should remember that they portray applicable results, *regardless of what indicator or indicators are used to portray need and fiscal capacity*. Use of other indicators could change information presented for particular jurisdictions, but it will never alter the basic

Table 9.1 FISCAL OUTCOMES, LOCAL CONTROL (STATE AVERAGE = 100)

Jurisdiction	Capacity[a]	Need[b]	Effort[c]	Revenue[d]	Percentage of Need[e]
Enclave	300	60	30	90	150%
Average	100	100	100	100	100
Poor	50	200	100	50	25
Aspiring Poor	50	100	150	75	75

a. Capacity $= \dfrac{\text{capacity measure of district (e.g., assessed value)}}{\text{capacity measure of average district}} \times 100$

b. Need $= \dfrac{\text{need measure of district (e.g., pupils)}}{\text{need measure of average district}} \times 100$

c. Effort $= \dfrac{\text{tax rate of district (e.g., 1.1\% of value)}}{\text{tax rate(s) of average district}} \times 100$

d. Revenue $= \dfrac{\text{capacity index}}{100} \times \text{effort index}$

e. Need $= \dfrac{\text{Revenue}}{\text{Need}} \times 100$

disparities among local governments in fiscal capacity and need that are illustrated here. Thus in table 9.1, need and capacity are presented as index numbers, with the state average set equal to 100.

ISSUES IN STATE FINANCING OF LOCAL SERVICES

Total Reliance on Local Funding

The base case for considering options for state aid and takeover of local functions is an environment in which the state leaves local governments totally dependent on their own resources to provide for a function. This pattern is found for practically every function in New Hampshire and is common for parks, police and fire, water supplies, and other local functions. The situations of the sample jurisdictions are shown on table 9.1.

This table portrays situations that are not unusual in local finance. Enclave, left to its own devices, provides a higher standard of services than average while levying taxes at less than one-third of those in the rest of the state. The Poor jurisdiction reaches only 25 percent of the state average in services while maintaining average taxes. The Aspiring Poor jurisdiction maintains services that are 25 percent below average only with taxes that are 50 percent above average.

Common Approaches to State Financing of Local Services

Even with the indicator(s) of needs unspecified, the situation of total reliance on local funding provides some clear disparities that most states have acted to reduce. The state action inevitably carries consequences for two aspects of local finance: tax burdens on residents and spending policy and spending levels. *Both effects on revenue and effects on spending must be considered to reflect the economics of any state options affecting local finance.* This section analyzes the impact of certain state aid arrangements and different types of communities.

State Assumption of Part of Program Costs, Flat Grants. One approach is for state government to assume a portion of program costs. It does so by two primary mechanisms: cost sharing, whereby the percentage of the state share of total costs is fixed and the total costs are determined by the local jurisdiction; and flat grants, whereby the state contribution to total costs is fixed and the state share of total program costs, which are set locally, depends upon the local costs.

The flat grant is simply an amount that is paid in relation to units of need without regard to fiscal capacity. It is commonly found in state support of local public health departments, libraries, and aging programs and in the minimum guarantee portions of school aid programs. For example, a state might provide a grant earmarked for public health of $2 per capita per year.

The effect of using state taxes to finance flat grants is to minimize fiscal disparities among local governments. Assuming, for the moment, that the state tax base is comparable to the local one, a state tax will produce three times as much revenue for the state from taxpayers of Enclave as from taxpayers of the Average jurisdiction and six times as much from Poor. Distributing assistance in relation to need will produce twice the allocation to Poor as to Average and 133 percent more to Poor than to Enclave.

The result is strongly equalizing. Assume that the state provides 50 percent of need. The tax aspects of this decision will cut the tax capacity of Enclave to 150 and cut the need to be met from local funds to 30 from 60. If Enclave maintains its tax effort at 30 percent of Average, it will collect 45 in revenues from local taxes and 30 in revenue from the state. The total of 75 will meet 125 percent of need, down from 150, and the state and local tax effort will be 100 percent of half the tax base (which is taken by the state) and 30 percent of half, for a net of 65 percent effort, up from 30 percent. Thus, in Enclave, this state intervention has drawn the tax effort of local taxpayers up toward the state average and has drawn the percentage of need met down toward the state average. The reverse effect occurs in both Poor and Aspiring Poor. In Average, the policy change makes no difference.

This impact of state takeover of costs is obvious when the state takes over the program entirely. In that case, 100 percent of need is met in all local governments and *100 percent of capacity is used to fund the program* in every jurisdiction.

The flat grant does not alter the marginal cost of additional spending at the local level. To raise spending above the level financed by the flat grant will require 100 percent local funding. But local government may well not be able to continue to respond at the past level. For example, Poor was meeting 25 percent of need when the function was locally funded, but it now can meet 50 percent of need without any local funding. Rather than continue past allocations for the function and meet 75 percent of need, it may choose to distribute its tax revenues over more functions, meeting, say, 30 percent of the need for the aided function and raising other functions from 25 percent of need to 30 percent. Enclave may choose to adjust its local effort upward to continue to meet the same high percentage of need that was being met before. To the taxpayers of Enclave, there will be an added burden. But this burden will be perceived by taxpayers as a reduction in local taxes accompanied by an increase in state taxes. If Enclave taxpayers do not relate the two changes, they will see local government providing the same level of service for less local tax and state government providing no extra services by levying higher taxes.

From the perspective of state officials seeking to increase spending on the program aided by these resources, the flat grant may appear less than optimal. As a practical matter, some of the state resources are likely to result in substitution of local revenues for some other function and a reduction of local effort for the aided function. To fight such a tendency, state and local aid programs are often drafted with maintenance of effort requirements, although the available evidence suggests that such requirements are largely ineffective in practice.

In broad terms, the impact of state intervention with flat grants is to cause what is called an income effect but no substitution effect for the local government. The income effect occurs because half the need is now met by state aid. This income effect is greatest in Poor, with the highest need, and lowest in Enclave. The income effect, so long as local officials ignore the effect on taxpayers of paying the new state tax burden, is likely to lead to overall higher spending in the local government and/or somewhat lower local taxes. But there is no substitution effect as the cost of meeting every local need, including the subsidized one, at the margin is still one dollar in local taxes for one dollar in added spending.

State General Revenue Sharing and Unearmarked Revenues. The discussion above does not specify a particular type of aid (e.g., for education). It is equally applicable to the overall need of a jurisdiction for unearmarked revenue, the need of a special district, or the need for a particular function within a multifunction government, such as law enforcement for a municipality. Although the definitions of need and fiscal capacity are somewhat more difficult to formulate in a politically acceptable fashion, the equalization effects of state revenue sharing grants are the same as other forms of assistance discussed in the section above and the sections that follow.

State Cost Sharing. Because grant formulas are often controlled by those interested in more spending on a particular function (e.g., state health departments, local public health officials, health committees in the legislature, and health-oriented lobbying groups), the method of state aid chosen is frequently one designed to increase total spending on the aided function rather than simply to mitigate fiscal disparities among local governments. The instrument of choice to achieve this objective is state cost sharing, which has significantly different effects than flat grants.

Let us assume that the state adopts a program that provides 50 percent of the actual expenditures of local government in meeting the needs in question. Given the initial assumptions and no change in local spending, the total costs of this program will be about the same as those achieved by local funding or local funding and state flat grants. However, the distribution of resources will be quite different. Poor would receive aid of 100 from the flat grant, but because of its low local effort, it would receive only 25 from a cost-sharing arrangement. Enclave would receive aid of 50 even though it had less need because of the large revenue it was devoting to meeting the need by virtue of its rich tax base. Thus the cost-sharing arrangement is often less equalizing than the flat grant.

This result is the fundamental reason why federal programs such as Aid to Families with Dependent Children (AFDC) and Medicaid tend to provide substantially more per capita in New York and Rhode Island than in Alabama and Mississippi, despite the higher need for such assistance in Alabama and Mississippi and their lower fiscal capacity.

The cost-sharing arrangement creates an income effect comparable to that of the flat grant, with adjustments appropriate to the different levels of aid involved for each jurisdiction. But cost sharing creates a substitution effect for each local government. Without cost sharing, a dollar of local revenue was needed to fulfill a dollar's worth of need; with cost sharing, only 50 cents is needed. This decrease tends to increase consumption of programs to meet the need for exactly the same reason that purchases of merchandise on sale tend to increase. Within a budget constraint, local officials tend to spend more on the aided function and less on unaided functions. With no budget constraint, they tend to increase total spending, with special emphasis on the aided function. This tendency is particularly true in the example; the budget can fund more needs without a local tax increase because some need is now being funded with state aid.

At the state level, the introduction of the new cost-sharing program may reduce allocations to other programs or it may cause tax increases. If tax increases are involved, there is an income effect on the taxpayer whose take-home pay is now reduced. That reduction should be felt in both a reduction of consumption of goods and services from the private economy and reduced willingness to pay additional taxes to any level of government.

Because the cost of the local decision to meet the aided need is now less, the overall consumption of resources for meeting this need can be expected to increase. Thus the state allocation will grow because total spending will grow and the state is committed to a fixed percentage of that growing total.

A State Foundation Program. The state flat grant in relation to need suffers from the problem that it provides the same amount of assistance per unit of need (e.g., per pupil) in rich districts as it does in poor ones, reflecting no equalization of capacity at all unless one also considers that revenues are disproportionately raised from rich districts to fund the state contribution. The cost-sharing program may provide greater assistance per unit of need in the rich districts than the poor ones, again before considering where the taxes to pay for the program come from. These features are often seen as major disadvantages. As a result, most states have adopted foundation-like programs for their major category of state aid to local government, support of the public schools. Unlike flat grants and cost sharing, the foundation program encompasses both tax capacity and need in the distribution.

A foundation program guarantees a minimum attack on needs and presumes a minimum local tax effort. To keep state costs within bounds, foundation programs typically build their foundations at a level well below averages in meeting needs. For the sake of illustration, we will assume the state wants to guarantee that every jurisdiction meets 80 percent of need and is willing to require that every jurisdiction must levy taxes at 80 percent of average to meet that need. The math for Poor, Average, and Enclave is shown in table 9.2.

This calculation shows that to guarantee a foundation spending level of 80 percent of need with a local effort that is 80 percent of the statewide average, the state would need to pay 120 to Poor. The minus number shown for Enclave suggests that if the logic of the program is followed to its conclusion, Enclave has excess revenue that should be captured by the state and used to finance assistance to poor districts. Although this option was recently discussed in Vermont and has been tried in a few states, state decisionmakers have generally found it too difficult to explain the diversion of local taxes in this manner. As a result, Enclave would typically receive no aid from the foundation formula but would be allowed to keep any of its excess tax revenue rather than having its spending leveled to nearer the statewide average.

The advantages and disadvantages of the foundation formula are clear from the examples above. By definition, the foundation program achieves the objective of ensuring that all districts, even the poorest ones, can maintain the level of spending that the state has defined

Table 9.2 THE EFFECTS OF A FOUNDATION PROGRAM ON DIFFERENT TYPES OF JURISDICTIONS

	Enlave	Average	Poor
Need	60	100	200
Foundation (80 percent need)	48	80	160
Capacity	300	100	50
Revenue (80 percent capacity)	240	80	40
Net need (Foundation less revenue)	− 192	0	120

as the minimum. The only possible hitch is that local officials and the voters in some districts will refuse to make a tax effort that is 80 percent of the statewide average. A solution often used by states is to require a minimum local effort, which can be the effort assumed in the state foundation program or somewhat below it.

The disadvantage of the typical foundation program is that the disparities in fiscal capacity that previously affected the entire local program, although disappearing at the foundation program level, are unmitigated at the extremes. That is, Enclave can still go above the minimum program with a much lower incremental tax effort and with an overall tax rate well below that of other jurisdictions. On the other hand, Poor needs a comparatively massive tax effort (and thus above-average local taxes) to achieve even the statewide average of meeting need.

Power Equalization. There is a way to eliminate completely the fiscal disparities among local governments. This is done by putting the equivalent of the same tax base behind each unit of need (e.g., assessed value per pupil, property valuation per capita) by a version of state cost sharing that calculates the state share of cost based upon the fiscal capacity of each district. Thus, the incremental cost to local taxpayers of an incremental dollar of spending is equal in the richest and poorest districts. This point can be illustrated by a policy to bring the poorest district to a level comparable to the average district. The state average of one unit of revenue-raising capacity for one unit of need would be guaranteed. As a result, a revenue-raising increment of one unit of effort would produce one unit of local revenue in Average. In Poor, with half the capacity of Average, the unit of tax effort would produce only 0.5 units of local money but the state would supplement by providing the other 0.5.

The rub in these formulations comes in dealing with Enclave. So long as the state guarantee falls short of the revenue-raising capacity of the richest district in the state, the attempt to equalize tax bases will always fail. In the example, the state would have to provide 250 units of revenue to Poor for every 50 raised by Enclave and 200 units for every 100 for Average to guarantee that an extra increment of tax effort in those districts would raise as much as it would in Enclave. Such a policy would massively increase spending in the state by making spending cheap, in local revenue terms, for poor districts and cheaper for every district but the richest and, as a result, would increase state taxes by a substantial margin.

But the concept of doing something to distinguish Aspiring Poor suggests going beyond the foundation approach to reward local effort above the designated minimum levels in some fashion. One approach is to apply a power equalization concept to some increment of tax effort. For example, it could be done in the range between 80 percent of the tax effort used in the foundation program and, say, 110 percent of that effort. The result is a reduction in the marginal cost of an additional unit of spending from 1 to 0.16 in the poorest district, providing a substantial incentive. As a compromise with fiscal reality, the tax base being guaranteed may not be that of the richest district but some other base such as 130 percent or even 100 percent of the state average.

Back-Door State Financing. To this point, this analysis has assumed that the only option open to state government in dealing with state-local fiscal relations is the state grant. But the state also has the option of finding a way to subsidize the local taxpayer rather than the local government. Such a subsidy, in theory, reduces local effective costs in the same way as a grant and has the same general effects on local spending decisions. That is, a local taxpayer would see no economic difference between a state program sharing 50 percent of the cost through a grant and a state program that rebated 50 percent of all taxes paid to support the same program.

In fact, the dynamics are considerably different. If the program is offered as a state action to reduce taxes, the location of credit and blame can differ. Unlike a grant, the stated local tax rate must reflect the full costs of the program. Taxpayers may not consider the impact of the state offset in considering whether to hold local officials accountable for tax rates. In addition, the local government may not get the credit for the state-financed spending. Some states have explicit procedures to ensure that local governments do not. For example, a property tax bill may calculate the tax owed and then subtract and thereby explicitly identify a portion of taxes being paid on behalf of the taxpayer by the state. Thus the extent of impacts on local spending patterns, taxpayer behavior, and therefore state costs is indeterminate, as is the impact of federal tax deductibility of taxes on state and local tax decisions.

There are two real ways and one illusory one by which state governments reduce the tax burdens of local government. The illusory one occurs when the state eliminates some portion of the tax base— such as adopting a homestead exemption or exempting or charging a lower property tax rate for business inventories. Such a move, without corresponding compensation to local government, will tend simply to redistribute the costs of raising any given amount of local revenue.

One real way to reduce local tax burdens is for the state, in effect, to buy out local governments from a particular revenue source. Alabama, where hundreds of municipalities have adopted local option sales taxes, is examining the possibility. The option being considered by state officials is to replace a penny or more of the local option taxes and replenish the lost revenues from the proceeds of a state sales tax increase. Comparable actions have taken place in Illinois with repeal of the tangible personal property tax and in Ohio with repeal of the intangibles tax on stocks, bonds, and other financial instruments. Conceptually, the state is paying local governments the revenue they would have received had the tax base not been narrowed. Practically, it is never possible to calculate what the tax base would have been, so the distributions are frequently tied to what they were at the time the tax scheme was altered. Although imperfect in achieving what they seek to do, these programs do have an impact of providing some state cost sharing because they allow local governments to levy taxes on what amounts to a phantom tax base and receive revenues from the state as though that tax base existed. However, the incentive effect of encouraging local taxes that are higher than they would otherwise be is probably limited.

A local tax-sharing measure with somewhat more impact is the circuit breaker and its equivalents. The concept is that a tax that is measured on one tax base is inequitable when viewed in terms of another tax base and that, in this situation, the presumed inequity should be remedied in the base and structure of the second tax. This concept is not unusual in state taxation. For example, some states have provided for a credit in their income taxes that conceptually offsets the regressive aspects of the sales tax as applied to food.

The most common circuit breaker affecting local tax revenues considers the real property tax in relation to income. From the taxpayer's perspective, the real property tax is paid to local taxing authorities in full. However, in filing the state income tax, there is a calculation that compares the real property tax bill (or a presumptive real property tax bill in the case of renters who are covered in some states) to the reported income of the taxpayer. If the property tax is too high as a percentage of income, the excess is, in effect, credited against the state income tax liability.

The economics of this approach is simpler than the politics. Economically, the provision has the most impact on the taxpayer whose relationship between income and property taxes and other eligibility criteria (e.g., over age 65 in some states) puts the household in the zone of getting the circuit breaker. To a taxpayer in this setting, the cost of a local property tax increase is zero. Therefore someone in this setting would be expected to support, or at least not oppose, such increases. This point accounts for the popularity of the concept among school spending advocates who fear that the income-poor, property-rich elderly persons without children will defeat property tax levies. To the local government, new taxes are free when applied to those eligible for the circuit breaker, but they carry full costs for those not in this category. For the state, the program represents 100 percent cost sharing for those who have already passed the eligibility threshold, partial cost sharing for those passing the threshold because of new local taxes, and no cost sharing for other taxpayers. Politically, it is not clear that taxpayers and city and state officials perceive the economic factors involved.

In-Lieu Payments. State rules for property taxation typically exempt the property owned by state government and state instrumentalities, such as universities and turnpike authorities, from local taxation. Local officials correctly point out that such property would be eligible for property tax if privately owned, and tax exemption creates service burdens on localities that have to provide road access, fire prevention and control, and so on. Some states have programs to make payments in lieu of taxes, but the concept is not popular for two reasons. First, as applied to state facilities, property taxes based on value are not closely related to the costs of the local service provided. Second, many state officials note competition for state facilities among local officials and conclude that, all things considered, location of a state facility in a local area is a blessing, not a burden.

Other Approaches to State Aid

There are a variety of other mechanisms for state assistance. They are generally rare, primarily because they reflect uncontrollable items in state budgets, which are discouraged by state fiscal authorities, and 100 percent reimbursement of local incremental costs, which obviously tends to eliminate local fiscal responsibility and drive up state costs without limit.

Funding Deficits. In this approach, the state funds the difference between some cost that is considered reasonable for local governments to pay and the total cost actually incurred by local governments for the assisted function. Such mechanisms are frequently used in dealing with deficits in mass transportation programs and in funding certain school activities, such as special education and school transportation.

Cost Reimbursement. The cost-reimbursement device is essentially the same as funding deficits except that no local contribution is required. It is most commonly used in connection with what amounts to the purchase of services, such as those of social service workers' determining eligibility for state-administered payments.

Capitation Payments. This is basically a fee-for-services approach as well, but fixed prices rather than cost reimbursement are used. Examples are the fees paid local jailers for holding state prisoners and monies paid to community mental health agencies based upon the number of patients served.

Customary Fees and Charges. States often pay local governments for services local governments provide in the private market. These payments are not generally considered aid, and the marketplace, supplemented by any state regulation of that marketplace, is considered adequate discipline over charges. Examples are municipal gas, electric, and water utilities and the services of county hospitals rendered to mental health patients, foster children, inmates and other wards of state government.

Hybrid State Aid Allocations. Allocations of state resources among governments result from a political process carried out by legislatures whose members each represent distinct geographic areas. In such a context, it should not be surprising that actual allocation formulas frequently reflect compromises among formula types and the grandfathering of old formulations within the context of the new. For example, it is not unusual in school aid formulas to have districts taking on a capitation basis—some by "hold harmless," reflecting allocations of an outdated formula, and some on the basis of the current formula.

One popular compromise in formulas is to use multiple formulas, with local governments given the choice to select the most beneficial formula.

More on Need and Fiscal Capacity

The discussion above assumes the existence of an objective need that can be measured. This notion is clearly true in the sense that state legislatures can and do adopt state allocations based on such indicators as full-time equivalent higher education students, average daily membership or average daily attendance of elementary and secondary students, number of aged persons, and population. There is no limit to the room for disagreement over need factors. Arguably, a low-income aged person presents need for aging programs 1.5—or is it 1.6 or 2.0?—times as great as a middle-income elderly person; high school students cost more than kindergarten students, and so on. These issues must be fought out on a state-by-state basis, but their resolution does not affect the general economics and politics of the state fund allocation procedures described in this chapter.

A few quirks in the process of determining need are sufficiently common to merit attention. The first is that it is possible to work within the confines of a definition of need to create what amounts to a cost-reimbursement formula. For example, the obvious unit of need for schools is students. So long as this indicator is used in a foundation formula, a district gains financially by having lower-paid teachers rather than higher-paid ones and larger classes rather than smaller ones. States can, and do, attempt to offset these incentives by state mandates. But they can also be restricted in the formula itself by, for example, reimbursing a district for a teacher unit composed of a given number of students but making the reimbursement either the actual cost for that unit or the cost authorized by the state formula, whichever is less. This rule provides automatic 100 percent state reimbursement for cost increases up to the state ceiling.

Some formula designers use a concept of need that is net of the local effort expected to be expended. This formulation can be quite misleading in certain contexts. An example arises in school foundation formulas; there is often a choice between raising the foundation level of need and prorating aid to, say, 95 percent of entitlements and leaving the foundation level lower but paying 100 percent of what the formula suggests the state should pay. Although these alternatives look alike, the former is immensely better for average districts and the latter much better for poor districts.

The absolute anchor for the measurement of fiscal capacity is the tax base that a district actually has to meet the particular need for which a formula payment is being made. The simplest case is school districts that have no tax base except the property tax; here the obvious measure of fiscal capacity is the tax base of the district as measured by the property's assessed value, excluding properties not taxable by reason of exemptions. Even in this relatively simple case, there is considerable room for argument. For example, does property that is assessed for taxation count even if the taxpayer is not making current tax payments because the property is abandoned or the taxpayer is in bankruptcy proceedings? Should revenues from the federal government in lieu of property taxes (e.g., impact aid and certain payments made for Indians living on reservations) be counted in fiscal capacity?

Another more complicated problem arises when logic requires increasing the fiscal capacity counted in a formula but the local taxing authority cannot, as a practical matter, reach that tax base. School districts around Atlanta are an example. The tax-administering jurisdictions (e.g., counties) set the valuation levels. But to avoid a group of districts milking a state aid formula through artificially low valuations (and thus local effort requirements), the state recalculates the local effort requirement as though the assessments reached the statewide standard as a percentage of market value.

This calculation affects the state aid but not what, as a practical matter, the districts can collect with their actual property tax. Thus districts can levy the appropriate amount, collect their state aid, and still be short of the revenues promised by the foundation formula.

The formulation becomes more complex for local governments that have options of mixing local revenues among property taxes, user fees, and other taxes, such as local option sales taxes. A decision must be made on how to calculate the mix of revenue resources, and difficult statistical problems are presented in the estimation of the tax base for jurisdictions that can but do not levy taxes on that particular base.

Problems also arise because of overlapping local governments. For example, taxpayers of central city school districts also pay higher municipal and urban county taxes than taxpayers outside most central cities. Center city school leaders argue that the true fiscal capacity of the school district is the total taxpayer capacity minus the bite of that capacity already taken by overlapping governments.

Understanding State-Shared Revenues

Most states share revenues in one fashion or another, but nomenclature is a frequent obstacle to understanding the economic and political substance of these programs. A program can be called revenue sharing that has nothing in reality to do with the donor government's revenue flow. General revenue sharing (GRS) is a good example. The amounts made available did not fluctuate with federal revenues generally or with revenues from any particular source. In the sense of sharing a portion of federal revenue from a particular tax source, federal highway aid and unemployment compensation administrative cost grants are more like revenue sharing than the GRS. Actual percentage sharing is applied to user charges for cutting timber on federal lands, grazing fees, and certain mineral extraction activities, but these fees are often viewed as payments in lieu of taxes.

In some instances, something called state revenue sharing is, in effect, a political commitment that may be difficult to change. For example, many Massachusetts state leaders have pledged that local governments will get 40 percent of the increases in state revenues. Carrying out this pledge depends on politics. Ohio jurisdictions get some percentage of the state income tax receipts, but the figure can be changed by legislation. Calling this money shared revenue rather than grants may or may not affect the politics of the program, but it does not affect the economics.

Often the legal niceties are overlooked both in the politics of the situation and in the statistics reporting on it. One-third of the revenue from the Maryland personal income tax goes to the counties where it is raised. Economically, this arrangement is the turnback of one-third of the state revenue, but legally it is a local option tax. Legally, Virginia income taxpayers are liable to their counties for state taxes, so the counties could be said to share their revenues with the state.

The critical questions in what is often called state revenue sharing are two: how much should the state distribute, and how should the distribution be made?

Some state programs share state revenue by designating a certain portion of total revenues for return (or retention, as the case may be) in the community where those revenues are raised. The most common form of this assistance is found in transportation user charges—whereby a portion of vehicle registration, operator license, and registration fees is returned to the areas of origin for use in road construction and maintenance. Many states also share the revenue from their motor fuel taxes. The rationale for these programs is typically relatively simple. State officials, reluctant to give local officials the authority to tax the same base that the state is taxing, want to provide local officials with road revenues provided by user charges. The place of origin of such user charges is viewed as a good proxy for the needs for road maintenance and construction, and it satisfies a certain sense of equity in returning user charges in the places where the users are located.

The federal highway program provides an example of a hybrid

formula. The allocation logic for the basic program relates to needs and not at all to places where user charge revenue is raised. This allocation tends to favor places with difficult road maintenance problems and little traffic, such as the sparsely settled western states. But representatives of other states have created another formula element that overrides the first allocation—requiring that a stipulated percentage of federal highway money be allocated to the state in which it is raised.

Alternative Approaches to Local Finance

Consolidation of Local Units Into One Government or State Takeover of Everything. The root of fiscal equalization problems of local governments is the segregation of tax bases and needs into jurisdictions with extraordinarily high or low tax bases, high or low concentrations of needs, or, frequently, the common combinations of substantial resources and low needs and of high needs and low levels of resources.

When the fiscal disparities problem is defined this way—as major deviation from statewide averages—the solution is obvious. *Every fiscal disparities problem would disappear if all taxes and spending were handled on a statewide basis, either by state takeover of financial responsibility for all functions or by massive consolidations of local governments.*

This solution, however, is not a practical one in the United States of the late twentieth century. If one looks more broadly than fiscal disparities to other factors, such as citizen control and tailoring programs to local needs and tastes, it may not even be a desirable outcome. Nonetheless, it is important to keep in mind because many of the remedies, other than state grant programs, for dealing with disparities are simply ways to move in the direction of state funding and local government consolidation.

Limited Consolidation. In public finance terms, and only in those terms, consolidation of local governments is one of the cleanest ways to avoid fiscal disparities. Consolidation of the poor district and the average district in our example would eliminate a district with 50 percent of the average state fiscal capacity and replace it with a district with 75 percent of that capacity while eliminating a district with twice the average need and replacing it with a need 50 percent higher than average. Consolidation of the Enclave and the Poor districts would eliminate the extremes in the state's local finances by creating a district with a capacity 75 percent (rather than one 200 percent above and one 50 percent below) of the state average and with needs only 30 percent above average. Although these moves alone do not solve all fiscal disparities, they substantially reduce the impacts and lower the costs of state policies to eliminate or mitigate them further.

State policy can require consolidation, as some states have done with school districts. In the extreme case, the state simply refuses to accredit programs in districts with less than x students or refuses state funding to districts that do not maintain a high school. But there are more subtle techniques that tell local voters that they can maintain separate districts but they must meet reasonable state standards, even if doing so as a separate district would be prohibitively expensive. Examples are a minimum of required and elective courses (e.g., physics, two foreign languages offered in high school) offered by the system.

Where consolidation is the objective, a clearly identifiable state policy with considerable appeal on its face is not to reward or punish a district for its size. Following this logic would deny state funding for administrative personnel in a small district unless the same student counts would call for the same personnel in a larger one. For example, if a student count of 200 triggered an allocation of one-tenth of a principal's salary and one-twentieth of a superintendent's and an assistant superintendent's, the small district would get the same allocation, thereby forcing it to use 100 percent local resources if it desired to maintain a full-time principal and a full-time superintendent.

The state can also provide incentives for consolidation. Examples are defraying the costs of feasibility studies of consolidation, holding harmless certain taxpayers during transition to a consolidated district, giving consolidated districts the option of taking funds from the school aid formula based on the separate characteristics of two merging districts during a transition period, and the like. These alternatives are all cost saving for the state in the long run if the resulting district has a higher fiscal capacity than one of the merging districts because the form of the school aid foundation formula rewards low-capacity districts.

There is substantial opportunity for consolidation of municipalities, but the institutional barriers to such consolidations often prevent them. City-county consolidations are also difficult, but some major ones have been accomplished. Examples are the consolidation of municipalities and Dade County (Florida), Indianapolis and other municipalities and Marion County (Indiana), and Nashville and Davidson County (Tennessee).

Annexation Policy. In retrospect, many problems of central cities in the Northeast and Midwest could have been avoided by state policies to permit easy annexation and by local foresight to annex unincorporated areas anticipating their development, even when the costs of serving them may have appeared to exceed the revenue gain in the short run. Pursuing vigorous annexation policies explains why cities like Columbus (Ohio) and Kansas City (Missouri) have less substantial fiscal and service problems than cities like Saint Louis, Chicago, Cleveland, and Boston.

No one can accurately predict the growth of medium-sized and small urbanized areas in the United States, much less which rural areas may blossom into metropolitan areas, much as Silicon Valley and Orlando have done. But state officials in some states have acted, for example, to bar incorporation of unincorporated areas within x miles of an existing municipality without the consent of that municipality. For many areas of the country, this matter is largely one of shutting the barn door after the horses have fled.

Tax-Base Sharing. The alternatives of consolidation and annexation achieve some values in reducing disparities in both needs and fiscal capacity, but only at the expense of some other valued factors, such as local control, and in some cases, black control of central city governments. But the objective of reducing fiscal disparities can be achieved short of consolidation if a way can be found to share the tax base, the extremes of service needs, or both.

Tax-base sharing is probably most appropriate in the limited number of circumstances in which a central city (or cities) anticipates that major growth in the metropolitan area will take the form of new investments in single-story, space-consuming industrial facilities and commercial developments, such as shopping centers, located on major beltways. In many areas, this growth will be captured by small suburbs or rural areas favored by the decisions of entrepreneurs. But there are also prospects for revival of central city tax bases built upon revival of construction of office buildings for service industries such as finance and communications. This development leaves some doubt over who the long-term winners and losers might be if tax bases are shared. Also helpful in this environment is a community and business leadership that believes the metropolitan areas will sink or swim as a unit and a state legislature willing to act on the preferences of metropolitan leadership.

The concept of tax-base sharing is relatively simple. Property that is likely to be unevenly distributed in relation to population is identified—principally industrial and large commercial investments. New valuation of property of that type is viewed as a resource of the entire metropolitan area, an aggregate tax rate is applied to the property, and the resulting revenues are distributed on some basis acceptable to the participants. Variations in the property covered, the amount shared, and the formula for revenue distribution are obviously possible. The prime example of this form of tax-base sharing is provided by the Twin Cities area in Minnesota.

A special problem arises in the case of massive investments in a single plant, for example, power plants valued in the high hundreds of millions and billions of dollars and located in rural areas. Without rule changes, such investments will enable the local governments serving them to reap immense returns while sharply lowering tax rates. The burden of the taxes will tend to fall on the consumers of the plant's output, not the residents of the jurisdictions that happen to play host to it. Many states have considered mechanisms that would share this tax base. One alternative is statewide assessment of such property, just as rail property is now assessed statewide. The difference is that the revenues would go into a statewide pot for distribution across a wider area than a few local governments.

A variation on this theme developed in the West, particularly when major energy-related investments (e.g., mine mouth power plants, lignite mining facilities, and coal gasification plants) were under consideration or construction. Impact fees associated with these investments and certain severance tax revenues could be applied to the development needs caused by the facilities and their workers. Often these impacts and the schools, courthouses, and roads associated with them were located, or considered likely to be located, outside the taxing jurisdictions where the major investments were contemplated. Impact taxes were collected and distributed by state governments.

Needs Sharing. Sharing needs so that low-wealth, high-problem jurisdictions export some of their problems to jurisdictions more able to take care of them sounds like an impossible idea in a nation where local governments can opt whether they want to assume the problems of other jurisdictions. But the concept seems more practical when specific policy options are examined. For example, the net effect of federal desegregation orders affecting Saint Louis and Kansas City is to spread the burdens of educating many central city children to the more affluent suburbs. In New Jersey, the effect of the *Mount Laurel* decision is likely to force suburban jurisdictions to take more low-income persons (and thus their service needs) than they would otherwise take.

Shifting Service and Cost Responsibilities to Higher Levels of Government. The mismatches of needs and resources found in some municipalities and townships are often mitigated in the service mix required by citizens of the county that serves them and the resources constituting the county tax base. There are significant examples around the country of counties assuming responsibility previously provided by central cities—zoos, parks, art museums, support of cultural activities, and other facilities and programs serving a broader area than the central city. State support, is also a move in this direction, but it moves the tax base beyond the metropolitan area.

Regional Bodies. Mismatches of needs and services can also be dealt with by moving the problem and its costs from the level of one or two municipalities, or even a central county, to a regional body serving an entire metropolitan area. The Port Authority of New York and New Jersey provides one of the oldest multistate examples. There are many in-state major examples. Two—the Metropolitan Sanitary District and a regional transit authority—serve the Chicago area. Regional park boards are common. Also common are regional planning bodies and economic development agencies, although they do not generally have taxing powers.

Revising the Local Tax Base. One of the most persistent local calls for relief from states concerns restrictions on the taxing powers of local officials. There are really three issues at stake, although they are often decided together. The first is the extent to which local governments will be able to take more from taxpayers. This issue is shown most vividly in the states that restrict the growth of local spending, regardless of the revenue source used to fund the increase. It also appears in local opposition to state taxation rules that require certain local tax increases to be approved by the voters. Changes in these measures do not deal with fiscal disparities.

A second issue concerns the flexibility of local governments in taxing their own residents. Examples include allowing an income tax levy by certain midwestern school districts, sales tax authorization for local governments not having it, and a variety of other revenue-raising measures. Local support for the option often reflects a desire to find a more palatable revenue source. However, the revenue source does not cut the real (but may cut the psychological) burden of taxes on local residents. For example, meeting the financial needs of a school district by a residential income tax in a rural district may shift a portion of the burden compared to the alternative of a property tax. But if the same amount is raised, the same burden will appear somewhere in the local economy. Thus it will be raised on high-income people with small property holdings and lowered on farms, the income of the retired, and businesses.

From the standpoint of dealing with mismatches of fiscal capacity and needs, however, the most exciting prospects for opening up additional local revenue sources lie in what local officials might do to fiscal capacity. In this regard, the taxes of interest are primarily those that can most comfortably be exported. Examples for central cities include income taxes levied on commuters from outside the city, a city sales tax accompanied by excise taxes on items such as cigarettes and soft drinks, a head tax on employees working in the city, and hotel and motel taxes.

But shifting from one tax base to several will not necessarily raise the fiscal capacity of all jurisdictions in a state. For example, requiring school districts to shift from 100 percent reliance on the property tax to 50 percent reliance on sales taxes will increase the tax base of a central city. But it will also cut the tax base of a suburban bedroom community hosting few taxable sales.

STATE AID WITHOUT FISCAL DISPARITIES

Much of the discussion above considers state aid and state and county takeover of functions in the context of reducing fiscal disparities. Although this is an important topic in state-local financial relations, it is by no means the only important issue. Another is the question of when a state should assist a local function if fiscal disparities are involved—because they have been mitigated or resolved by consolidation, they are offset by a general revenue sharing program, or a major state program, such as a school foundation program, offsets the major disparities.

If there were no financial disparities, there would be few reasons for any state financial aid to local government. State aid for equalization purposes would be unnecessary; it would simply reflect routing money through the state capitol that could be collected and spent locally. This statement would be true even if the state aid were equalizing within a function. For example, two jurisdictions might have average fiscal capacity and average needs across all functions but unequal resources or needs in two functions, say, road maintenance and schools. But a state attempt to redress such disparities is not likely to work symmetrically, except by chance, because the process of deciding on the road program will be largely divorced from the process of deciding on school aid. As a result, the state might pursue a highly equalizing program in one area and a less equalizing one in another. The result could be less equalizing than the starting point.

This chapter provides a general introduction to the options that states may choose among in structuring financial assistance to local governments. It also analyzes how specific state approaches affect jurisdictions with different financial bases or levels of need. These types of considerations must be taken into account in designing equitable state aid formulas.

Chapter Ten

REFORMING STATE POLICIES THAT AFFECT LOCAL TAXING AND BORROWING

Daphne A. Kenyon

This chapter provides a framework for examining reforms and re-visions of state policies that affect local taxing and borrowing, and briefly examines several reform proposals. First, the nature and range of existing state policies are described. Next, the changing context within which these state policies must be examined is explored. This context includes the shift to an increasingly service-based econ-omy, recent changes in the market for tax-exempt debt, and the pas-sage of the Tax Reform Act of 1986. Recent developments in public finance as well as the traditional criteria for judging reform of state policies that affect local taxing and borrowing are discussed. Finally, the advantages and disadvantages of several reform proposals are presented.

State policies affect local government finances in several ways. States restrict local taxing powers by placing limits on property taxes or by limiting the types of taxes that localities may levy. At the same time, many states spend a significant amount of their budgets on property tax relief. State governments pursue a similar mix of carrot-and-stick policies with respect to issuance of local debt. States often limit the amount of debt a locality can issue; they also allocate the volume of certain types of tax-exempt debt allowable under federal law. On the other hand, by creating bond banks or issuing debt on behalf of their localities, state policies enhance local borrowing pow-ers.

STATE PROPERTY TAX LIMITS

In part because of the longstanding unpopularity of the property tax, states have regulated local property taxation through a number of avenues. The basic features of the existing property tax and revenue limits are illustrated in table 10.1, which distinguishes among six basic types of limits the states impose on property taxation:

□ *overall property tax rate limits*: setting a *maximum rate* that may be applied against the assessed value of property, taking into account all local governments (e.g., municipalities, counties, school districts, special districts), without a vote of the local electorate
□ *specific property tax rate limits*: setting a *maximum rate* that may be applied against the assessed value of property by one type of government or for one type of service
□ *property tax levy limits*: setting the *maximum revenue* that may be raised from the property tax by a jurisdiction
□ *general revenue limits*: setting the *maximum revenue* that may be raised from all sources by a jurisdiction
□ *limitations on assessment increases*: forcing increases in statutory tax rates in order to raise revenue, and
□ *full disclosure requirements*: requiring advertisement and public hearings on proposed rate increases, also known as truth in property taxation.

Limits on assessment increases and full disclosure requirements seek to improve government accountability as well as to limit tax levels. Limitations on assessment increases force government officials to raise tax rates in order to raise revenues instead of relying on general increases in property values, especially during inflationary times. Full disclosure rules require advertisement and public hearings on proposed rate increases.

Other limits place direct restrictions on revenue-raising powers. The narrowest limit is a stipulated maximum property tax rate that can be levied by a particular government or for a particular service. An overall property tax rate limit, which applies a maximum rate to the assessed value of property taking all units of local government into account, or property tax levy limits, which specify a maximum amount of property tax revenue that may be raised, have broader applications. General revenue limits, which apply to taxes other than the property tax, have the most comprehensive impact.

The most common state limitation on local property taxation, the specific property tax rate limit, imposed by 31 states, was enacted prior to 1978 in almost all cases. The limitations that have been popular more recently are the property tax *levy* limits, limitations on assessment increases, and full disclosure requirements. A number of property tax limits were adopted after the passage of Proposition

Table 10.1 STATE-IMPOSED LIMITS ON LOCAL GOVERNMENT PROPERTY TAXATION, 1985

Region and State	Overall Property Tax Rate Limits	Specific Property Tax Rate Limits	Property Tax Levy Limits	General Revenue Limits	Limitations on Assessment Increases	Full Disclosure Requirements
New England						
Connecticut						
Maine						
Massachusetts			P			
New Hampshire						
Rhode Island						
Vermont			X			X
Mid-Atlantic						
Delaware		X	P			
Maryland				P	X	X
New Jersey			X			
New York		X			P	
Pennsylvania		X				
Great Lakes						
Illinois		X	P			P
Indiana			P			
Michigan	X	X	P			P
Ohio	X		X			
Wisconsin		X				
Plains						
Iowa		X			P	X
Kansas			X			
Minnesota		X	X	X	P	
Missouri		X		P		

(continued)

Table 10.1 STATE-IMPOSED LIMITS ON LOCAL GOVERNMENT PROPERTY TAXATION, 1985

Region and State	Overall Property Tax Rate Limits	Specific Property Tax Rate Limits	Property Tax Levy Limits	General Revenue Limits	Limitations on Assessment Increases	Full Disclosure Requirements
Nebraska						
North Dakota		X	P			
South Dakota		X				
Southeast						
Alabama	P					
Arkansas		X	P			
Florida	P	X				X
Georgia		X				
Kentucky	X	P				P
Louisiana		X	P			
Mississippi		X	P	P		
North Carolina		X				
South Carolina						P
Tennessee						X
Virginia						
West Virginia	X	X				
Southwest						
Arizona			P	P		
New Mexico	X	X	P		P	
Oklahoma	X	X				
Texas		X				P
Rocky Mountain						
Colorado		X	X			
Idaho		X	P			P

Montana		X				X
Utah		X				
Wyoming		P				
Far West						
California	P	X			P	
Nevada		X	X			
Oregon	X	X	X		P	
Washington	X	X	X	X		
Alaska	X	X				
Hawaii						X
Total	12	30	22	5	7	13

Source: Adapted from Advisory Commission on Intergovernmental Relations 1986, table 78, pp. 116–17.
Note: X = limit imposed before 1978; P = limit imposed after 1978.
1

13 in California in 1978. Since then, there has been little action on the property tax front, although three states acted in 1987 to ease property tax limits: Massachusetts eased its override provision on Proposition 2 1/2, and Nevada and North Dakota raised their property tax lids (Benker 1987, p. 10).

Property Tax Relief

States also have major effects on local property taxation through several forms of so-called property tax relief, illustrated in table 10.2:

□ *Classification systems:* assessing different classes of property at different rates
□ *Homestead exemptions:* providing property tax exemptions to certain classes of individuals, such as elderly or disabled individuals or veterans
□ *Residential deferral programs:* deferring a beneficiary's tax but generally charging the market rate of interest on the deferred tax reliability
□ *Circuit breakers:* providing property tax relief as a function of individual income by rebating some part of an individual's property tax payments through the state income tax, and
□ *Agricultural use-value assessment mechanisms:* basing property taxation on the value of property in its current use rather than on its market value.

Circuit breakers provide direct aid to individuals and thereby provide indirect aid to local governments. Because state policies that qualify as property tax relief for individuals limit individual property tax payments, they impose limits on the financing abilities of local governments. They include classification, homestead exemptions, and agricultural use value assessment.

Table 10.2 labels these forms of property tax relief as statutory forms of state property tax relief to make an important point. Certain forms of so-called property tax relief result in a reduction in the effective "price" of local services faced by taxpayers. This reduced price can in some cases substantially increase the desired level of public services. A few recent research studies examined this propensity, and in some cases they found that so-called property tax relief stimulates desired local spending by so much that it even results in a net increase in the overall property tax burden (Bell and Bowman 1987).

Table 10.2 MAJOR STATUTORY FORMS OF STATE PROPERTY TAX RELIEF, 1985

Region and State	Classification	Homestead Exemptions	Residential Deferral	Circuit Breakers	Agricultural Use Value Assessment
New England					
Connecticut		X	X	X	X
Maine		X	X	X	X
Massachusetts		X	X		X
New Hampshire		X	X		X
Rhode Island		X	X	X	X
Vermont		X		X	X
Mid-Atlantic					
Delaware		X	X		X
Maryland		X	X	X	X
New Jersey		X	X		X
New York				X	X
Pennsylvania		X	X	X	X
Great Lakes					
Illinois		X	X	X	X
Indiana		X			X
Michigan		X	X		
Ohio	X			X	X
Wisconsin				X	
Plains					
Iowa	X	X		X	X
Kansas	X			X	
Minnesota	X	X		X	X
Missouri	X			X	X
Nebraska		X			X

(continued)

Table 10.2 MAJOR STATUTORY FORMS OF STATE PROPERTY TAX RELIEF, 1985

Region and State	Classification	Homestead Exemptions	Residential Deferral	Circuit Breakers	Agricultural Use Value Assessment
North Dakota	X	X		X	X
South Dakota				X	X
Southeast					
Alabama	X	X			X
Arkansas		X		X	X
Florida		X	X	X	X
Georgia		X	X		X
Kentucky		X			X
Louisiana	X	X			X
Mississippi	X	X			X
North Carolina		X			X
South Carolina	X	X			X
Tennessee	X		X	X	X
Virginia					
West Virginia	X	X		X	X
Southwest					
Arizona	X			X	X
New Mexico		X		X	X
Oklahoma		X		X	X
Texas		X	X		X
Rocky Mountain					
Colorado	X	X	X	X	X
Idaho		X		X	X
Montana	X	X		X	X
Utah	X	X	X	X	X
Wyoming		X		X	X

	Col1	Col2	Col3	Col4	Col5
Far West					
California	X	X	X	X	X
Nevada	X			X	X
Oregon		X	X	X	X
Washington		X	X		X
Alaska		X	X		X
Hawaii		X		X	X
Total	18	40	21	32	46

Source: Adapted from Bowman and Mikesell 1987, pp. 33–35.

The regional pattern of these property tax relief measures is shown in table 10.2. Whereas the use of homestead exemptions and agricultural use-value assessment is nearly universal, the regions differ strongly in their reliance on the other property tax relief mechanisms. For example, the New England and mid-Atlantic states have not adopted classification systems, but most of those states do have circuit breakers and residential tax deferral programs. In contrast, none of the Plains states makes use of residential deferral, but nearly all rely on both classification and circuit breakers.

Local Revenue Diversification

States also affect local taxing powers in a significant way by allowing or disallowing local general sales and income taxes. Of these two tax sources, the one of most current importance to localities is the general sales tax. In FY 1985–86, general sales taxes accounted for 11 percent and income taxes accounted for 5.9 percent of total local government tax revenues (U.S. Bureau of the Census 1987, table 29).

As of 1987, localities in 28 states levied general sales taxes. The number of localities in each state levying this tax and the percentage of total local taxes it accounted for in 1986 are shown in table 10.3. A greater proportion of local governments levied general sales taxes in the Southwest than in any other region; no local governments in New England currently levy this type of tax.

Localities in only 11 states levy income taxes, but certain local governments in an additional three states levy employer payroll taxes. More than three-quarters of the local governments levying income taxes are in Pennsylvania, where cities, boroughs, towns, townships, and school districts do so. In most cases, local income taxes employ structures very different from those of the federal government or the states; the local income tax base often consists only of wages and compensation (see table 10.4).

Not all local governments that are allowed by their states to levy income or general sales taxes in fact choose to levy them. For example, Arkansas cities and Georgia cities and counties are authorized to levy income taxes, but none of those local governments does. The decision to forgo an available revenue source often results from conditions placed on the tax authority. State law prohibits Georgia counties and municipalities from levying income taxes if they adopt general sales taxes. This provision helps explain why Georgia localities have not adopted income taxes even though they are authorized to do so.

Table 10.3 LOCAL GENERAL SALES TAXATION

Region and State	Counties Number levying tax, 1987	Percentage of total 1986 taxes	Municipalities Number levying tax, 1987	Percentage of total 1986 taxes	Special districts
Mid-Atlantic					
New York	58	50%	26	16%	1 transit district
Great Lakes					
Illinois	102	5	1,271	30	2 transit districts
Ohio	79	23	n.a.	n.a.	2 transit districts
Wisconsin	12	0	n.a.	n.a.	
Plains					
Kansas	60	17	108	21	
Minnesota	n.a.	n.a.	3	2	
Missouri	114	52	474	29	69 transit districts
Nebraska	n.a.	n.a.	22	26	
North Dakota	n.a.	n.a.	3	5	
South Dakota	n.a.	n.a.	111	51	
Southeast					
Alabama	56	34	326	50	
Arkansas	35	42	76	22	
Georgia	143	39	a	6	1 transit district
Louisiana	63	36	192	50	47 school districts
North Carolina	100	29	n.a.	n.a.	
Tennessee	95	38	10	17	
Virginia	95	10	41	11	
Southwest					
Arizona	2	0	74	54	
New Mexico	28	22	100	53	
Oklahoma	16	1	457	79	
Texas	n.a.	n.a.	1,023	28	6 transit districts
Rocky Mountain					
Colorado	31	14	193	62	1 transit district
Utah	29	18	219	40	
Wyoming	15	21	n.a.	n.a.	
Far West					
California	58	7	380	30	7 transit districts
Nevada	7	2	n.a.	n.a.	
Washington	39	17	268	30	
Alaska	6	4	87	18	

Sources: Advisory Commission on Intergovernmental Relations 1987, vol. 1, p. 57; and U.S. Bureau of the Census 1987.
Note: n.a. = not available.
a. Georgia's state government collects all local general sales taxes on a county-area basis and returns the tax revenue to counties and to cities within the counties. To levy a local sales tax, both the county and any cities within the county must approve the tax.

Table 10.4 LOCAL INCOME TAXATION, 1987

Region, state, and type of government	Number of governments with income taxation	Tax base	Notes
Mid-Atlantic			
Delaware			
city	1	Wages and compensation	Wilmington
Maryland counties	24	State income tax liability	20–50% surcharge on state tax
New York cities	2	For residents, state taxable income/state tax liability; for nonresidents, earned income	New York City and Yonkers
Pennsylvania cities, boroughs, towns, townships, and school districts	2,782[a]	Wages and compensation except for Philadelphia, which also taxes unearned income	
Great Lakes			
Indiana counties	51	County adjusted gross income	
Michigan cities	18	Earned income	

	Number	Tax base	Notes
Ohio			
Cities	482	Wages and compensation	
School Districts	6		
Plains			
Iowa			
school districts	57	State income tax liability	
Missouri			
cities	2	Wages and compensation	Kansas City and Saint Louis
Southeast			
Alabama			
cities	10	Wages and compensation	
Kentucky			
Cities	85	Wages and compensation	
Counties	25		
Total (excluding Pennsylvania)	763		
Total (including Pennsylvania)	3,545[a]		

Source: Advisory Commission on Intergovernmental Relations 1987, vol. 1, pp. 46–49.
Note: Only those regions and states with local income taxation are included. Localities that are authorized to levy income taxes but do not levy them are Arkansas municipalities and counties and Georgia municipalities. In addition, payroll taxes are levied on the total payroll of employers in Los Angeles, San Francisco, Newark and certain Oregon counties.
a. Estimated.

Limits on Local Borrowing Power

The ability to borrow to finance capital projects is a key financing tool of local governments. Localities as well as states have the option of either (1) directly levying taxes or fees to pay for a capital project or of (2) issuing bonds to borrow the necessary funds, and levying taxes or fees at a later time to finance the necessary payments of principal and interest. Because the interest on most state and local debt is exempt from federal income taxation, state and local governments can typically borrow at lower interest rates than can corporations or individuals.

Although there have been few defaults or near-defaults on state and local debt in recent years, during the earlier years of our country, there were several periods when many state and local governments defaulted on their debts.[1] Most current state limitations on state and local borrowing power are derived from reforms put in place after these earlier periods of default or debt repudiation.

Two major types of tax-exempt debt are general obligation bonds (GOs) and revenue bonds. The distinction between them is that GOs are backed by the full faith and credit of the issuing government, whereas revenue bonds are backed only by the particular revenue stream generated by the project being financed. As late as the 1960s, general obligation bonds accounted for most long-term tax-exempt debt issued. In recent years, the use of revenue bonds has increased dramatically so that during the 1980s they have accounted for about three-quarters of tax-exempt bonds issued (Petersen 1986, pp. 762–5).

Although revenue bonds have become the predominant type of tax-exempt debt, the limitations that states have placed on local government debt usually apply only to general obligation bonds.[2] The most important limit on local debt issuance is the requirement, imposed by 42 states, for voter approval of general obligation bond issues (Government Finance Officers Association 1987, pp. 39–44). In addition, 45 states impose a cap on the amount of their local governments' outstanding general obligation debt. In most cases, these caps limit outstanding debt to some percentage of local property values. In a few states, a broader tax base is taken into account. In Connecticut, for example, debt is limited to 2.25 percent of the locality's latest tax receipts.[3] These limits on the level of outstanding debt often have no practical effect because actual debt levels fall far below the cap (Government Finance Officers Association 1987, p. 40). In other cases, a binding cap means that the affected locality will merely alter the form of debt it issues, that is, it would issue revenue bonds instead of general obligation bonds.

Other State Policies Affecting Local Borrowing Powers

Certain state policies can enhance local borrowing powers. Because interest costs are inversely related to credit risk and the credit rating received by the state will affect the ratings of its local governments, state policies designed to maintain a high state credit rating will tend to lower local borrowing costs. States can also act in a more direct manner to lower local borrowing costs. Through a bond bank, under which the state borrows on behalf of its localities and thereby lends both its credit rating and its financial expertise to its local governments, local borrowing costs can be further reduced. Another variant is for the state to insure local debt. For example, New Jersey provides insurance for local government school bonds by maintaining a reserve equal to a certain percentage of the outstanding local government school debt. The effect of this insurance program is to obtain a AA rating for local government school bonds even when they are issued by communities with a general credit rating less than AA.

State policy will eventually affect local government borrowing in another important way. Private-activity tax-exempt debt, issued for industrial development, housing finance, and other purposes, is limited by volume caps included in the federal tax code.[4] Although no states have come up against the federal caps yet, under the more stringent volume cap described below, some states are likely to find their caps constraining within the next few years. Congress gave state legislatures the power to set the allocation systems for allowable private-activity debt. In the absence of state legislative action, however, the allowable volume is divided equally between state and local issuers and then allocated to local issuers on the basis of relative population levels.

Having described the most important state policies directly affecting local taxing and borrowing, we turn to the changing context within which these state policies must be evaluated.

STATE TAX POLICY AND THE MOVE TO A SERVICE-BASED ECONOMY

Each year, a larger proportion of U.S. employment is in the service sector rather than in manufacturing, and a larger proportion of total economic activity is accounted for by services rather than products. From 1960 to 1985, for example, the value of services as a proportion of gross national product rose from 10 to 16 percent (Economic Report of the President 1987, p. 256). Because of this trend toward an increasingly service-based economy, a general extension of state sales taxation to services seems inevitable. And because most local governments are tied to the state sales tax base and the sales tax is an important revenue source for local governments, the extension of state sales taxation to services will be an important positive development for a number of local governments. As shown in table 10.3, in many states, general sales taxes account for as much as 20 percent of total county or municipal tax revenue. In several states, general sales taxes account for over 50 percent of total county or municipal tax revenue.

The effort to extend the sales tax to services was of intense interest in 1987, when Florida tried and failed to extend general sales taxation to a broad range of personal and professional services.[5] Currently, 20 of the 44 states levying general sales taxes do not include services under their general sales tax base. At the other end of the spectrum, only six states (Hawaii, Iowa, New Mexico, South Dakota, Washington, and West Virginia) levy what Gold (1988) terms either general or broad taxation of services. Despite Florida's difficult experience in attempting to broaden its taxation of services, a number of other states recently either considered or passed measures that broaden sales taxes to services. They were motivated by the need to fund projected deficits or by an interest in funding property tax relief. In 1987, Arkansas, Minnesota, and Texas all broadened their sales tax bases to include certain services (Benker 1987, p. 66).

THE CHANGING MARKET FOR TAX-EXEMPT DEBT

The market for municipal debt has changed dramatically during the past 20 years. For example, the volume of long-term debt issued annually by state and local governments has increased enormously—from $18 billion in 1970 to $145 billion in 1986.[6] A second major development, noted above, is the growth in the volume of revenue bonds issued and the increased importance of revenue bonds relative to general obligation bonds.

Related to the growth in the proportion of tax-exempt debt that is accounted for by revenue bonds is the increase in the volume of debt that is issued for nontraditional purposes. In 1970, education, transportation, water and sewage, public power, and certain other general government purposes accounted for 95 percent of total long-term tax-exempt bonds issued. By 1983, these same categories accounted for only 34 percent of all long-term tax-exempt bonds. The remainder included bonds issued for private purposes such as housing, industrial development, and student loans and for nonprofit hospitals and educational institutions (Petersen 1986, figure 2.3, p. 761). Although there is much disagreement about the appropriate dividing line between public and private-purpose bonds, it is clear that the purposes for which tax-exempt bonds were issued in recent years differ from those for which most bonds were issued two decades ago.

Most of these nontraditional types of tax-exempt bonds are not issued directly by state or local governments but are issued by creatures of these governments, that is, by statutory authorities or special districts. In the late 1960s, approximately 26 percent of tax-exempt bonds were issued by statutory authorities; in 1983, the percentage of total annual issuances accounted for by statutory authorities had risen to 54 percent (Petersen 1986, table 2.4, p. 763). As Petersen (p. 762) wrote:

The significance of the statutory authority borrowing is that these entities are typically established to accomplish purposes that are beyond the normal purview of governmental activity. To put it more bluntly, they frequently are created solely for the purpose of financing activities in circumvention of various debt, tax, or expenditure limitations and referendum requirements that restrict general units of government. In some cases, the authority device may simply be a backdoor device to tap into tax collections; but in many cases, the device acts as a conduit for financing private-purpose activities by use of tax-exempt securities.

The tax-exempt bond market continues to change rapidly. Some of the most recent developments, such as the increased use by state and local governments of taxable rather than tax-exempt debt, were prompted by the changes in federal tax-exempt bond law included in the Tax Reform Act of 1986, to which we now turn.

THE IMPACT OF FEDERAL TAX REFORM ON STATE AND LOCAL GOVERNMENTS

The Tax Reform Act of 1986 has been described as the most sweeping reform of federal tax law since the federal income tax was enacted (Wilkins 1986). The broader federal income tax base and reduced federal marginal tax rates affect state and local taxation in both the short and the long run. One part of the base-broadening efforts placed important restrictions on the issuance of tax-exempt debt.

Effects on the issuance of tax-exempt debt. The Tax Act made significant changes in federal law that affect the tax-exempt bond market across the board. Discussion of many of these changes, such as the changes affecting the demand for tax-exempt bonds, reporting requirements, and restrictions on advance refundings and the ability to earn arbitrage, are beyond the scope of this paper. The aim here is to describe briefly the manner in which the Tax Act will affect the allowable purposes for which tax-exempt bonds may be issued.

Although the changes in tax-exempt bond law enacted in 1986 were far-reaching, given the U.S. Supreme Court's 1988 decision in *South Carolina v. Baker* that state and local governments have no constitutional right to issue tax-exempt bonds, these changes may be only a harbinger of more significant changes yet to come.

Under federal tax law, municipal bonds are exempt from income taxation if they can be classified as either governmental bonds or as allowable private-activity bonds. Many governmental bonds are also general obligation bonds, and many private-activity bonds are revenue bonds, but the match between the categories is not perfect. For example, veterans' bonds, which are issued in five states (Alaska, California, Oregon, Texas, and Wisconsin) in order to help finance veterans' land purchases at less than market interest rates, are simultaneously general obligation and private-activity bonds.

One major change in the federal law is a tightening in the general rules that divide governmental bonds from private-activity bonds. Tax-exempt bonds generally no longer qualify as governmental bonds if over 10 percent of bond proceeds are used directly or indirectly in any trade or business—the trade or business test—*and* more than 10 percent of the payment of principal or interest is secured directly or indirectly by payments or property used in a trade or business— the security interest test. The dividing line for the security interest and trade or business tests under prior law was 25 percent.

An example of the application of this test is the construction of a municipal recreation building with a private concession, such as a fast-food restaurant. If more than 10 percent of the bonds used to finance construction of the recreation building is used by the fast food restaurant, and if more than 10 percent of the interest or principal is secured by the restaurant the bonds will not qualify as governmental bonds. Unless there were a special provision for such an issue under the rules on private-activity bonds, these bonds could not be issued on a tax-exempt basis. (In fact, under current federal law, construction of a fast-food restaurant could not be financed with tax-exempt bonds.)

A second general dividing line is labeled the private loan rule. Under the new law, if an amount exceeding 5 percent or $5 million, whichever is smaller, of the proceeds of a bond issue is used to make loans to individuals, the bond does not qualify as a governmental bond. State and local bonds issued to buy land that is later sold to developers are most likely to run afoul of the private loan rule.

The Tax Act will also directly affect debt issuance by changing the sunset dates for two major types of private-activity bonds. Mortgage revenue bonds are issued to provide below-market interest rates for certain first-time homebuyers. The sunset date for these bonds was delayed by one year to the end of 1988. Small-issue industrial development bonds (IDBs) are issued to provide a tax benefit to businesses to generate economic development. The sunset date for small-issue IDBs issued for manufacturing establishments was also delayed by one year until the end of 1989. These sunset dates have been delayed before, however, and the postponements included in the Tax Act may not be the last ones.

Further, the Tax Act has created a tighter limit on the total amount of private-activity bonds that can be issued, in the form of a lower unified volume cap. Under prior law, there were two important state-by-state volume caps: one on mortgage subsidy bonds and the other on IDBs and student loan bonds. The new law combines those prior law volume caps. The initial cap is set at the greater of $75 per capita or $250 million for 1987 and is lowered to the greater of $50 per capita or $150 million beginning in 1988. When states begin to come up against this tighter cap, the allocation of the cap among the remaining allowable purposes could become an important political issue.

Table 10.5 provides a detailed summary of how the Tax Act affects each category of private-activity bonds. It indicates which bonds become taxable under the new law and, if still eligible for tax-exemption, whether they are subject to the unified volume cap and what sunset date, if any, applies.

Federal tax reform affects the level and mix of state and local taxes as well as the level and form of debt that state and local governments issue. In the discussion below, we distinguish between the short-run and the long-run effects of federal tax reform on state and local taxes for the simple reason that the two types of effects appear to be

Table 10.5 TREATMENT OF PRIVATE ACTIVITY BONDS UNDER PRIOR LAW AND AFTER THE TAX REFORM ACT OF 1986

Type of bond	Prior law[a]				Tax reform act of 1986[b]			
	Taxable	Cap	No cap	Sunset	Taxable	Cap	No cap	Sunset
Multifamily			X			X		
Sports		X			X			
Convention/trade show		P	G		X			
Airports, docks, and wharves		P	G		P		G	
Mass commuting facilities		P	G		P	G		
Parking		X			X			
Sewage		X					G	
Solid waste		X				P		
Electric energy and gas		X				X		
Pollution control		X			X			
Water		X				X		
Hydroelectric		X		12/88		X		12/88
Heating or cooling		X				X		
Hazardous waste	X					X		
Industrial park		X			X			
Small-issue industrial development bonds		X		nonmfg 12/86 mfg 12/88		X		nonmfg 12/86 mfg 12/89

	12/87	12/88
Student loans	X	X
Mortgage revenue	Separate	X
Veterans	Separate	Separate
Redevelopment	no provision in code[c]	X
Nonprofit hospital and educational facilities	X	X[d]

Notes: P= privately owned; G= governmentally owned.

a. Prior law had three separate caps:

Qualified mortgage bond cap = greater of $200 million or 9% of average mortgage originations for preceeding three years.

Qualified veterans' mortgage cap = average annual issuance between 1/79 and 6/84 for each of five states.

Industrial development bond/student loan bond cap = greater of $200 million or $150 per capita ($100 per capita after 1986).

b. The new law retains a separate veterans' bond cap and combines mortgage and IDB/student loan bond caps. Cap = greater of $75 per capita or $250 million for 8/15/86 to the end of 1986 and for 1987. Beginning in 1988, cap = greater of $50 per capita or $150 million.

c. Under prior law some of what are now called redevelopment bonds are taxable bonds, others are governmental and thus tax exempt and uncapped. Under new law certain redevelopment bonds will be tax exempt and under cap.

d. $150 million per organization limit on outstanding non hospital bonds.

different in nature. Whereas many states and a few localities had the opportunity to receive short-term windfalls as a result of federal tax reform, the long-term effects of federal tax reform on state and local governments are likely to be negative, not positive. As discussed below, the most likely major long-run effects include an increase in interjurisdictional tax competition and a reduction in the level of state and local taxes willingly supported by voters.

Short-Run Effects on State and Local Taxes. The impact of the changed federal tax law that was the initial focus of interest in the aftermath of the passage of the Tax Act was the so-called windfall in state individual income tax revenues. Because the income tax base of 30 states is linked in some way to the federal tax base, unless their legislatures acted to decouple from the federal tax base or to lower their rates, it was predicted that state individual income tax revenues would rise $5.9 billion in FY 1988. As of September 1987, with all but two state legislatures having taken action, the cumulative effect of state legislative actions was to return about 80 percent of the potential individual income tax windfall to taxpayers (Benker 1987, p. 13).[7]

Income taxation plays a much smaller role in local taxation than it does in state taxation. The local governments that levy income taxes and their respective tax bases were shown in table 10.4. In terms of our interest, those local income taxes that are linked to the state base are important. According to this table, in combination with estimates of potential state individual income tax windfalls, local governments in three states were potential recipients of income tax windfalls as a result of federal tax reform. Now that states have decided to return the bulk of their potential windfalls, no local governments appear to receive significant windfalls. Maryland counties, for example, could potentially have received increases in their income tax revenues of over 5 percent, but after the state acted to return most of its potential windfall, the counties, which piggyback on state tax liability, will probably receive less than a 2 percent boost in income tax revenues.[8]

The Longer-Term Effects. One can make a persuasive argument that a year or two from now, income tax windfalls from federal tax reform will be of little interest. Federal income tax reform did not change the essential fiscal capacities of either state or local governments. The changes in the tax bases that arose as a direct effect of the federal tax law can, and may well be eventually, completely undone by state legislative efforts.[9]

The lasting effects of federal tax reform are more likely to come from resulting changes in the net cost to taxpayers of state and local services. This can be viewed from two vantage points.

Many studies have shown that both individuals and business firms take the level of taxes and spending into account when choosing where to live.[10] One unambiguous effect of the federal Tax Act is to increase interjurisdictional tax differentials. In some cases, this change will put pressure on high-tax states and localities to reduce their tax levels.[11] Take, for instance, an individual who is indifferent between the government services and other amenities of two suburbs in a large metropolitan area: Green Acres and Walnut Creek. Suppose that before federal tax reform, the taxpayer was an itemizer in a 50 percent tax bracket living in Green Acres and that local taxes in that suburb totaled $3,000 and in Walnut Creek, $2,000. The net cost of local taxes to this taxpayer, after federal tax deductibility, was $1,500 in Green Acres and $1,000 in Walnut Creek. Although Green Acres was clearly the more advantageous community for this taxpayer, the difference in net tax burdens ($500) might not have been sufficient to induce the taxpayer to relocate. Suppose that after tax reform, this taxpayer no longer itemizes his taxes. Now the yearly difference in tax burdens is $1,000. It is possible that this increased tax differential will induce the taxpayer to relocate.

State and local tax differentials have increased for individuals as a result of federal tax reform for three reasons: fewer taxpayers itemize their taxes, federal marginal tax rates are reduced, and state and local general sales taxes are no longer deductible. State and local tax differentials have also increased for business firms and are likely to have a similar effect on business location incentives.

Even if individual taxpayers are not inclined to relocate because of family commitments or other reasons, in the long run they are likely to support slightly lower spending levels in response to the increased "price" of state and local services. Whereas the top-bracket individuals who itemized deductions on their federal tax returns used to pay 50 cents of every extra dollar of state and local taxes, after tax reform, if they are in the 28 percent tax bracket, they will now pay 72 cents of every extra dollar. This general increase in the effective price may eventually lead to a reduced appetite for state and local services on the part of taxpayers.

There have been several estimates of the quantitative impact of this potentially reduced demand for state and local services. Kenyon (1988) estimated that tax deductibility increased aggregate state and local spending by approximately 3 percent over what it would otherwise have been prior to federal tax reform, but the overall stimulus was reduced to approximately 1 percent after tax reform. Courant and Rubinfeld (1987) estimate that the Tax Reform Act of 1986 will reduce aggregate state and local spending between 0.9 and 1.9 percent.

As is often the case, the aggregate estimates mask a considerable variability in effects among governments. Gramlich (1985) produced estimates for local governments in Michigan and found that *eliminating* tax deductibility would have had no effect on the demand for state and local spending in Detroit, that it would have decreased demand by slightly over 10 percent in the suburbs of Detroit and Lansing, and that it would have reduced demand 6–10 percent in the rest of the state.

A final long-run impact of federal tax reform is its effects on state and local revenue mix. Federal tax reform has reduced the relative attractiveness of income and property taxes by reducing the proportion of taxpayers who are itemizers and by reducing marginal tax rates; it reduced the relative attractiveness of sales taxes by eliminating sales tax deductibility. This change may add further impetus to the recent trend toward increased reliance on user charges instead of tax financing. Despite the fact that sales taxes continue to be less unpopular than property and income taxes, in the long run, there may be some shift away from sales taxation as a result of disallowing federal deductibility of general sales taxes.

Because property taxation is far and away the most important revenue source for local governments, this possibility raises the issue, which has yet to be adequately addressed, of the impact of federal tax reform on property tax revenues. Courant and Rubinfeld (1987, pp. 94–95) outline the important factors serving both to increase and to decrease property tax bases, but are unable to predict the overall direction of change. For example, they note that owner-occupied housing receives less favorable treatment now than it did before federal tax reform because fewer taxpayers itemize and they generally face lower marginal tax rates. Furthermore, rental housing receives less favorable tax treatment as a result of the new limitations on passive losses and other provisions. On the other hand, it appears that housing may still be relatively favored because of the limits the Tax Act placed on other types of capital investment.

IMPACT OF RECENT STATE INCOME TAX REFORMS

Nineteen eighty-seven proved to be a major year for state tax reform, "with more important reforms enacted than in any year within recent memory " (Gold 1987).[12] The most important impetus to the year's state income tax reforms was the passage of federal income tax reform. Those states with an automatic linkage to the federal tax code had a choice between unlegislated and legislated changes. Probably all state legislatures were attracted to tax reform to some degree because congressional enactment of what was perceived to be a successful tax bill indicated that tax reform could be a politically popular issue.

State tax reforms paralleled the federal reform in at least three respects. First, the theme of broadening the income tax base and lowering marginal tax rates, in particular the top tax rate, was echoed at the state level. Thirteen states reduced tax rates, and many states terminated certain deductions and exemptions.

Second, the goal of taking poor and moderate-income households off the income tax rolls was achieved by 11 states as well as by federal tax reform. As at the federal level, one of the chief means of accomplishing this change was to increase personal exemptions and the standard deduction.

Third, states acted to simplify the structure of their income taxes. When fully phased in, federal income tax brackets will be reduced to 3 from 14. Minnesota and New York both moved to two tax brackets and Colorado adopted a flat tax.

State income tax reform affects certain localities that are linked to the state tax base, as noted above. More important, though, by removing poor households from the income tax rolls, 13 states increased their commitment to redistribution to low-income households and thereby reduced the potential burden faced by local governments.

RELEVANT DEVELOPMENTS IN PUBLIC FINANCE

Two developments in the public finance literature cast new light on the evaluation of proposed reforms of state policies affecting local taxing and borrowing. One is the development of a new theory of competitive federalism, and the other is the growing empirical literature indicating the quantitative importance of tax and expenditure capitalization.

According to the new theory of competitive federalism recently developed by researchers working at the intersection of politics and economics, just as effective competition is essential to our economy, effective competition among federal, state, and local governments is essential to our federal system of government. The basic logic of the theory is that when governments are required to compete for support, they will be more responsive to citizen demands. In turn, governments will be more likely to produce the type and amount of goods and services that citizens desire and to produce these goods and services efficiently.[13] These achievements in efficiency must, of course, be balanced against a concern for equity. Intense intergovernmental competition tends to reduce the state and local role in maintaining a safety net for the poor and makes it difficult to maintain a progressive tax system at other than the federal level. Despite this important caveat, the heightened appreciation for the potential benefits of interjurisdictional tax and policy competition, brought about in part by the literature on competitive federalism, has important policy implications. One of the most important is that previous recommendations for consolidating local governments and for establishing areawide governing bodies are brought into question. Another implication, especially relevant in the context of this chapter, is that strong forces of competition among local governments may reduce the necessity for state regulation of local government taxing and borrowing.

The second important advance in the public finance literature is the growing body of evidence on the importance of tax and expenditure capitalization and the growing appreciation for the implications of the phenomenon. The concept of tax capitalization is based on the mathematical relationship between a present value and a perpetual annuity. An example can put this idea in everyday terms. Suppose that two families, the Gordons and the Kushners, purchase single-family homes that are identical in every respect except that the Gordons' house is subject to $2,000 more in property taxes every year. At an interest rate of 8 percent, with full tax capitalization, we expect that the Gordons will pay $25,000 less for their house than will the Kushners. An accumulation of empirical studies over the last 15 years has established that tax, and to some degree, expenditure capitalization are substantial. In a review of 20 studies of property tax capitalization, Bloom, Ladd, and Yinger (1983) concluded that interjurisdictional differences in property taxes are 50 to 100 percent capitalized into property values.

The implications of capitalization are quite broad. For one example, consider a family that is apparently overburdened by its local property tax relative to property taxes paid by similar families in other communities. The capitalization phenomenon is crucial to evaluating the potential inequity of that household's situation. In the example above, once the Gordons and the Kushners move into their respective homes, it will appear that there is a property tax disparity problem because the Gordons will be paying $2,000 more each year in property taxes. However, because the Gordons paid a lower price for their home than did the Kushners, the Gordons have already been compensated for their differentially high property taxes. The relatively high property tax burden of the Gordon family is *not* inequitable.

We can now move to an examination of the traditional criteria for evaluating alternative reform proposals.

CRITERIA FOR JUDGING ALTERNATIVE REFORM PROPOSALS

The traditional criteria for evaluating reform proposals are equity, efficiency, adequacy and accountability, and the balance of fiscal authority between state and local governments. Each will be discussed briefly in turn.

Equity. It is important that state and local tax policies aim for both horizontal equity (equal treatment of equals) and vertical equity (treatment of those with greater ability to pay taxes appropriately relative to those with less ability to pay taxes). Insofar as it is possible, for example, two individuals who have the same incomes should pay the same amount in taxes for any given level of services. Furthermore, it is generally agreed that high-income individuals should pay more in taxes than low-income individuals, although the previous general approval of progressive taxation has come under intense scrutiny in recent years, and some would support proportional or even regressive taxation at the local level.

We noted above the manner in which the phenomenon of capitalization affects the general concern with property tax disparities. The existence of capitalization of debt burdens also has equity implications. One of the usual arguments in favor of financing long-term capital projects with debt rather than on a pay-as-you-build basis is that the pattern of tax liability under current financing of capital improvements appears inequitable. An individual moving out of a community after a capital improvement is built and financed appears to have been subject to a disproportionate tax burden, whereas new entrants into the community appear to be paying too little for the benefits of the same capital improvements. However, to the extent that property values reflect debt and tax burdens of a community, there is no inequity. The outmigrant's house will sell at a higher price because of the low future debt and tax burden that results from the fact that the capital improvement has already been paid for. The inmigrant's future share of the benefits of the capital improvements is paid a higher price for the house. To the extent that the debt and tax levels are fully capitalized, it does not matter whether capital expenditure is debt-financed or financed on a current basis.

Efficiency. Efficiency has many facets, some of which have been alluded to already, such as producing the mix and level of goods and services desired by voters in the least-cost way. Another facet is budgetary efficiency, whereby the state achieves its goals in the least-cost way. For example, budgetary efficiency is not achieved when property tax relief is so poorly targeted that a substantial proportion of the tax relief goes to high-income individuals for whom the policy was not designed. Furthermore, good tax policy should minimize distortions of the private sector or achieve neutrality. Sales tax differentials in adjoining towns that cause commercial development to relocate in the low-tax town are examples of a harmful private sector distortion. In addition, citizens, policymakers, and academics have all become increasingly concerned about institutional structures that induce excessive public sector growth.

With respect to the issuance of public debt, cost minimization is of particular interest. That is, when deciding whether to issue bonds or to pay directly through taxes or fees, policymakers should take into account the relative costs of the two methods. Furthermore, and just as important, the state should safeguard its credit rating as well as the credit ratings of its local governments in order to minimize the cost of future bond finance. In fact, to the extent that the market for bonds is a segmented one, the state should also be concerned with the overall volume of debt issued by all governmental entities within its boundaries. In a segmented market, individuals and institutions tend to purchase debt from a particular state or group of states. Thus a weak credit rating for a particular local government can raise interest costs to some degree for all bonds issued within the state in which that local government is located.

Adequacy and Accountability. State policies must also be judged against the criterion of adequacy. At a time when localities are still adjusting to relatively recent cuts in federal grants and when they must cope with burdensome federal and state mandates, local policymakers are justly concerned about the adequacy of their tax bases.

The choice between issuing debt on a general obligation basis by general purpose governments versus issuance by special authorities, generally in the form of revenue bonds, raises issues of accountability as well as adequacy. Some argue that certain needs, such as buildings for housing state bureaucrats, would never be approved by the voters in a state referendum. These individuals argue that adequate support for certain state needs requires the issuance of debt by special authorities. On the other hand, this avenue for debt issuance reduces government accountability to the voters and, because of the limited revenue source for repaying the bonds, increases the cost of debt finance.

Balance of Fiscal Authority Between State and Local Governments. One of the most difficult goals to achieve is maintaining an adequate balance of fiscal authority between state and local governments. In small states like Hawaii and Nevada, it may be appropriate for the state to wield greater control over local governments than in a larger state like Minnesota. Even so, each state faces a difficult problem of determining the appropriate balance between state and local fiscal authority. An implication of the theory of competitive federalism is that if a state government gains a near monopoly on government power within the state, it will curtail the effective competition among levels of government, thereby weakening an important factor encouraging all levels of government to be more responsive to their citizens.

EVALUATION OF PROPOSALS FOR REFORM

Diversification of Local Revenue. A perennially favorite reform proposal is for states to provide increased tax authority to their local governments. It is specifically suggested that many local governments could benefit from the ability to levy income or sales taxes in addition to property taxes as a way to increase local fiscal capacity or to reduce fiscal disparities. For administrative costs and distortions of the private sector to be reduced, it is often recommended that localities adopt the state's tax base or that a common tax rate be adopted over a wide area, such as a county.

The advantages of broadening local tax authority are the potential for improving a local government's fiscal capacity, reducing the regressivity of the local tax burden, and reducing the economic distortions that come from relying too heavily on one particular tax source. Ladd and Bradbury (1985) have examined the ability of large central cities to export taxes to nonresidents and thereby increase their fiscal capacities. According to their estimates, because of the relatively greater ability to export income taxes to nonresidents, increasing tax revenues by raising property taxes costs city residents an average of 25 percent more than if an equal amount of revenue were raised through income taxation.

The policy of local revenue diversification has several problems, however. First, can local revenue diversification in fact increase local fiscal capacity or reduce fiscal disparities? Whether these goals can be achieved is likely to vary with individual circumstances. A tourist town may be able to enlarge its tax base by gaining access to a general sales tax base, but another community with a poor property tax base may also have poor general sales and income tax bases.

Furthermore, some argue that placing a limit on allowable tax bases can serve as a useful guard on excessive public sector growth. They favor limiting local governments to property taxation and even favor a prohibition against a state income tax. From their point of view, forcing all local governments to levy an income or general sales tax in order to serve the needs of some local governments is likely to contribute to excessive government spending. The alternative of allowing local governments to adopt income or general sales taxes at their option does not appear particularly attractive either because of the resulting distortion of private economic activity that can easily occur.

Revision of Tax and Debt Caps. Most states could benefit from a periodic reevaluation of the usefulness of any tax and debt caps that they place on their local governments. In some cases, caps are placed on inappropriate bases. For example, with reduced reliance on property taxation by local governments a cap on property taxes alone may not place the desired restraint on local government spending. The natural reaction of local officials when faced by a binding cap is to devise creative solutions to circumvent the limit. After the passage of Proposition 13 in California, for example, many local governments turned to financing through user fees, which were not under the original revenue limit. Similarly, local governments constrained by limits on issuing general obligation debt can turn to debt financing through revenue bonds or to use of lease purchase agreements. To reform the ineffective limits, the obvious solution is to broaden the base of the cap. Property tax caps can be replaced by general revenue caps, and debt limits can be extended to forms of tax-exempt debt other than general obligation bonds.

Easing of Tax and Debt Limits. Alternatively, states may want to reexamine the need for any tax or debt limits. A change could help further the goal of revenue adequacy for some localities. Because of the effectiveness of interjurisdictional tax and policy competition, even without state-imposed limits, local governments will be constrained in their levels of spending and, less so, in the amount of tax-exempt debt they can issue.

Improved Targeting of Property Tax Relief. Budgetary efficiency is an important issue in the design of reforms of state property tax relief for local governments. It is plausible that benefits of agricultural use value assessment go to recently converted gentleman farmers as well as to the family farmer the policy is designed to help. Likewise, homestead exemptions may primarily benefit the wealthy elderly. Furthermore, because of the existence of tax capitalization, certain property tax relief measures will not achieve the desired equity goals. For example, instituting a property tax circuit breaker will benefit even those households that have been compensated for their especially high property tax burdens by especially low purchase prices for their houses. A partial answer to this dilemma is to attempt to target any circuit breaker program to the less mobile, less informed taxpayers living in central cities, where property tax capitalization is less likely to compensate effectively for high property tax burdens.

Allocation of Authority to Issue Private-Activity Debt. Some states have always limited local issuance of private-activity debt. Limits can be beneficial because a high volume of bond issuance by any entity within a state tends to drive up interest costs for all governments within that state. Realizing this fact and believing that clearly public purpose debt should receive first priority, certain officials have supported state-imposed limitations on private-activity or private-purpose debt. With the newly tightened federal volume cap on private-activity tax-exempt bonds, states may want to reevaluate their local debt policies. Although the currently depressed tax-exempt bond market makes this cap less of a problem currently, eventually there will be a need to examine the current systems for allocating the allowable volume of private-activity debt or to institute such a system if the state does not now have one. Some states now allow a first-come, first-served system, and others attempt to rank bond proposals according to a number of criteria, including, for example, the number of jobs created or retained. The success of these systems should be evaluated as lessons for other states.

CONCLUSION

At all levels of government, with respect to both tax and expenditure policies, individually sensible policies adopted over time often do not make for overall fiscal policy that is wise. That fact is part of the reason for periodic reform efforts. This review of state policies affecting local taxing and borrowing is intended to provide a conceptual framework as well as a brief evaluation of a few suggested reforms that can be useful for states and localities considering periodic reform efforts. First, we examined a range of state policies affecting local taxing and borrowing, from limits on local taxation and state-financed property tax relief to state policies either limiting local debt issuance or augmenting local borrowing powers. Any reforms of state policies affecting local financing must take into account the changing environment, including the recent federal tax reform, the move to a service-based economy, and continuing developments in the market for tax-exempt debt. The application of the traditional criteria for judging potential reforms—equity and efficiency—is altered somewhat given the growing appreciation of the benefits of interjurisdictional tax and policy competition and increasing empirical evidence on the importance of the capitalization phenomenon. An examination of available policy options produced a mixed evaluation of the usefulness of local revenue diversification and of state caps on local debt and taxes. A reevaluation of the effectiveness and targeting of state-financed property tax relief and of state limits on local issuance of private-purpose debt were called for.

Notes

1. The most notable of these periods were the recessions of 1837 and 1873, the repudiation of debt by southern states after the Civil War, and the depression in the 1930s. See Aronson and Hiley (1986).

2. Some states prohibit their local governments from issuing revenue bonds. Ac-

cording to Wilson White (1985, p. 27), Connecticut, Delaware, Maine, Maryland, Massachusetts, New Hampshire, New Jersey, New York, North Carolina, and Rhode Island permit local governments to issue general obligation bonds only. This ban means that the proportion of tax-exempt debt issued by local governments accounted for by general obligation bonds will be somewhat higher than 25 percent.

3. For a detailed state-by-state table, see Advisory Commission on Intergovernmental Relations (1987, table 43).

4. Private-activity debt has a specific definition under the Internal Revenue Code that was last modified by P.L. 99-514, the Tax Reform Act of 1986. Private-activity debt includes industrial development bonds (IDBs), student loan bonds, and mortgage subsidy bonds, among others. (For a more complete list, see table 10.5 later in the chapter.) Private-purpose debt is a related, nonlegal term often used to refer to many of the same types of bonds.

5. The total projected FY 1988 revenue gain for this proposal was $721 million (Benker 1987, p. 66).

6. The 1970 figure is from Calkins (1984, table 6–1, p. 117). The 1986 figure is from U.S. Office of Management and Budget (1987, table F–17). Both sources begin with publicly reported bond volume and adjust those figures upward for unreported small IDBs.

7. The potential for a state corporate income tax windfall has only recently received serious analysis. Robert Aten (1987) of the U.S. Treasury estimated the total potential corporate windfall at about $3.2 billion for 1987. As of the end of 1987, eight states reduced corporate tax rates to offset some of the windfall, but a majority retained the windfall (Vlaisavljevich 1987).

8. Preliminary estimates obtained from the State of Maryland, Office of Fiscal Services.

9. William Niskanen (1987) has argued that these short-term windfalls may be of some lasting interest. He draws on the flypaper concept from the literature on federal grants to state and local governments to make this point. The empirical literature has generally shown that state and local spending rises by more when income flows directly to those governments in the form of grants than when income goes into the hands of the taxpayers. This behavioral response was named "the flypaper effect" because "money sticks where it hits." Niskanen argued that the state appropriation of a significant proportion of the total individual and corporate windfall was consistent with the previously found flypaper effect. There is no implication that this effect will disappear over time.

10. See Kenyon (1988) for a recent literature survey.

11. The situation will depend on the evaluation of the benefits of state and local expenditures. This point is made at some length in Kenyon (1988).

12. Much of the following description of state income tax reforms is based on Gold's paper.

13. See Breton (1985) for an excellent exposition of this theory.

References

Advisory Commission on Intergovernmental Relations (ACIR). 1986. *Significant Features of Fiscal Federalism.* Vol. 1. Washington, D.C.: ACIR.

Aronson, Richard, and John L. Hilley. 1986. *Financing State and Local Governments*. Washington, D.C.: Brookings Institution.

Aten, Robert H. 1987. The Magnitude of the Additional State Corporate Income Taxes Resulting from Federal Reform. *Tax Notes* (3 August): 529–34.

Bell, Michael E., and John H. Bowman. 1987. Minnesota Property Tax Relief Policy and Issues. *Hamline Journal of Public Law and Policy* 8 (Spring): 197–213.

Benker, Karen. 1987. *Fiscal Survey of the States*. Washington, D.C.: National Association of State Budget Officers and National Governors' Association.

Bloom, Howard S., Helen F. Ladd, and John Yinger. 1983. Are Property Taxes Capitalized into House Values? In *Local Provision of Public Services: The Tiebout Model After Twenty-Five Years*, edited by George R. Zodrow. New York: Academic Press.

Bowman, John H., and John L. Mikesell. 1987. *Local Government Tax Authority and Use*. Washington, D.C.: National League of Cities.

Breton, Albert. 1985. Supplementary Statement. In *Report of the Royal Commission on the Economic Union and Development Prospects for Canada*. Ottawa: Canadian Government Publishing Centre.

Calkins, Susannah E. 1984. Tax-Exempt Bonds. In ACIR. *Strengthening the Federal Revenue System: Implications for State and Local Taxing and Borrowing*. Washington, D.C.: ACIR.

Courant, Paul N., and Daniel L. Rubinfeld. 1987. Tax Reform: Implications for the State–Local Public Sector. *Journal of Economic Perspectives* 1 (Summer): 87–100.

Gold, Steven D. 1988. Florida's Sales Tax on Services: Aberration or Innovation? *State Legislatures* 14 (January): 12.

Government Finance Officers Association, Government Finance Research Center (GFRC). 1987. *Constitutional, Statutory and Other Impediments to Local Government Infrastructure Finance*. Washington, D.C.: GFRC.

Gramlich, Edward M. 1985. The Deductibility of State and Local Taxes. *National Tax Journal* 38 (December): 447–65.

Kenyon, Daphne A. 1988. Interjurisdictional Tax and Policy Competition: Good or Bad for the Federal System? Paper Submitted to the Advisory Commission on Intergovernmental Relations, 7 January, Washington, D.C.

———. 1988. Implicit Aid to State and Local Governments Through Federal Tax Deductibilty. In *Intergovernmental Fiscal Relations in an Era of New Federalism*, edited by Michael E. Bell. Greenwich, Conn.: JAI Press.

Ladd, Helen F., and Katherine L. Bradbury. 1985. Changes in the Fiscal Capacity of U.S. Cities, 1970–1982. In 1984 *Proceedings of the*

Seventy- Seventh Annual Conference on Taxation. Columbus, Ohio: National Tax Association–Tax Institute of America.

Niskanen, William. 1987. How State Reforms Look from the Nation's Capital. Paper Presented at the Conference on State Tax Reform: Agendas for the Next Five Years, 22–23 October, Washington, D.C.

Petersen, John E. 1986. Recent Developments in Tax-Exempt Bond Markets. In *Federal-State-Local Fiscal Relations*, Technical Papers 2. Washington, D.C.: U.S. Department of the Treasury.

U.S. Bureau of the Census. 1987. *Government Finances in 1985–86.* Ser. GF-86, no. 5. Washington, D.C.: Government Printing Office.

U.S. Office of Management and Budget. 1987. *Special Analyses, Budget of the United States Government, Fiscal Year 1988.* Washington, D.C.: Government Printing Office.

Vlaisavljevich, Michael. 1987. Federal Impacts on State Business Taxes: How Can States Handle Them? Paper Presented at the Conference on State Tax Reform: Agendas for the Next Five Years, 22–23 October, Washington, D.C.

White, Wilson. 1985. *The Municipal Bond Market.* Jersey City, N.J.: Financial Press.

Wilkins, John G. 1986. The United States Tax Reforms. Remarks before the Institute for Fiscal Studies, Conference on International Tax Reform, 24 November, London.

ABOUT THE CONTRIBUTORS

Jack A. Brizius, a partner in Brizius and Foster, is a consultant specializing in public management and policy development. Prior to becoming a consultant, he served as the director of policy research at the National Governors' Association. He has also served as the director of state planning and economic development in Pennsylvania, deputy director of the Bureau of the Budget in Illinois, and director of human services planning in New Jersey.

Stephen B. Farber is chairman of Concordia Group, a public policy consulting firm. From 1975 to 1983, he was executive director of the National Governors' Association. He previously served as assistant to the president of Harvard University and executive assistant to the governor of New Jersey. His published work deals with fiscal and intergovernmental affairs.

R. Scott Fosler is vice president and director of government studies for the Committee for Economic Development. He is editor of *The New Economic Role of American States* and has served as an elected county council member in Montgomery County, Maryland.

John Stuart Hall is a research professor of public affairs at Arizona State University. He is the author of numerous books and articles on U.S. intergovernmental and urban affairs. His publications include several national studies of domestic policy that have been published by The Brookings Institution, the Woodrow Wilson School of Princeton University, the National Academy of Sciences, WESTAT, Inc., The Urban Institute, and other organizations.

Harold A. Hovey is the editor of *State Policy Reports* and *State Budget & Tax News* as well as a consultant on state and local fiscal issues. He has been the chief financial official of Illinois and Ohio and has been employed by the federal Office of Management and Budget and Battelle Memorial Institute.

Daphne A. Kenyon is a research fellow at the Lincoln Institute of Land Policy. She is the author of several papers on the effects of the Tax Reform Act of 1986 on state and local governments, on federal deductibility of state and local taxes, and on tax-exempt bonds. During the past year, she participated in state tax studies in Nevada, New Jersey, and Texas. Her role in these studies included an examination of state policies with respect to local borrowing.

E. Blaine Liner is the director of the State Policy Center at The Urban Institute. He has been involved in the design, management, and evaluation of state and local economic development programs for 25 years. He has been a staff member of the governor's office in New York and North Carolina and has served as an adviser and consultant to the Coalition of Northeastern Governors, the Southern Governors' Association, and the Western Governors' Association.

Charles J. Orlebeke is the director of the School of Urban Planning and Policy, University of Illinois at Chicago. During the Ford administration, he was assistant secretary for policy development and research in the Department of Housing and Urban Development. He is the author of *Federal Aid to Chicago* and numerous other publications in the areas of national urban policy, intergovernmental finance, and housing.